T0339801

The Egyptian Revolution

The Egyptian Revolution

Between Hope and Despair:

Mubarak to Morsi

Mohamed El-Bendary

Algora Publishing
New York

Library of Congress Cataloging-in-Publication Data —

El-Bendary, Mohamed, 1966-
   The Egyptian Revolution: From Hope to Despair, Mubarak to Morsi / Mohamed El-
Bendary.
      pages cm
   Includes bibliographical references and index.
   ISBN 978-0-87586-990-2 (soft cover: alk. paper) — ISBN 978-0-87586-991-9 (hard
cover: alk. paper) — ISBN 978-0-87586-992-6 (ebook) 1. Egypt—History—Protests,
2011- 2. Egypt—Politics and government—1981- 3. Mubarak, Muhammad Husni, 1928- 4.
Mursi, Muhammad, 1951- 5. Islam and politics—Egypt. 6. Social conflict—Egypt. I. Title.
   DT107.87.E42 2013
   962.05'6—dc23
            2013009045

Front Cover: Tahrir Square, Cairo, Egypt, © Monique Jaques/Corbis

Printed in the United States

TABLE OF CONTENTS

Chapter 1. The 2011 Egyptian Revolution: An Introduction

> The more I travelled through the Middle East, the more I came to appreciate Egypt—the home to one of every four Arabs. For all its forgotten glory and crippling economic problems, Egypt is very special. It is multilayered, and the more you peel away, the more there is to discover. —DAVID LAMB, *The Arabs: Journeys Beyond the Mirage* (2002)

The year 2011 was epochal in the history of Egypt. No one expected a revolution to take place in the Land of the Nile, but it did. And it all played out at a breakneck speed like a video reel with the whole world watching. On Tuesday January 25 of that year, thousands of protesters poured into Tahrir (Arabic for "Liberation") Square in central Cairo and in other major governorates across Egypt such as Alexandria, Suez, and Ismailia. On that day, which was a public holiday known as National Police Day, Egyptian demonstrators—many of them young people—launched the first salvo of an eighteen-day battle to topple Egyptian President Hosni Mubarak, dissolve parliament, and draft a new constitution. Three protesters died in Suez, which is located in the north-eastern part of the country, and one policeman was killed in the Egyptian capital as a result of clashes between demonstrators and riot police. Washington and European states called on both the Mubarak government and demonstrators to exercise restraint, but clashes continued. By the time Mubarak stepped down from power on February 11, more than 300 Egyptians were reported dead or missing—though many at the time questioned the validity of such number. A government-established fact-finding commission stated on April 19 that the death toll was much higher: 846. More than 6,000 people were also reported injured.[1]

During the eighteen days of protest, Mubarak spoke to protesters three times to seek their support and ease tension. The first speech was on January 28, when he declared a new government; the second was on February 1, when he appointed a prime minister to engage in dialogue with protesters and called on Parliament to amend articles 76 and 77 of the Egyptian Constitution. Then, on February 10, the embattled president promised he would hand power to his prime minister, reform the Constitution, and cancel the emergency law once the crisis eased.

After Mubarak's resignation was declared on the following day, power was handed over to the Supreme Council of the Armed Forces (SCAF), which soon dissolved Parliament, suspended the Constitution and created an eight-member panel to draft amendments to key articles related to presidential elections. A poll for the referendum was run on March 17. Elections for the People's Assembly were scheduled for September, and the presidential elections later in the year or in early 2012. Parliamentary elections were not, however, held until November 28 and planned to be complete by March 11, 2012; presidential elections were also rescheduled for mid-2012; the first session was held on May 23 and 24 of that year.[2]

In the first day of protests, the streets in the city I live in, Benha, about forty miles north of Cairo, were less crowded; there was a sense of bewilderment mixed with fear dancing on people's faces. On the following day, Wednesday, January 26, popular Arabic-language satellite television stations such as Al-Jazeera, Al-Arabiya, BBC Arabic, and France24 began showing images of Egyptian youth demonstrating in Tahrir Square—despite police warning on that day that protesters would be detained. Anti-government activists posted messages on Facebook and Twitter urging people to continue with their demonstrations. During the first a few days, the state-owned print and broadcast media reported little on what was going on the streets and the human losses that took place, particularly on Friday, January 28—known as the "Friday of Anger." On that day a curfew was imposed from 6:00 p.m. to 7:00 a.m. in major cities. Infuriated by what they called "police brutality" against demonstrators on January 28, Egyptians rejected Mubarak's promise to pursue political and economic reform in the television speech he delivered later on that day. From that time on, we began to see the wave of street protests spreading across the country, and not just in Cairo, Alexandria, and Suez. The curfew spread on the following days to include cities such as Ismailia and Mansura, among others, where there had been demonstrations. Protests were also seen in different parts of the Egyptian capital, home of twenty million inhabitants, and not just in Tahrir Square. There were demonstrations in front of the Syndicate of Journalists and major state-owned press houses such as Al-Ahram, Al-Akhbar, and Dar Al-Tahrir in rejection of their coverage which protesters denounced as "pro-government."

The number of protesters at Tahrir Square during the first day of the revolution was large and well-coordinated—more than any police officer could have ever imagined; it did take the security police by storm. Yet police mockingly put the number at 10,000, although protesters said it was much higher: 100,000. Indeed, there were tens of thousands of people and the number kept rising at a shocking rate over the next seventeen days. Protesters were determined and refused to leave Tahrir Square despite the bitter cold Cairene nights in winter. Protesters, many of whom were tech-savvy middle- to upper-class youth, were demonstrating not just against rising food prices, reduction in government subsidies, and high unemployment but also against rigged elections, rampant corruption, lack of employment opportunities, and oppression of free speech. They demanded dissolving Parliament and reforming the Constitution, and they did it all peacefully, with police showing restraint on the first day of protests.

From the second day on, we saw security police starting to jump to subdue demonstrations. Among the protesters were writers, poets, actors, movie directors, talk-show hosts, and renowned public figures. Some sang the national anthem; others shouted slogans: "The people want to bring down the regime," and "We want freedom and human dignity." Minister of Interior Habib El-Adli, who was later imprisoned, issued a statement on the first day saying that the Ministry respected the rights of peaceful demonstrations and of protesters to "voice their demands and exercise their freedom of expression." But it warned them, especially those affiliated with the Muslim Brotherhood, not to "damage public property" or throw stones at police.

Protesters who stayed for days at Tahrir lived in tents and formed their own media center. They compiled footage and produced and distributed videos to the media (and posted them online) that showed their struggle against police brutality. They carried large signs that called for their rights, most prominent of which was: "Bread, freedom, social justice, and human dignity." Some of the demonstrators were veteran protesters who had marched in other anti-government demonstrations over the past years.

By the time Mubarak resigned on February 11, the protests had claimed hundreds of lives despite their peaceful march. One protester compared the January 2011 Revolution to the July 1952 one in which Egypt gained its independence from British occupation. Yet during the 2011 Revolution there were certainly more puzzling questions on people's minds: Would Egypt move toward a real democracy? Could state instability threaten the country's future? How much influence would their revolution have on other Arab states in their struggle to liberate themselves from autocratic rule? Where would the United States stand on all this? There was little or no fear of the SCAF and its generals holding power until elections were held.

The speed with which the Egyptian January 25 Revolution took place enthralled the Arabs and the world. It ignited questions about the future stability of other Arab countries. To some extent, the revolution reminded me, as I sat in this Cairene suburb, of the fall of the Berlin Wall and the political changes that took place in Eastern Europe thereafter. However, Galal Amin, a distinguished political analyst and an economics professor at the American University in Cairo (AUC), cautioned that the fall of the ruling regime "does not mean the culmination of the revolution because we are still at its onset. The revolution has numerous demands other than the departure of Mubarak. The 1952 Revolution did not come to an end with the departure of King Farouk but had other goals, such as agricultural reform, abolishing titles, implementing a republican system of government, and nationalizing the Suez Canal." The AUC professor stressed that the 2011 Revolution—unlike that of 1952—began as a revolution and not as a move by a few individuals that later turned into a revolution with the public joining in.[3] In an interview with the BBC in April, Nabil Fahmy, a former Egyptian ambassador to the United States, called it a "revolution in progress, an ongoing revolution."[4]

Why Did It Erupt?

The Egyptian revolution, in my opinion, broke out primarily because a large number of Egyptians have not benefited from the economic growth which the country enjoyed in the decade prior to the January 25 Revolution. Then comes the issue of lack of personal freedom. The series of economic reforms that began in the 1990s weakened the status of workers and their rights, with many private owners not only offering their employees low pay but also declining to grant them full jobs with benefits. Many private companies cut the number of staff to increase profit. This, together with low salaries, resulted in workers demonstrating for their rights in the weeks that followed Mubarak's resignation. Trade unions had conducted their own sit-ins on and off over the five years that preceded the 2011 Revolution. There were textile workers' strikes in 2006 calling for the right to their own independent unions and for raising the country's minimum wage. There were also demonstrations on April 6, 2008, against skyrocketing food prices.

Egypt adds a million-plus annually to its population. Since 1952 the country has increased its population from 21 million to 83 million by 2011, and that has resulted in higher unemployment, particularly among youth. The country has a large youth population, a "youth bulge," 20 percent are between the ages of fifteen and twenty-four. According to figures released by international non-governmental organizations and the U.S. State Department, half of the population is below the age of twenty-five. A total of 90 percent of those unemployed are youth. The literacy rate is about 58 percent of the adult population.[5]

Rapid population increase has made the Land of the Nile more dependent on food imports and hence accumulating a huge public debt. Political corruption, a dilapidated health care system, squandering of public money, and government reluctance to raise the minimum wage have made things worse for Egyptians and increased the level of poverty in the country.[6] This was taking place even though the Egyptian economy was improving by between 5 to 7 percent during the four years that preceded the January 25 Revolution. Many Egyptians were wondering why their living standards were not improving.

There was also the issue of the "rigged" People's Assembly elections of November 2010. The winning of the ruling National Democratic Party (NDP) of 420 seats out of the People's Assembly's 518 seats (ten of which are appointed by the president) was considered fraudulent by many Egyptians. The Tunisian Revolution, which led to the ousting of President Zine el-Abiden Ben Ali on January 15, 2011, without a doubt injected a rush of adrenaline for the Egyptian revolution and triggered a roller coaster of sentiments.

The growing youth population in Egypt was generally absent from public life; they were utterly disengaged from the political process prior to the revolution. But the middle class strata among them were becoming more engaged than in the past, according to Prof. Amin. These youth have also become more ambitious than young people during the 1950s because of the spread of education. Their self-confidence was higher, added the AUC professor. Access to the Internet and modern mass media has further empowered them. Nations of the Western world, noted Amin, have supported their cause, unlike in the past when they often supported the English and outside nations that were occupying Egypt.[7] In short, Amin said, the causes of the revolution had accumulated over the past three decades, including increasing unemployment, rising prices and low wages, the absence of social justice, and the spread of corruption. He added that some reasons go back to six years ago, such as what happened to Khaled Said (a twenty-eight-year-old who was tortured to death by police in Alexandria), the fraudulent 2010 parliamentarian elections, the advent of former United Nations nuclear watchdog Mohamed ElBaradei on the political scene and the warm welcome he received, and earlier events in Tunisia.[8]

Protests against the Egyptian government's policies on the domestic level first erupted in December 2006 when textile workers in the city of Mahalla took to the streets. We then saw a few other protests taking places, most prominent of which was the one on April 6, 2008, against skyrocketing food prices. Ordinary Egyptians were angered by how blatantly the Mubarak regime catered to the rich. Consider this, for example. It was an established routine that government pays for medical treatment for actors and top government officials, many of whom are rich. This was infuriating to the ordinary Egyptians whom I spoke with. Some of them often shouted: "What about the poor? Forget them!" Such disappointment heightened over the past six years of Mubarak's rule due to the haphazardly-run open-market economy policies championed by Prime Minister Ahmed Nazif's government and buttressed by Mubarak's son, Gamal. During those years, which I have witnessed myself, I saw the gap between the haves and have-nots dramatically widen. Community subsidies were slowly eroding. It was easy to buy subsidized bread when I came back from abroad to live in Egypt in 2004, but that had become like fighting a battle in the last three years of Mubarak's rule. All this had led some Egyptian intellectuals and legal experts to predict a revolt of the masses, an eruption similar to that of Tunisia. Hisham El-Bastawisi, a judge who at the time of this writing was considered a presidential hopeful, left his post in 2005 and moved to Kuwait after leading a campaign by judges against the Mubarak regime. In 2008, he wrote about the possibility of a revolution taking place in Egypt against the Mubarak rule. He came back to Egypt in 2011 and joined the anti-Mubarak protest in Tahrir hours before Mubarak's downfall.[9]

Influence of the Tunisian Revolution

If Tahrir Square is the epicenter of the Egyptian revolution, the Tunisian revolution is the epicenter of Arab uprisings. On December 17, 2010, a young Tunisian man named Mohamed Bouazizi set himself on fire after police confiscated the cart which he used to sell his fruit and vegetables to earn a living. His tragedy inflamed ordinary Tunisians, and an uprising broke out leading to the ouster of President Ben Ali after 23 years in power. And the Egyptians were watching closely, to the extent that when I was once walking in a street in downtown Cairo late in December 2010, I heard Egyptians (known for their sense of humor) shouting in laughter: "We should do as the Tunisians did." And, indeed, they did; they followed the path of the Jasmine Revolution.

There is no doubt that the Jasmine Revolution had an agenda-setting effect on Egyptians, but the Tahrir revolution was more powerful and of higher magnitude due to Egypt's strong socio-economic role in the Arab world. The country is also seen as the historical hub of intellectual life in the Arab world. Egypt has a greater strategic weight to the United States and the world than Tunisia, and this echoed well in the words of Tunisian President Moncef Marzouki when he said on May 23, 2012, the day Egypt was holding its post-revolution presidential elections, that Egyptians today "will determine the destiny of the Arab world." Not only did Egypt's eighteen-day liberation battle shake the world, it also inspired

Arabs to follow in its footstep and march for freedom. Once Mubarak stepped down, many Arab states followed the path and attempted to topple their bureaucratic regimes, borrowing many of the slogans coined in Tahrir Square. We began to see protests and "revolutions" erupting in Yemen, Bahrain, Libya, Oman, and Syria, among others. Some Bahrainis even said they want to change the name of their "Pearl Square" to "Tahrir Square." The effect of the Tunisian revolution even spread as far as China, and in late February we saw Chinese going out on the streets in Shanghai to hold their "Jasmine" demonstration.

But we must stress, once again, that Egyptians were galvanized by the Tunisian revolution. From early on, Egyptian protesters cited the Tunisian uprising as an inspiration for their march for freedom. The outcome of Jasmine Revolution was immense; it was an agenda-setter, with the suicide occurrence moving very rapidly from Tunisia to Egypt. After Bouazizi sat himself ablaze, there were reports in Egypt of an increase in the number of Egyptians trying to set themselves on fire. Two days before the revolution broke out, Fathi Sorour, the then-Speaker of the Egyptian Parliament, even asked the People's Assembly's Religious and Social Affairs Committee to discuss the issue. In short, the Tunisian revolution fueled the Egyptian revolt, with the latter greatly influencing the political atmosphere in the broader Arab world. Definitely, said Lewis Greiss, former chief editor of Egypt's *Sabah El-Kheir* magazine, the Arab uprising began in Tunisia but the success of the Egyptian people meant the "winds of change" were felt in the entire Arab world.[10]

The self-immolation of the young Tunisian had huge ramifications in the Arab world, as we began to see similar suicide attempts made by young Arabs, many of whom were living hand to mouth in an undemocratic, despotic environment. Those desperate young people believed that pouring petrol on their bodies and setting it afire was a method to get their message heard and liberate their countries from the "tyranny" of their rulers. They wanted jobs, justice, liberty, and an end to the practice of rigged elections.

Why Tahrir Square?

The January 25 Revolution has turned Tahrir Square into a symbol of unity; it has taught Egyptians—Christians and Muslims—once again that they must stand united and protect each other's rights and beliefs as they have done in the past. To the outside world, Tahrir has become a historic place, an icon of the Egyptian revolution; British Prime Minister David Cameron even asked to visit it during his trip to the Land of the Nile late in February. The U.S. Secretary of State Hillary Clinton, French Foreign Minister Alain Juppé, and Chairman of the U.S. Senate Foreign Relations Committee John Kerry also toured Tahrir in separate trips in March.

In the early days of the revolution, Tahrir Square to me resembled China's Tiananmen Square. The question is: Why Tahrir? Without a doubt, the Square has always had a fascination about it that draws Egyptian and non-Egyptians alike. Now in my mid-forties, I developed a passion for it as a sightseeing place when I was ten and during a school visit to the Egyptian museum located on one of its corner. Ever since, I have became a frequent visitor to the square and the museum, so that every time I was in downtown Cairo I would go and have a look at it and the many captivating, culturally attractive, and intellectually stimulating places located around it. These include the American University in Cairo, established in 1919 and relocated to New Cairo in 2008; the country's biggest government employment body, Mogamma, founded in 1951; the Arab League headquarters; and the Nile Hilton hotel—both established also in the 1950s. Located close to Tahrir are also the Shura (Consultative) Council, People's Assembly, Ministry of Interior, and a number of fancy hotels. In a way, the Square and its neighborhood resemble London's Westminster and Big Ben or the Place de la Concorde in Paris. In short, it is an Egyptian utopia.

The Square has six entrances to major, popular streets. It was first named "Ismailia Square" after the grandson of Mohamed Ali Pasha,[11] Ismail, who served as khedive of Egypt from 1863 to 1879. Khedive Ismail invested deeply to create a luxurious, distinctively modern European-style quarter with a French influence shown in boulevards, gardens and palaces scattered around in what is known today as Garden City; this is where the British and American embassies are located. When Britain occupied Egypt in 1882, it stationed its soldiers at Ismailia Square. The Egyptian Museum was built by a prominent French architect in 1902. After the 1952 coup d'état, which liberated Egypt from British rule, Ismailia Square was renamed Tahrir (Liberation) Square. Since Egypt became a republic, Tahrir has become a center for demonstrators to gather in. When President Anwar Sadat tried in 1977 to lift subsidies on essential products, particularly bread, ordinary Egyptians took over the Square in protest.

Undoubtedly, the sight of teeming masses of Egyptians in Tahrir during the eighteen days of the January 25 Revolution captivated the world. The Square has became a symbol of freedom, pride, patriotism, community, compassion, truth, solidarity, patience, end of corruption, hope for change, and at times even worrisome uncertainty, chaos, and martyrdom. There is today a "Tahrir" in the heart of every young Egyptian. When a major demonstration breaks out in a public square in any part of the world today, inhabitants and journalists sometimes call it a "Tahrir-style demonstration." In that sense, Egypt's Tahrir Square has become more emblematic of protests and revolutionary minds than China's Tiananmen Square.

Egypt's Influence on Arab Culture

Egypt is a huge country—the most populous country in the Arab world and the second-most populous nation in the continent of Africa.[12] Politically and geographically, it has always been the hub of the Arab world and has a strong cultural influence on Arabs; some call it the "Hollywood" of the Arab world. Other Arabs try to imitate Egyptians, sometimes as a form of humor and at other time as a form of admiration. As the popular Egyptian anthropologist Gamal Hamdan wrote in his 1967 Arabic-language masterpiece *Egypt's Personality*, "Egypt is more than just a huge part in the Arab body; it is the head—an influential and inspirational head indeed—and its effective central nerve system."[13] By the roots of its "grandfather," Egypt is "pharaonic" but it is also "Arab" by the name of its "father."[14] Of homogeneous and Hermitic origin, Egyptians have had a powerful influence on Arab literature, with novelist Naguib Mahfouz being the first Arab to win the Nobel Prize for literature. Egyptians have also played a central role in the promotion of various areas in the socio-political fields in the Arab world, including the media, as noted by Mustapha Bakri, a former member of the People's Assembly and chief editor of the weekly paper *Al-Osboa*, in an interview with the state-owned television station Al-Oula.[15]

Abbas El-Tarabilli, a columnist at the daily paper *Alwafd*, described Egyptians as people "with endless patience, but when they revolt they become like a ferocious tsunami rising above all and sweeping away everything; no one can stop it." He cited the 1919 Revolution[16] as an example and spoke of how the British thought that after the Ahmed Urabi 1882 Revolution[17] it would take Egyptians more than half a century to rise again. But they were shocked by the nationalist movement advocated by Mustafa Kamil (1874–1908),[18] and which later culminated in the 1919 Revolution. And that, added El-Tarabelli, is exactly what the Egyptians did on January 25, 2011, after thirty years of oppression. They revolted against tyranny.[19] And, yes, Arabs were watching, to the extent that on the day of Egypt's first post-Mubarak presidential elections the Lebanese newspaper *As-Safir* wrote, in May 2012, that Egyptians are not just voting for a president for their country but "a president for all the Arabs."[20]

America's Reaction

Egypt is considered America's closest partner in the Arab world; it is the second major recipient of U.S. aid—after Israel—receiving some $1.3 billion annually, mostly for military use. Since its signing of the Camp David Accords with

Israel in 1978, the country has received $60 billion in military and development aide. During his three-decade rule, Mubarak was considered a close ally of the United States and he paid an official visit to Washington on an annual basis—except during the younger Bush's second term in office, a change which was seen as a sign of his resentment of Bush's polices in the Middle East. Thus, America was watching developments in the Land of the Nile with closer eyes than it did with the Tunisian revolution.[21]

While the American people showed great encouragement for Egyptian protesters from the moment the revolution erupted on January 25, the U.S. government's stance was somewhat unclear. Washington was prudent in its first observations on the Egyptian uprising; after all, President Obama's relationship with Mubarak—as his Cairo speech on June 4, 2009, had shown—was strong. Hence, some Middle East experts argued that Obama feared taking a stance against Mubarak which he might regret in the future. During the first a few days of protests, the White House's reaction was neutral, urging all sides to refrain from violence. Although the Obama administration called on the Egyptian government and police to respect people's rights for peaceful demonstrations and for a free and democratic system of government, it did not call on Mubarak to resign as protesters demanded.

On the day protests began, the White House stated, "The Egyptian government has an important opportunity to be responsive to the aspirations of the Egyptian people, and pursue political, economic, and social reforms that can improve their lives and help Egypt prosper." In the statement, White House spokesman Robert Gibbs made reference to Obama's speech. "More broadly, what is happening in the region reminds us that, as the President said in Cairo, we have an unyielding belief that all people yearn for certain things: the ability to speak your mind and have a say in how you are governed; confidence in the rule of law and the equal administration of justice; government that is transparent and free of corruption; and the freedom to live as you choose—these are human rights and we support them everywhere."

The U.S. State Department issued a statement on January 25 urging all parties to refrain from violence. "The United States supports the fundamental right of expression and assembly for all people. All parties should exercise restraint, and we call on the Egyptian authorities to handle these protests peacefully." The statement added, "The United States is a partner of Egypt and the Egyptian people in this process, which we believe should unfold in peaceful atmosphere." In a news conference with Spanish Foreign Minister Trinidad Jimenez on the same day, Secretary of State Hillary Clinton said the United States believed Mubarak's government was not under threat. "Our assessment is that the Egyptian government is stable and is looking for ways to respond to the legitimate needs and interests of the Egyptian people," said Clinton. Two days after the demonstrations began, U.S. Vice President Joseph Biden stated that he would not refer to Mubarak as a "dictator." Later, however, the U.S. administration urged the Mubarak government to carry out real reform. From the beginning of February we started to see the Obama administration—as a number of major U.S. dailies reported—united around a "Mubarak-must-go-now" position and the handing of power to a transitional government headed by Vice President Omar Suleiman with the backing of the Egyptian military, including the chief of the armed forces, Lieutenant General Sami Enan, and Field Marshal Mohamed Tantawi, the defense minister. America's most senior foreign policy figure, ex-presidential candidate John McCain, was, nonetheless, the first American politician to call on Mubarak to step down.

On February 1, and minutes after the Egyptian president delivered his second speech, Obama told Mubarak over the phone that he must begin transition of power. "What is clear, and what I indicated tonight to President Mubarak, is my belief that an orderly transition must be meaningful, it must be peaceful and it must begin now," Obama said in a televised address to his nation minutes later. "We have borne witness to the beginning of a new chapter in the history of a great country and a long-time partner of the United States," he said. While noting that "it is not the role of any other country to determine Egypt's leaders," the U.S. President commended the Egyptian military for its restraint in dealing with protesters, stressing that Mubarak had told him that the status quo "is not sustainable." The U.S. President added, "The voices of the Egyptian people tell us that this is one of those moments. This is one of those times."

Obama's televised speech came out after he met with his national security advisors for one hour at the White House on January 29, right following Mubarak's firing of his government and naming his intelligence chief Suleiman as vice president—a post that had been vacant for thirty years. On February 3, Biden spoke by phone to Suleiman, urging that "credible, inclusive negotiations begin immediately in order for Egypt to transition to a democratic government that addresses the aspirations of the Egyptian people." In spite of Washington's support of Suleiman for what it described as his constructive role in the Arab–Israeli peace process, Egyptians rejected him as "another Mubarak." Ordinary Egyptians alleged that he was tough in his dealing with Hamas and pro-Israeli in Mideast peace talks. There were also those who said that Mubarak's appointment of a vice president came too late. On the day Mubarak resigned, Obama observed, "Egyptians have inspired us, and they have done so by putting the lie to the idea that justice is best gained through violence. . . . We must educate our children to become like young Egyptian people."

Egyptian public opinion on America's stance toward the revolution carried mixed signals, between those who praised Washington and those who did not; yet most Egyptians were appreciative of the American people's support for their cause. An Egyptian magazine commented that Obama's statement on February 11 saying Egyptians "have inspired us" suggests that American society has been astonished by the action of Egyptian youth, and that he truly "wants to encourage them. But there is also the possibility that Obama is facing opposition from inside his government and hopes that this will result in a stronger move toward his victory."[22] A fifty-year-old Egyptian told me during the second week of the revolution that he "has an unyielding belief" that the Obama administration did not desire to show that it wanted to force Mubarak out of office. Mubarak, he said, was after all the "stronghold" of U.S. policy in a chaotic Middle East.

Stance of the European Union

Similarly, the European Union was critical of the Mubarak regime and called on Cairo in a statement released on the evening the uprising began to respect the "yearnings" of its people and their "legitimate wish" for change. "Today, thousands of Egyptian citizens have gathered in the streets of Cairo to declare their wish for political change," said the EU Foreign Policy spokeswoman Maja Kocijancic, stressing that Brussels was closely watching the situation in the Egyptian capital. There were, of course, those on both sides who believed that the EU stance toward the Egyptian revolution was not consistent, particularly during the first days of the revolution. The EU did not play a more vital role in the revolution, noted former NATO Secretary General Jaap de Hoop Scheffer in an interview with a Dutch television on February 13. Scheffer stated that while the United States was monitoring things closely, "Europe's position was inconsistent." Later, on March 21, the EU ministers decided to freeze the assets of Mubarak and eighteen of those close by him, including his wife and two sons.

Among the popular quotes made by European leaders on the revolution, and which Egyptians cherished and printed and hung on their doors, are those by the prime minister of Norway, British prime minister, the French president, the Italian president, and the president of Austria. Here is what each of those European leaders said respectively:

"Today, we are all Egyptians." (Jens Stoltenberg)

"We must consider teaching the Egyptian Revolution in schools." (David Cameron)

"France calls on all Egyptians to continue their march towards liberty." (Nicolas Sarkozy)

"Nothing new in Egypt . . . The Egyptians have made history — as usual." (Silvio Berlusconi)

"The people of Egypt are the greatest people on earth, and they deserve a Nobel Prize for Peace." (Heinz Fisher)

Goal of This Book

The fall of the Egyptian regime confused many, even the Egyptians themselves; after all, bringing down a regime in eighteen days should capture media attention across the world. The aim of this book is to cover Egypt's January 25, 2011, Revolution and its aftermath—a period which the author witnessed firsthand. It offers both a chronicle and a critical analysis of the revolution and the major events that erupted thereafter—from Hosni Mubarak's departure to the first eight months of Mohamed Morsi's presidency. It documents the "how" and "why" behind the revolution and tries to define the dimensions of the "Egyptian Dream" and how it can be accomplished. To be more concise, the book performs a discursive analysis of public opinion as expressed in the Egyptian media; and it presents and analyzes what the Egyptian media tell us about Egyptian public opinion on the revolution. In doing so, we draw on viewpoints from the growing diverse Egyptian media and commentaries by various distinguished political analysts and journalists in Egypt. The time period which this book examines is roughly two years—a couple of days from the time the revolution erupted on January 25, 2011, to late in February of 2013 when President Mohamed Morsi pushed forward the date of the start of parliamentary elections. Throughout the book, and since Egypt under Mubarak was America's stalwart ally in the Arab world, the text also touches on American–Egyptian relations and the question of whether Egyptians can achieve their dream of establishing a stable democratic state without U.S. economic assistance or "U.S. meddling" in their country's internal affairs. When using the word "media" we basically mean Arabic newspapers, magazines, television, radio, and the Internet. At times we use the word "press" to figuratively refer to the media as a whole. Similarly, when the terms "press" and "journalism" are used, they refer to both print and broadcast media. Furthermore, the book examines how coverage of major events by Egypt's privately-owned (independent) and partisan (opposition) press differed from the state-owned (national) press and played an essential role at times in uniting Egyptians during and after the revolution.

Under Mubarak, as we have stated above, Egypt was America's stalwart ally in the Arab world and the momentous events in Egypt raise questions about the future of U.S.-Egyptian ties—a topic which we will also try to touch on in the book. A naturalized U.S. citizen of Egyptian descent, in 2004 I returned to the

North African state, a nation whose future is of vital importance to the Arabs and Africans. And there was nothing easy about being a writer in Egypt at the time Arab uprisings (Arab Spring) began because the startling speed of events in the region left one flooded with information. During the early months of 2011, one felt that there was a "plague of revolutions" in the Arab world. "Yesterday it was Tunisia, today Egypt, and tomorrow Libya and then Yemen," that is how one Egyptian summarized to me in mid-March of that year the winds of change that were sweeping the region at the time. No one could have forecasted that uprisings and revolutions would spread so quickly in the Arab world—not just in Libya but in Yemen, Bahrain, Oman, Syria, Morocco, Jordan, and Algeria. This book also touches on the repercussions of these seismic political changes in the Arab world on stability and peace in the Middle East and how the West should deal with them.

In conclusion, I wish to draw the attention of the reader that Friday is the beginning of the Muslim weekend where Muslims are required to go out for the noon prayer at mosques, so it should be of no surprise that many of the major protests and events that took place, and which this book discusses in details, were held on Fridays—such as the "Friday of Anger," "Friday of Departure," "Friday of Victory," and "Friday of Purification." Furthermore, most of Mubarak's speeches and statements were often delivered on Fridays. It is also important to cite here that all the individuals and media channels we refer to in the book are Egyptians; or else we state their background and ownership. The book consists of two parts and a total of eleven chapters, with Chapter 1 serving as an introduction and Chapter 11 as a conclusion. Part I has five chapters and focuses on the revolution; Part II is formed of four chapters and covers the revolution's aftermath. Below is a summary of the book's chapters.

Chapter 2 tackles the pivotal role the social media played in the success of the revolution and how the tech-savvy youth of Egypt—like their counterpart in Tunisia—organized their protests via digital platforms, from Facebook and Twitter to the video-sharing Website YouTube. It also offers an overview of the shape and structure of Egypt's three different media systems and how they generally covered the series of episodes that took place during the eighteen-day revolution, and thereafter. Chapter 3 examines the events of Friday January 28—the Friday of Anger—a day that Egyptians would never forget, a day in which mass protests swept the country and violent clashes erupted. Riot police used rubber bullets, water cannons, and tear gas to disperse crowds in Tahrir Square but there were later reports of use of life ammunition. In face of heavy attacks from police and members of the State Security Intelligence Agency (SSIA), anti-regime protesters used stones to defend themselves. Others spoke of being trapped in battles with police for four hours on the renowned Qasr El-Nil Bridge located on one side of Tahrir Square. These clashes broke out not just in Tahrir but in many parts of the Egyptian capital. The chapter also looks at how the Mubarak regime tried to disseminate the conspiracy theory in the fabric of the Egyptian society, claiming that "foreign elements" were behind the protests.[23] Protesters, on the other side, accused the regime of releasing prisoners on that day to terrorize them.

The hard-hitting day of looting and vandalism was Saturday January 29, and Chapter 4 focuses on the state of disorder that engulfed the country following police withdrawal. In it, we try to record Egyptians' feelings and reactions to that environment of chaos by analyzing news materials published or broadcast on the couple of days that followed. Chapter 5 examines the hours-long violent clashes between pro- and anti-Mubarak government supporters at Tahrir Square on Wednesday February 2, a day which is often referred to among Egyptians as "Black Wednesday" or "Battle of the Camel." That Egyptian-against-Egyptian battle—in which thugs entered the Square mounted on camels and horses attacking protesters with sticks, stones, and knives—left many killed and injured.

Chapter 6 unveils the state of euphoria—the clapping, yelling, and cheering—that overwhelmed Egyptians following the demise of Mubarak on February 11, together with the state of fear echoed by some who saw their country without a ruler for the first time in five thousand years. On that evening, the author went out on the streets of Benha and saw how some Egyptian men were sitting in coffee shops celebrating and enchanting "God bless Egypt" and offering each other hot drinks. But there was also that sense of bewilderment on the faces of some; yes, there was that fear about the future. Chapter 7, on the other hand, examines the constitutional referendum of March 19 and the fierce debates that erupted on whether the Egyptian Constitution should be amended or a new one be written altogether since, they argued, amending the constitution was not enough because it was the brainchild of an "autocrat" and thus needed to be abolished.

Chapter 8 covers the trial of the deposed President Mubarak and his two sons on August 3, and how their stand behind bars shocked the eyes of Egyptians and the world over. It documents how the Egyptian media recorded the extraordinary scene both in images and in the written word. Chapter 9 is on the presidential debate that was held on May 10, 2012, between presidential hopefuls Amr Moussa and Abdel Moneim Aboul Fotouh. It offers a thorough analysis and examination of the issues raised in the debate and how each candidate's views on them were. Chapter 10 records how the public received the victory of Morsi as Egypt's first, post-revolution civilian president. It examines whether or not public opinion was satisfied with the result at a time clouded by suspicion of SCAF's role and fear by liberals of Islamists rising to power. Chapter 11 serves as a conclusion, offering a broad analysis of what we found in the book and how a healthy political system that insures people's rights could mean for Egypt—and the Arab world—if achieved. The author ruminates over Egypt's future, the obstacles the country will face, and are facing, and the tools needed to overcome them. We tackle the issue of tension in U.S.–Egyptian relations as a result of Egyptians' intrusion into the U.S. embassy in Cairo in September 2012 due to a U.S.-produced film which Muslims viewed as blasphemes to their religion. We also offer an analysis of the main challenges that Morsi faced in his first eight months in office, particularly the protests which began in early December of 2012 and were still continuing when this book was completed in late February of 2013. Demonstrators are calling for his downfall because his accumulation of power, which seems hardly different from previous regimes, and because of the controversial amendments to the draft constitution which Egyptians say were imposed on them.

One should mention here that at the conclusion of each chapter I try when possible to inject a piece of Egyptian humor, because Egyptians have long been famous among the Arabs for their gripping sense of humor—particularly at times of crises. Yes, Egyptians' sense of humor is the most sophisticated among Arabs and skits about the revolution and parodies were often echoed in the media. So, be prepared for a smile, for a piece of political humor, at the end of some of the book's chapters.

PART ONE: THE REVOLUTION

CHAPTER 2. SOCIAL MEDIA: TWEETING THE TURMOIL

Egyptian protesters and revolutionaries skillfully used cyber technology in getting their message out and gathering momentum in their struggle to topple the Hosni Mubarak regime during the January 2011 Revolution. They were well-organized and used the immensely popular social-networking website Facebook as their operation room, the center from which they raised the spirit of their cause. And they did it so well and so skillfully that no one could have ever anticipated it, including those who were living close by them. A large amount of materials such as videos and photos came in to the mainstream Egyptian media from Tahrir Square—and from many parts of Egypt—over the Internet via Twitter and Facebook. The Mubarak government and the ruling National Democratic Party (NDP) did not realize, as some experts argued, the "power of the Facebook youth, or what we now call the 'Facebook State,' which has managed to bring down the government of [Prime Minister Ahmed] Nazif in a couple of days, because those youth felt it was a government of businessmen who did not feel the pulse of the public and of limited income individuals."[24] This is the first revolution in Egypt's history in which technology plays a crucial role, said Mohamed Hasseinein Heikel, a distinguished journalist who served as advisor to President Gamal Abdel Nasser, in an interview with the privately owned Egyptian satellite TV station "Dream" on the day of Mubarak's downfall.

This book consists of two parts. Part I tackles the pivotal role the social media played in igniting and organizing the revolution. Part II offers an overview of the structure of the Egyptian media, which we believe will assist the reader in comprehending media coverage of the series of episodes that took place during the eighteen-day revolution, and thereafter.

Social Media

New media technologies—social media, blogging, mobile news—and all participatory forms of journalism made it possible for the Tunisian and Egyptian revolutions and for ensuing Arab uprisings to take place. Social networking avenues have become icons of uprising. The capability of the web to mobilize support for the January 25 Revolution was enormous. From the moment protests began in Egypt, they received significant attention on blogs, Facebook, and Twitter; they were symptomatic of the social media generation. Activists used social networks and text messages to organize the protests; they blogged about the future of freedom in their homeland. Egypt is ranked at the top of social networking users in the Arab world, with close to nine million Facebook users and one million on Twitter.[25] According to Naila Hamdy, a journalism professor at the American University in Cairo, the country has a "unique and distinctive" blogosphere which has been effective in engaging the public in debates.[26] A generation of youth, which Egyptian actor Hamdi Ahmed described as tech-savvy, "surprised" the billionaires in government and the NDP with their grouping via SMS messages.[27] These tech-savvy youth did it via digital platforms, from Facebook and Twitter to the video-sharing website YouTube. To disperse police, they cunningly advertized on the social media their January 25 protest marches in twenty different places around Cairo. Security forces knew about the protests but said that they expected only a few hundreds of demonstrators, similar to what had taken place in April 2008, but they were shocked when they found hundreds of thousands of demonstrators gathered in Tahrir Square, let alone those on the streets of other major Egyptian cities, particularly in Suez. Security police must had been unaware that Internet use in Egypt had dramatically risen over the past two years, reaching 23 million in 2010,[28] and this has resulted in an increase in people's digital connectivity.

If technology is taking over the mainstream Egyptian media, social media are changing the face of the journalism industry—what the head of Al-Jazeera English Online labeled as a new "journalism ecosystem."[29] The digital media outlets have empowered Egyptian and Arab protesters and offered them a voice for political participation, while they have also been viewed as "enemies" by some Arab autocratic regimes. Within this context, one can argue that the Egyptian revolution is the outcome of the Internet age; the will of the cyber generation was strong in changing the political map in the Land of the Nile. Egypt is considered the fastest growing country in terms of Internet users in the Middle East and

North Africa, with its websites viewed as the most professional in the region. The majority of Egyptians use the Internet for e-mailing and social networking purposes.[30] Mumtaz El-Kot, chief editor of the state-owned *Akhbar El-Yom* newspaper, claims that Egypt is among the top five countries in the world in terms of Internet users, Facebook, Twitter, and other forms of social media and exchange-of-information vehicles.[31] In his doctoral dissertation, Ahmed Samir Hammad of Egypt's Al-Azhar University studied the dimensions of Arab networking by examining the activities of over one hundred Arabic-language social networking groups on Facebook, Myspace, Yahoo, among others. He found that Arab social networking showed strong adherence to prominent global issues of cultural values—such as freedom, democracy, human rights—and practical values such as the ability to build a cooperative society founded on social participation.[32]

With police forces defecting on January 28, the Mubarak government decided to cut off the country's Internet connection for five days (it was restored on February 2), but in important respects in the cyber age connectivity cannot be stopped. During the Internet shutdown, the mobile industry boomed to such an extent that when I went to charge my mobile I found that the cost had shot higher.[33] The country's mobile networks were also severely disrupted—if not brought down altogether on a couple of days at least, especially on January 28, known as the "Friday of Anger." Text messaging services were down. The government's order to shut down Internet access was criticized by world leaders and by social networking giants and rights groups. Attempts to help protesters connect and pass their message across were made, with Telecomix—which is formed of a global community of online activists—offering Internet connection to Egypt via a dial up number. Google's SayNow and Twitter teamed up and created a Speak-to-Tweet service which gave protesters a voice by letting them use phones to leave voice mail messages that automatically generated Twitter messages. And, yes, I heard of Egyptians using those services. In that sense, and from what I witnessed, one can argue that the Internet blackout and disruption of mobile services led Egyptians to be more determined in their mission of bringing down the Mubarak regime. It also resulted in Egyptians seeking more news from Arabic-language satellite television stations—particularly Al-Jazeera, Al-Arabia, Abu Dhabi, BBC Arabic, and France24—which offered their viewers reliable images of embattled protesters. Newspapers also managed to print, though there was a bit of delay, with reporters using other communications means to deliver their stories to their editorial rooms. Emad Eddin Hussein wrote in the privately-owned paper *Al-Shorouk Al-Jadeed* on January 29 that the government thought that "because we had gotten used to produce and receive all materials for our newspapers via e-mail, we would not be able to put our papers to bed. Yes, they succeeded in delaying our work, but we did produce our papers with journalists using faxes and telephones to deliver their materials to us." He wondered for how long the government would shut down the Internet and disrupt Mobile services, an act which he denounced as a sign of weakness. "The government feels that it is actually threatened," added Hussein, and "its behavior exhibits that it is truly failing.[34] Magd Khadr criticized the three mobile phone providers in Egypt (Mobinil, Etisalat, and Vodafone) for shutting down their services during the "early days of the revolution," and he accused the businessmen who own them of siding with the Mubarak regime.[35]

The fierce clashes that erupted on January 28 were, in many ways, between a generation of social networking and police using tear gas. The seeds of change sprouted quickly in the Arab world and they persisted with the help of the social media, which also helped Arab protesters to garner support from the international community. The power that the social media showed in strengthening protesters' voice and promoting the revolution was enormous. Everyone around me was telling each other of things he or she had read on Facebook. Whenever I went on the Internet, everyone was twitter-tattling about the Egyptian revolution, with some calling it the uprising of the Facebook–Twitter generation. Thus, the social media were used as tools against oppression and despotism, with protesters posting updates and footage of their demonstrations on their blogs, together with news and editorials from the world media. Or as Yousra Zahran of *Al-Fagr* mockingly put it, "Mubarak did political activists in Egypt the greatest service: The Internet."[36] Political commentator Rafaat El-Said wrote on March 12 in the state-owned paper *Al-Ahram* that many Arab rulers never thought that that growing blogging community could "penetrate the walls of silence" and get its message to the public. "But the popular revolution came from where they never thought; it crawled to them from windows that could not be shut." El-Said further cautioned Arab rulers, "This lesson will be repeated, so those who remain in power should take note."[37]

The "Facebook Revolution"

Undoubtedly, Facebook has become an arena for the expression of Egyptian youth's demands to end political corruption and show pain for their lost ones in the January Revolution. Many believe that it was Facebook which helped in accelerating the momentum of the revolution with 80,000 people saying they would attend the protests at Tahrir on January 25. "Via Facebook and the Internet, the youth of the Egyptian governorates managed to group together in masses on January 25," said Galal Amin, a professor of economics at the American University in Cairo (AUC).[38] The January Revolution is not the product of television programs but of "Facebook," asserted Hussein Amin, an AUC mass communications professor.[39] And one can only agree with the two AUC professors, because wherever one went during the eighteen days of the revolution, he saw the word "Facebook" written on signs and street walls and tee-shirts. As a column in the state paper *Al-Gomhuria* proclaimed, Facebook was certainly the "main instigator" of the January Revolution.[40] "Praise to the Facebook youth," cried a column in the party paper *Alwafd* immediately following Mubarak's ouster.[41] When Essam Sharaf was appointed as prime minister in mid-March in place of Ahmed Shafiq, Mubarak's last prime minister, he said he would connect with Egyptian youth via Facebook. The youth of Facebook and satellite television had a different culture, a modernized one that prefers connecting with the world.[42] Hisham El-Bastawisi, an anti-Mubarak judge who later ran for the presidency, believes that Facebook did not "ignite" the revolution but "helped in its organization" by being a medium for its groups to post information about times and dates of protests.[43]

The influence of Facebook is "strong," cautioned Hossam Fahmi, a professor of computer engineering at the Cairo-based, state-owned Ain Shams University. "Those at Tahrir Square and at other Egyptian squares should take their steps carefully and only cry out what they feel and not what others feel." There are 17 million Internet users in Egypt, according to Fahmi. Facebook has over 450 million members worldwide, with 3.5 million of them in Egypt.[44] As of late February 2011, Facebook had more than 500 million users and Twitter, the microblogging site, had more than 80 million users, making the former a much bigger and better-organized group. Many of Egypt's anti-Mubarak groups, such as the April 6 Movement (named after the April 6 protest it organized in 2008),[45] began on Facebook.[46]

By late afternoon of January 25, there were reports that Facebook had been blocked in Egypt, something which the Egyptian government denied. There were also reports that evening that other social networking groups had been blocked. A day later, the April 6 Movement urged Egyptians "to carry on with what we began on January 25." The group asked its Facebook members to connect and continue with their protests via Twitter and Flickr, a photo-sharing site, until their demands were met.

Another powerful public group on Facebook is called *Kulluna Khaled Said* (Arabic for "We Are All Khaled Said"). In June 2010, Egyptians were infuriated by the images of the disfigured corpse of twenty-eight-year-old Khaled Said, an Egyptian from Alexandria who was allegedly beaten to death in the street by Egyptian police. The graphic images of his "brutal death" shocked the nation. Thirty-year-old Google Middle East executive Wael Ghonim created the Facebook group, which contributed to the growing discontent toward the police and government prior to the January Revolution.[47] Other Egyptian opposition groups said to have employed social networking sites, particularly Facebook, include the Popular Democratic Movement for Change, Justice and Freedom Youth, Association for Change, and the Revolutionary Socialists. Even the Supreme Council of the Armed Forces (SCAF) established a page on Facebook on February 18, donating it as a gift to the "Egyptian youth" of the January 25 Revolution. There were roughly 70,000 visitors to the SCAF page on the day it was founded. An alternative media Facebook page called the "Ten Minutes News," which was launched shortly before the revolution and focused on issues it claimed the mainstream media did not cover well, has given a voice to youth, centering on issues relating to the revolution such as presenting a photo documentary of the bombing of the Two Saints Church (or "Al-Qidisayn Church" in Arabic) in Alexandria on the New Year's Eve of Egypt's Copts, which some following the revolution claimed was the work of the minister of interior.

To sum up, the social media have empowered Egyptian protesters in their struggle to liberate their nation from oppressive rule, particularly after realizing that it was all too possible in the tiny state of Tunisia. They were asking: "If they were able to do it, so can we." We have the same social media they used to group together. And the Egyptians did it, followed by the Libyans. Like the Mubarak government, the Gadhafi regime shut down the Internet for weeks. People in all parts of the Arab world were tweeting messages and becoming more frequent users of Facebook either to get informed or organize similar protests. There were protests in Syria, Bahrain, Yemen, Algeria, and Morocco. On March 5, the pan-Arab satellite television station Al-Arabiya even reported that members of the Iraqi cabinet, which had faced protests from Iraqis demanding better standard of living and an end to corruption, had established their pages on Facebook. At around the same time, a campaign on Facebook called for demonstrations to be held in front of Egypt's State Security Intelligence Agency (SSIA) building to demand the abolition of the notorious agency. The social media were also means for protesters camping with laptops at Tahrir[48] to know what was going on in their neck of the woods, be it a visit by a popular singer, actor, or poet, or even a couple deciding to hold their wedding at Tahrir. On February 6, a young couple of the protesters—twenty-eight-year-old Ahmed Zafraan and twenty-two-year-old Ola Abdel Hamid—got married at Tahrir. Protesters first heard about this story of their fellow couples getting married via Facebook and Twitter, and suddenly the young couple became celebrities among the thousands of people at Tahrir, with people all over Egypt speaking of them. "They sure have courage to celebrate their wedding at Tahrir," a senior woman told me in surprise. A young man, laughing, said: "Not a bad way to cut these ugly skyrocketing wedding costs." This sense of humor was often shown during this tumultuous time. For example, following the constitutional referendum of March 19 a "Fingers of Democracy" page was opened on Facebook, with over 5,000 participants showing photos of their fingers colored with phosphoric ink—a sign that an individual had voted. In the past, Egyptian rarely went to vote because they believed results were decided in advance, with members of the NDP always winning.[49] On March 11, I saw a colored poster on Facebook containing pictures of members of the Mubarak regime who were under arrest or charged with fraud. They were dressed like a football team with Mubarak placed at the top with the title "Team of Corruption." Written on the chest of each one was the amount of money he has (or rather stole), with all figures stated in billions of dollars. Mubarak is placed as the "chief executive" with the sum of $70 billion.

Egyptian Media

The Egyptian press constitutionally serves as the Fourth State after the executive, legislative, and judicial branches. The broadcast media have always been government owned, with radio being established in 1934 and television in 1960. Over the past decade we have begun to see, however, the emergence of privately-owned television stations. Until the 1952 coup d'état, which declared Egypt a Republic a year later, newspapers and magazines under the monarchy system[50] were owned by individuals. Egyptian newspapers are rich, advanced, and diverse; they have a history that stretches over a century: *Al-Ahram*, for example, was established in 1876. Currently, there are three types of newspapers: 1) national (state owned), 2) party (opposition), and 3) independent (privately owned). Almost all Egyptian magazines are owned by the government. The national press is owned by the Higher Press Council, created by President Anwar Sadat in 1975, and is chaired by the Speaker of the partially-elected Shura (Arabic for "Consultative") Council. In that sense, the Shura Council holds all ownership rights of the state owned press.

The Higher Press Council has the authority to endorse or reject applications for licenses of new publications and is seen as a tool by which the president and its ruling party—NDP, since Sadat's time—can exercise pressure on publications and journalists for self-regulation and censorship. It has over a dozen members on its board, each serving a four-year renewable term.[51] An Egyptian president holds, nonetheless, the authority to appoint board chairpersons of national press establishments, observed Lewis Greiss, former chief editor of *Sabah El-Kheir* magazine. Since Sadat's time, the Egyptian press has continued to operate on the same pattern "with a few changes here and there."[52] Party newspapers are owned by political parties with their coverage being critical of government since they express the views of their political parties which have been founded in opposition to the NDP. The Party newspapers were founded decades ago (*Al-Ahrar* and *Alwafd* were established in 1977 and 1984 respectively); while the oldest independent newspaper, *El-Dostour*, was launched in 1995.[53] The government does not have the power to appoint board chairpersons or editors-in-chief of party and independent papers the way it does with the national press. Party and independent newspapers make their profit from advertising and distribution, with the distinguished independent paper *Al-Masry Al-Youm* distributing up to 600,000 copies daily.[54] Independent newspapers, unlike party ones which tend to be staunch anti-government in their tone, are independent in their coverage and often focus on corruption and social injustice. *El-Youm El-Sabaa* is a prominent independent daily newspaper which began printing in mid-2011.[55] Prior to 2009, Egypt had nine major state-owned press establishments: Al-Ahram, Akhbar El-Yom, Al-Tahrir, Al-Hilal, Rosa El-Yossef, Al-Maarif, Al-Taawin, El-Shaab/October, and Middle East News Agency. In May 2009, the Shura Council issued a decree to merge one or two of those press establishments with the two massive Al-Ahram and Akhbar El-Yom. The country has up to half a dozen of state television stations that broadcast news and a number of privately owned ones.

Restrictions on the press in the North African state come through a combination of laws issued over the past half a century. When President Gamal Abdel Nasser nationalized the press in 1960, he issued a press law, known as the Press Organization Law, which made owners of newspapers and magazines the board chiefs of their publications. It stated that no newspaper could be published without permission of the country's sole political organization, known then as the National Union and renamed the Arab Socialist Union in 1962.[56] The Nasser government rejected those who said that what it had done was to nationalize the private press.[57] At that time, wrote eighty-two-year-old Greiss in March 2011, "we lived under the umbrella of a press law" that granted the Arab Socialist Union ownership of news publications. An individual was installed at each news establishment whose task was to monitor what was published. But President Sadat, he added, placed that responsibility on the editors-in-chief. There was an office at the country's ministry of information (which the January 25 Revolution dissolved)[58] from which recommendations from the Egyptian president were sent to the editors-in- chief. From that time on, President Mubarak placed the burden of the press and the media as a whole on the shoulders of seventy-eight-year-old Safwat El-Sherif, who had served as media minister for two decades before he was appointed secretary-general of the NDP. Mubarak, concluded Greiss, called on his media minister to allow "some freedom" to the print media but to "tighten censorship" on television and radio, because he believed people did not read newspapers as much as they watched television.[59] In short, a harsh penal code, a press law, and a publication law, together with an emergency law enacted in 1981 after Sadat's assassination, had blocked press freedom in the country under Mubarak's rule.[60]

State (National) Media

The way state media covered the eighteen days of protests—from January 25 to February 11—was in many ways disappointing; they were tools of relentless government propaganda with state television claiming that the protests were organized by outside forces.

State broadcast and print media offered an entirely different view, overlooking the large number of demonstrators and showing nothing of the events that documented police brutality. They were utterly pro-government. In the opinion of Professor Hussein Amin, the "Egyptian media were liberated on February 11 but their performance from January 25 to February 4 could be described as shameful; it will remain a mark of disgrace for us." After that day, the media slowly began to return to their right path in covering events, reaching the level of "complete freedom after February 11," added Amin.[61] The state media had been supportive of the corrupt government, and they—television in particular—continue to be pro-corruption, stressed Mohsen Radi, a former member of the Egyptian Parliament who represented the Muslim Brotherhood, in a meeting held in the Egyptian city of Benha on March 16. At the same meeting, Mohamed Mustapha of the anti-Mubarak Kifaya Movement said the "media have played a role in the state of division we face today." Writer Mohamed Barakah criticized the head of news at the state television, Mohamed El-Menawi, for keeping the cameras away from the "battlefield" on Qasr El-Nil Bridge (located on one side of Tahrir Square) on February 28. With a passion for "romanticism," Barakah mockingly wrote, the cameras of state television focused on "Qasr El-Nil during sunset when there is quietness, romanticism, and a strayed ray from the primary places it last kissed on the River Nile." He further criticized popular evening programs, such "Misr El-Naharda" (Arabic for "Egypt Today"), for inviting mostly Mubarak supporters to go on the air. He said that State broadcast and television stations are "scary media" that cannot function without directions. Barakah added that the solution would be to push aside all their current directors and chairpersons and replace them with skilled people from the second and third generation. "It is only then that the lies of Egyptian broadcast and television stations will vanish."[62]

During the first week of the revolution, or rather until the "Black Wednesday" clashes of February 2, state television and broadcast stations aimed mostly to please the regime and not offer their audience a fair and objective coverage. On the days that followed the upsurge of the revolution, a number of journalists at state television resigned. They rejected as false the feeling of stability in the country conveyed by state television stations, which rarely aired images of clashes between police and protesters or of security police beating protesters. They were laboriously trying to show that it was the anti-Mubarak demonstrators who were causing trouble. Alas, the state media offered little coverage of the protests or police violence against unarmed civilian protesters. We rarely saw, heard, or read of an Egyptian demonstrator being injured or killed. Instead, the state media were a strong voice of government, a propaganda tool of the Mubarak regime and the NDP. Such biased reporting deeply angered protesters that on the last days of the revolution they marched to the massive, Cairo-based radio and television building (known as Maspero building) and threatened to demolish it but the army intervened. On Saturday, January 29, and a day after Mubarak's speech, I went out to buy a number of national, party, and independent newspapers since the Internet was shut down and the only news I was getting was from television. I found at the newsstand I regularly go to that most major daily independent papers (such as *Al-Masry Al-Youm*, *El-Dostour*, and *Al-Shorouk Al-Jadeed*) and the party *Alwafd* paper were sold out; while state-owned ones were lying in piles. I did not see or hear anyone asking for the national press. I spent a couple of hours visiting newsstands looking for independent papers and *Alwafd* until I was able to get them. On the days that followed, independent papers, particularly *Al-Masry Al-Youm*, were also sold out fast.

Partisan Press

The Egyptian Constitution forms of Egypt a multi-party system. Up until 1976, the NDP was the single legal party in the country; it owned all major political newspapers. In 1977, President Sadat issued a law that permitted separate political parties to be established, and this allowed for possible changes in the structure of the press. A political party was granted the right to issue one or more newspaper without restrictions on gaining permissions as was the case with the privately-owned newspapers. Political parties and their papers view themselves as opposition parties and papers; they uphold certain ideologies, although under Mubarak their criticism of government was hardly visible. Thus since Mubarak stepped down and the constitutional amendments were made on March 19, many have spoken about the future of political parties. The head of New Wafd Party, El-Sayed El-Badawi, proclaimed on March 13 that the revolution has brought down the legitimacy of many things, including political parties.[63] Prior to the revolution, Egypt had over twenty political opposition parties with four of them considered main ones. Besides the three main parties, which we discuss below in more detail, there was also the Muslim Brotherhood that was banned under Mubarak. In April 2011, and after the SCAF introduced the

Political Party Law which makes it easier for parties to form, the Muslim Brotherhood was re-launched and renamed Freedom and Justice Party. Mubarak's three-decade ruling NDP was dissolved by a judicial decree on April 16 and its assets transferred to the government. Other political parties were established and about forty parties are in operation today, with some gaining rapid acclaim such as the secular Free Egyptians Party. The Freedom and Justice Party, along with other Islamist parties, will gain more votes, though, because the majority of Egyptians sympathize with the "oppression" they experienced under Mubarak's rule. This same argument—that Islamist political parties will win—can be applied to many other Arab states if free elections are to be held, as we have seen in Tunisia, for example. But one can also argue that the misguided and unsophisticated political decisions taken by leaders of Islamist parties in the future will weaken their standing and their public support.

The three key opposition political parties are New Wafd Party, Arab Nasserist Party, and the National Progressive Unionist Party (often referred to as "Tagammu" Party). The New Wafd Party, which publishes the daily *Alwafd* (The Delegation) newspaper, is a powerful opposition party that embraces liberal nationalist policies that somewhat represents the upper class of the Egyptian society. The New Wafd Party was first founded as the voice of Saad Zaghlul's Wafd Party in 1918 but was abolished after the 1952 Revolution.[64] It was re-established in 1983 under the name of the New Wafd. Coverage of the January revolution by *Alwafd* was, in my view, on equal footage with major independent papers such as *Al-Masry Al-Youm*, *El-Dostour*, and *Al-Shorouk Al-Jadeed*, though some have questioned its coverage in the months that followed and the claim that the Party allied itself with the Freedom and Justice Party to gain seats in the parliamentary elections.[65] The Arab Nasserist Party was founded in 1992 and launched its weekly paper *Al-Arabi* (The Arab) a year later. It had published several articles in the past about the political future of President Mubarak's son, forty-six-year-old Gamal, who was then believed to be in training to succeed his father. The Party, which derives its main ideas from the Nasserite political, social, and economic experience, embraces a revolutionary concept at times. It sees any deviation from these ideas in politics a matter of betrayal. Yet it does not neglect the deep changes that Egypt has experienced since Nasser's death. In the 2005 elections, the Party failed to win any of the 454 seats in the People's Assembly. The National Progressive Unionist Party is a leftist party and publishes the weekly paper *Al-Ahali* (The People). Prior to its current title, it was named the Progressive National Unionist Party. Its principles are founded on those which the 1952 Revolution promoted—supporting workers' rights and protecting social welfare programs. The Party boycotted the 2005 presidential elections and won only two seats in the legislative elections held in the same year.

From time to time, Egypt's main political parties stood in confusion during the eighteen days of protests and were unable to form a united stance. They even abandoned their parties' buildings during the protests; youth loyal to them went in disdain and opened some of them by force. With a sense of disappointment in the leaders of their parties, some youth used the buildings as centers for treating those injured at the protests. As Professor Galal Amin emphasized, during the Mubarak regime, political parties operated "under its wings."[66] Political parties—such as Wafd, Tagammu, Arab Nasserist—were weak, said Anwar Abdel Malk, a renowned political analyst and historian.[67] There were no active political parties on the streets but for the NDP—and those who benefitted from supporting it and its open market economies, as was stressed by Aisha Rateb (who had served as a minister of social affairs during President Sadat).[68]

But how will parties be formed now and on what bases? How will they gain their funding? These are questions that continue to occupy the minds of many Egyptian intellectuals, particularly after SCAF cancelled in late March government subsidies to political parties which had been in effect since 1979. In the law issued, SCAF also made it much easier for political parties to be established but not on religious or sectarian grounds. It will probably take political parties a few years to establish themselves and make their agendas known among ordinary people.

Those that are most likely to be popular and able to compete to some extent with the Muslim Brotherhood are the New Wafd Party, Arab Nasserist Party, and the National Progressive Unionist Party, and new ones such as the Free Egyptians Party as we have seen from the results of parliamentary elections that began in late November.

Independent Media

Independent Egyptian newspapers such as *Al-Masry Al-Youm*, *El-Dostour*, *El-Youm El-Sabaa*, and *El-Shorouk Al-Jadeed* offered, in my opinion, good coverage of the revolution—though there were slight differences among them, with *El-Dostour* ranking at the top. Of the country's many popular privately-owned television stations—such as Al-Hayat, Al-Mehwar, Dream 2—some were accused of exaggerating in their coverage; others were said to be utterly pro-government and hiding the truth the same way state television did. With the exception of ONTV, owned by Egyptian telecommunication billionaire Naguib Sawiris—I saw private television stations offering less voice to the embattled protesters than anticipated. Arabic satellite stations such Al-Jazeera and Al-Arabiya, France24, BBC Arabic, and Al-Hurra were showing police attacks on civilians while most Egyptian state-owned and privately-owned television stations ignored that. ONTV did, in my view, cover it better than any other Egyptian television, state- or privately-owned, but we later (in the second half of 2011) saw the rise of unique TV stations such as Al-Nahar and Al-Tahrir which have attracted many Egyptians with their balanced coverage in the post-Mubarak period, particularly its criticism of SCAF's handling of the subsequent protests.[69]

It is worth mentioning here that the battle in the airwaves between Egypt's highly established channels, such as ONTV and Dream 2, and pan-Arab satellite stations, such as Al-Jazeera and Al-Arabiya, was fierce at times. Al-Jazeera (and Al-Hurra), according to writer and author Mohamed Safaa Amer, covered the events in an objective manner.[70] However, one can argue, and judging from what he recorded, that both the Qatari station and Al-Arabiya's quote of the number of casualties was questionable at times, particularly by comparison to the numbers given by BBC Arabic and France24. While Al-Jazeera's coverage was in many cases welcomed by Egyptians who saw the Qatari station as offering the "true face of the story," others labeled it as "sensational" and "inflammatory," a station that embraces "yellow journalism."[71] The Qatari station said, for example, that Sawiris and his brother left Egypt. The telecom tycoon, who is highly respected among Egyptians for the charity work he provides inside and outside of Egypt, denied that. Speaking from Cairo, Sawiris said, "Al-Jazeera broadcast news about me departing Egypt merely to provoke people." The Qatari station is trying to "divide" Arabs, said one Egyptian in an interview with Nile News on January 31. Essam Kamel of *Al-Ahrar* claimed on the same day that in covering the protests the Qatari station "place poison in the honey" by overlooking the "positive" aspects of the youth protests and focusing instead on the "negative." It produced an "artificial and distorted picture of the Egyptian society."[72] Ali Ibrahim, chief editor of *Al-Gomhuria*, claimed that Al-Jazeera "did not stick to objectivity in its coverage of the 'boiling' events in Egypt. Al-Jazeera is not an objective pan-Arab television station but a mouthpiece of Qatar's foreign policy. He further accused it of promoting American foreign policy in the region.[73] Al-Jazeera did, however, receive the acclaim of many Egyptians and coverage in the independent press was supportive of it. Protesters at Tahrir, said Zahran, shouted on February 6: "Viva Al-Jazeera." She praised the station for backing political change in the Arab world. While the state television stations were showing pictures of street traffic running normal; the pan-Arab station was showing "images of angry protesters and dead bodies at the autopsy room." This, stressed Zahran, angered the Mubarak regime that the state-run satellite NileSat decided on January 27 to suspend its broadcasting with the minister of information issuing a decision three days later to shut down all its offices in Egypt.[74] Only the Al-Jazeera English-language television station was left in operation. In spite of that, up to a dozen of Arabic-language television channels offered to carry the content of Al-Jazeera's Arabic channel. Al-Jazeera journalists were also reported to have been briefly detained by the Egyptian police and military or attacked by pro-Mubarak supporters. Al-Jazeera officials stressed that their job was nothing but to cover the full story in a balanced way. "History shows that where Egypt goes Arabs follow it, and it is no wonder that Arab autocratic rulers are shivering as they witness the massive influence of Al-Jazeera on the Arab street," added Zahran.[75]

The Future

Since the revolution began, there had been an unrelenting demand by the public for a reshuffle of the state media. "Now We Want a Responsible Media," screamed the headline of a column by Dina Abdel Fattaah of *Al-Masry Al-Youm*. She charged the "current media, with all their forms, of fueling anger" under the claim of "transparency."[76] The main aim of the revolution was to purify and improve the standard of state media performance by changing their editorialship, said journalist Essam Zakaria of *Sabah El-Kheir* in an interview with Al-Masria television station on March 25. Yet until today the media have not been "cleansed" from their bureaucratic leadership.[77] On March 31, new appointments for executive and editorial posts of the state media were declared by the SCAF, and this—as one journalist told me—has been comforting to them.

In the week that followed Mubarak's resignation, state television coverage remained, in my view, biased and less supportive of the revolution, and as I am about to finish writing this chapter it continues to be pro-government and fully supportive of the SCAF (although one must give credit to Nile News because it struggled at times to be objective). Whether state television will reestablish credibility in the eyes of Egyptian viewers remains to be seen. What we know is that there have been some genuine attempts by its journalists to achieve credibility in coverage. While doing so, there is an urgent need to reform policies. Professor Hussein Amin stressed the need to turn the now-defunct ministry of information into an entity similar to the British Broadcasting Corporation (BBC) or the French state broadcasting (ORTF). He also made reference to America's Federal Communication Commission (FCC) and how Egyptians can learn from the vital mission it plays in regulating and supervising more than seven thousand satellites and fourteen thousand television stations. The role of the new establishment he proposes is to insure media independence and diversity in Egypt in a manner that suits the ongoing media revolution while maintaining "our identity and cultural heritage." Under the new establishment, he added, there will be "very a few" state-owned television stations. "We need to bring back people's trust in the Egyptian media," concluded Amin, proposing that the government owns only Channel 1 and Channel 2 (the latter sometimes referred to as "Al-Masria"), but privatize all Nile Television Network (NTN) channels in a manner that separates ownership from administration in order to insure accountability.[78]

Like Professor Hussein Amin, the popular television broadcaster Yousri Fouda of ONTV observed that the abolition of the ministry of information is a decision he strongly supported because there needs to be no restrictions on Egyptian television stations and the media as a whole. We need to "liberate the Egyptian media from these shackles after being involved in misleading people for many years," said Fouda, who characterized state television coverage during the early days of the revolution as "media shame." He cited the BBC as a "good model," among other superlative ones in the world, for our state media to embrace.[79] A staff member at the Egyptian state television with whom I conducted an interview in late March said the best solution for state broadcast and television at the moment is to sell the Maspero building and use the money to erect a new state television establishment at the Media Production district in 6th of October City. The aim, he said, would be to found a limited number stations with each of them focusing on a main topic such as hard news, movies and entertainment, education, and sports. Currently on leave and working for an independent television station, he complained of widespread bureaucracy at state television due to the large number of staff, which he claims to be roughly fifty thousand individuals. He stressed that the only way out would be to raise wages and push for early retirement—possibly at the age of fifty—while guaranteeing each employee full benefit.

Chapter 3. Friday of Anger

Friday January 28, 2011, in Egypt was a day etched deeply into the memories of all who were there. It was characterized as the "Friday of Anger," with mass protests (hundreds of thousands of people) sweeping the country following the noon prayers, and unprecedented violent clashes and street battles erupting later in major cities—from Cairo to the northern city of Alexandria and the canal city of Suez. Riot police used rubber-coated bullets, water cannons, and tear gas to disperse crowds in Cairo's Tahrir Square, but there were also later reports of the use of live ammunition. In face of heavy attacks from police and members of the State Security Intelligence Agency (SSIA), anti-government protesters used stones to defend themselves. Others spoke of being trapped in battles with police for four hours on the renowned Qasr El-Nil Bridge located on one side of Tahrir Square. Hundreds of people fought riot police which, according to eyewitness, was armed with tear gas, batons, and shields and did not hesitate to use them. When protesters tried to move forward toward Tahrir Square riot police started shooting tear gas at them. Angered by the action, protesters pushed it forward throwing metal barracks and tear gas canisters into the Nile River.

These clashes broke out not just in Tahrir Square but in many parts of the Egyptian capital. But it was the ones in Tahrir which, alas, looked like a war zone. Police and SSIA forces, as one protester told me, had never anticipated "our resistance" to be that strong at Tahri. All of a sudden Tahrir was taken over by protesters, and this led to the moral of police and state security going down as they were forced to withdraw from it and from the other places they were scattered in and asked to defend across Cairo. Protesters formed a camp full of tents, or rather a city of tents, occupied by a blend of people from all walks of life of the Egyptian society. Prominent Egyptian activist and former director of the International Atomic Energy Agency, Mohamed ElBaradei, was among a group of protesters targeted by police after leaving a mosque in downtown Cairo. "This is the work of a barbaric regime that is, in my view, doomed," said ElBaradei after being sprayed by a water cannon.[80] The Nobel laureate for his work with the UN agency to promote nuclear nonproliferation had been asking President Hosni Mubarak to step down from the first day protests erupted on January 25. ElBaradei called for respect of the Egyptian people's rights, including a change of government, rewriting the constitution, ending emergency law, and improving workers' rights and civil liberties.

With clashes spreading in many parts of the country, Egypt was truly in a crisis. Multiple deaths and many injuries were reported on the Friday of Anger, and almost all state institutions collapsed. At that moment most Egyptians knew that only one establishment remained that was capable of protecting their homeland and safeguarding them: the military. And it responded. The army stepped in later that day and went on the street to fill the security void in a scene filled with extraordinary human tragedy. It imposed a curfew from 6:00 p.m. to 7:00 a.m. from that day on. Egyptians, however, defied the curfew and continued their protests on the day after, with young and old, rich and poor, gathering on the streets of major Egyptian cities and not just in Cairo. It was truly a watershed moment in the history of modern Egypt; it was at that exact point in time that Egyptians began to speak of their "struggle" and their "revolution." We began to see children carried on their parents' shoulders with signs reading: "The Children of Egypt Want Mubarak Tried" and "Leave, Let Us Live." Yes, and as we have mentioned in Chapter 1, the most outstanding sign was the one that said: "Bread, Freedom, Social Justice, and Human Dignity."

Coverage of Protests

The Qasr El-Nile Bridge clashes broke out later in the afternoon; in the print press there was no mention of them at all on the following day. State-owned television stations, such as Channel 1, only showed the side of the bridge where there was slight clashes; while the privately-owned ones, such as ONTV, aired images of heavy clashes. Similar tactics were employed by state television—in contrast to the privately owned stations—to reduce the large number of protesters at Tahrir Square in the eyes of viewers. This biased method was distinct, and I witnessed it myself.

There was also wide dissimilarity in the way the different Egyptian press[81] covered the events of the Friday of Anger. As mentioned in Chapter 2, Egypt has three genres of newspapers: national (state owned), party (opposition), and independent (privately owned). Research for this chapter includes opinionated articles—op-eds, editorials, and columns—from major eight daily newspapers (four national, three independent, and one party) representative of the three press systems. Egypt's three main opposition parties are the New Wafd Party, Arab Nasserist Party, and the National Progressive Unionist Party. Of them, only the New Wafd Party publishes a daily paper, named *Alwafd*, and hence it was selected in the research as the sole party paper. The country's only other daily party paper is named *Al-Ahrar* and it is viewed as a weak paper published by Al-Ahrar or "Liberals" Party. It carried no opinionated pieces on the Friday of Anger events in its January 29 issue. In all, we analyzed 54 opinionated news items that were published in the eight selected papers on Friday January 29—the day that followed the Friday of Anger.[82]

The way the Egyptian press covered the Friday of Anger protests is varied and raises numerous questions for scholars of Arab journalism on how the country's diverse press systems operate at times of crises, and how such coverage changes over time as we shall see in the remaining chapters of the book. In examining the three press systems' coverage, we were first interested in finding out which system referred to the protests at that early stage as a "revolution," or the beginning of one. Here is what we found. Of the total 54 articles under study from the three different press systems only 7 articles (12.96%) talked about a revolution happening in Egypt. Though that number is small it is not insignificant, particularly when considering that the discussion on whether a revolution was occurring was debated in the press only four days after the protests began on January 25. Out of the 26 articles examined from the national papers none spoke of a revolution taking place in the North African state. Only 4 articles (21.05%) of the 19 articles scrutinized from independent papers and 3 articles (33.33%) of the 9 pieces studied from the party paper characterized the protests as a revolution. Table 3.1 below shows results in more details.

Table 3.1. Is there a revolution?

Press System	No N (%)	Yes N (%)	Total N (%)
National Press	26 (100)	0 (0)	26 (100)
Independent Press	15 (78.95)	4 (21.05)	19 (100)
Party Press	6 (66.67)	3 (33.33)	9 (100)
Total:	47 (87.04)	7 (12.96)	54 (100)

Journalists at the national press criticized government policies but focused their themes on how protesters should not commit what they described as "acts of violence." In an editorial titled "No to Violence and Vandalism," the editor of the national paper *Al-Ahram Al-Masae* pointed out that Egyptians have a right to express their views but not to "destroy" and harm their country because Egypt has achieved a "lot," thanks to the "democratic progress" it has been pursuing.[83] Journalist Abd El-Latif El-Menawy of that same paper lamented: "Egypt yesterday was in a state of confrontation with the shape of its future. Its sons and daughters were in a challenge to construct the nature of the road their nation will follow, a nation which I always desire to describe as an eternity. That will not be established, however, but with the hands of its people."[84] A piece in the national paper *Al-Ahram* called on Egyptians to demonstrate—as that is a right granted in the constitution—but not to destroy their country. It stipulated that citizens should ask themselves the question: "Have you ever in your life seen a civilized society in Europe burning buses, underground stations, hospitals, or restaurants while it demonstrates? Are we less than them?"[85]

The independent and partisan press, unlike the national one, was more vigorous and detailed in its criticism of government, often pointing out that Egyptians revolted—or declared a revolution—because of the sense of social injustice they feel. According to Mohamed Amin of the independent paper *Al-Masry Al-Youm*, government's lack of action (despite the statement by Safwat El-Sherif—head of the Shura "Consultative" Council and secretary-general of the National Democratic Party, or NDP—in which he promised his willingness to engage in dialogue with protesters) was ill-advised and has made a mockery of us that "we have to stand by the revolution."[86] Hassan Nafah, a Cairo University political science professor who often writes op-eds, argued, "The revolution which began on January 25 is initiated by youth, and people of all factions and backgrounds responded to it. It holds all the elements needed to persist and achieve its goals." His piece was titled, "And the Revolution Train Has Taken Off."[87] Similarly, the independent paper *Al-Shorouk Al-Jadeed* proclaimed: "Blackout of the Internet, phone services, and all means of modern telecommunications will not shut off change and all 'idiots' must realize that millions of revolutions took place prior to the invention of tools of telecommunications."[88] It was a foolish decision which turned Egypt into a "big prison."[89]

In a piece in *Al-Masry Al-Youm*, Osama Heikel believes there will be two teams of presidential consultants to Mubarak, one will try to convince him that there is nothing to worry about because the protests are blown out of proportion by the media, and that things will calm down and come back to what they were. The other team will caution the president that things can get violent with human casualties occurring if clashes erupt between the police and protesters;

hence, it will be wise to respond to their demands by dissolving Parliament—which is the product of rigged elections—and rewrite articles 76 and 77 of the Constitution[90] in order to allow for candidates outside the NDP to run for office and limit a president's term in leadership. Heikel wondered which team of presidential consultants the president would listen to.[91]

Though few in number, there were some commentaries in the independent papers that said directly or in directly that the protests are the outcome of people's anger at the sense of "humiliation" and "degradation" they feel for being dominated by other countries (fingers pointed at America and Israel). For example, Essam El-Erian, a member of the office of consultancy of the banned Muslim Brotherhood Party, spoke of Arabs leaders as "puppets" who resent responding to their people's demands.[92] Referring to how America has often supported dictators such as the Shah of Iran and Pervez Musharraf of Pakistan, Selim Azouz of the independent paper El-Dostour spoke of how the tone of U.S. speech regarding the protests in Egypt on the first day was different and softer in nature from that in the days that followed. He said that on the first day of protests, Secretary of State Hilary Clinton declared that the government in Egypt was stable but Washington later turned up the heat on the Mubarak regime.[93]

Writer and civil activist Sameh Fawzi insists that it was the bad economic conditions which pushed people to revolt against the regime.[94] Fahmi Howeidi, a popular columnist whose articles are published in many Arab papers, had a different take on the story in a piece he wrote for Al-Shorouk Al-Jadeed. He believes it is not economic difficulties that "mostly drive people to seek a revolution or go on the street to topple a regime," or else we would have seen revolutions by now in other countries where there is poverty, such as India and Bangladesh. What drives people to revolt, he said, is when their "dignity" is humiliated and "respect for themselves and freedom" is violated, and that is exactly what has been happening to Egyptians during Mubarak's thirty years of harsh rule. Hewadi surmised that those who rule the country do not know how humiliated Egyptians feel today after their homeland has been degraded on the world landscape. They live under an emergency law, fraudulent elections, and a political system stalled in corruption. To further elaborate his viewpoint, Hewadi claimed that Egyptians felt humiliated by the Mubarak regime's participation in the enforcement of the siege on Gaza and the building of a racist wall to protect Israel. "And what a shame and embarrassment that has been to Egyptians."[95]

In "No Life Without Change," Tariq Abbas of Al-Masry Al-Youm spoke of how Europe experienced its darkest Middle Ages when the "power of the church" exerted superiority over the "power of knowledge," but this later changed and Europe enjoyed the Renaissance by embracing developments in science. Egypt also changed after its 1952 Revolution, restructured itself and "exported its revolution to some Arab, African, and Latin American countries. But it committed a horrible mistake when it cancelled political parties and thus hindered the march for democracy."[96] The time has come to embrace "democratic and constitutional reform," wrote distinguished journalist Salah Issa—who serves as chief editor of the weekly independent paper *Al-Qahira* (Arabic for "Cairo")—in *Al-Masry Al-Youm*.[97] Wael Quandil, a renowned political commentator known for his anti-Mubarak viewpoints, lamented in *Al-Shorouk Al-Jadeed* the way the security police "bombarded" the honorable people of Suez (a governorate located in the north-eastern part of the country where there is the Suez Canal) known throughout history for their strong sense of patriotism and resistance to foreign occupation.[98]

The partisan press, as echoed in our analysis of the country's only major daily party paper *Alwafd*, was somewhat similar to that of the independent press but was more outspoken in espousing that a revolution is taking place in the Land of the Nile. In piece titled "The Masses and History," columnist Mustapha Shafiq said Egypt is witnessing a "public revolution against corruption and that has entirely changed the country's face in the eyes of the world."[99] He pondered, Does the president see any exit from this "flaming revolution?"[100] The men of the regime must realize that this revolution will not stop, observed Alaa Arebi.[101] The protesters are ordinary Egyptian citizens from different social strata, noted the party paper, and they are technologically well-equipped and mostly have no political affiliation.[102] Shutting down the Internet and phone services is a sign of "powerlessness" on part of government. It shows that problems which have not been solved over thirty years will not be solved, commented *Alwafd*. It proves that the regime and the government insist on being "obstinate and resistant to change."[103] The government has never really realized that members of the Facebook group *Kulluna Khaled Said* (Arabic for "We Are All Khaled Said")[104] have exceeded three hundred thousand and that the number of people calling for the downfall of the Minister of Interior Habib El-Adli has also been increasing.[105]

Government Reaction/First Mubarak Speech

The government statements made from the day the protests began to the Friday of Anger were seen by many as further intensifying youth's anger and leading to the breakout of violent confrontation later on that day. For example, Prime Minister Ahmed Nazif said there would be no job openings in government and cautioned youth of the consequence of their protests. El-Sherif said the Egyptian who set himself on fire in mid-January is not an issue worth discussing.[106] The seventy-eight-year old who served as minister of information for twenty two years added that suicide acts are the results of psychological reasons and should not be used for exploitation.[107] The president of Al-Fayoum University, a state institution, said whoever wants to burn himself is free to do so.[108] Foreign Minister Ahmed Aboul Gheit argued that talks of the transfer of the Tunisian epidemic to Egypt are nonsense,[109] a statement which many Egyptian intellectuals rejected, including Saadeddin Ibrahim, a prominent political activist who serves as a sociology professor and director of the Ibn Khaldun Center for Development Studies at the American University in Cairo.[110]

Late on the evening of the Friday of Anger, President Mubarak delivered his first televised speech which protesters denounced because they said it did not respond to their demands. The eighty-two-year-old President fired his cabinet but refused to step down, and on the following, Saturday, he appointed Intelligence Chief Omar Suleiman as vice president—a position which has been vacant since Mubarak assumed the presidency in 1981.[111] He also appointed Aviation Minister Ahmed Shafiq as prime minister. In the speech, Mubarak regretted the "loss of innocent lives" and said what Egypt needed was "dialogue not violence." He cautioned that there was a "thin line" between freedom and chaos and characterized the protests as part of a "bigger plot" to destabilize Egypt. "Egypt's youth are its most valuable asset and looting of public and private property, destroying what we have built, is not the route to follow," he said. He promised to "proceed" with political reform and the enhancement of the standard of living. But his words received little respond from the majority of Egyptians whom I spoke with; they often talked of how the content of Mubarak's speech could best be summarized in the English proverb: "Old wine in a new glass." Prominent anti-Mubarak youth movements, such as the April 6 Movement, deplored the speech, describing it as a false attempt to cool people's anger on the street. Hence, the protests continued on the days that followed with people yelling more loudly: "Down with Mubarak."

All articles in the country's three different press systems were critical of government and its policies, which they blamed for the breakout of protests, but none from the national press disapproved of President Mubarak himself. Only 5 articles (9.26%) from the total 28 articles studied from independent and party papers criticized Mubarak. Of the 19 independent paper articles examined, 3 (15.79%) were critical of the Egyptian President; while 2 (22.22%) of the 9 Al-wafd articles were critical of Mubarak. Articles which disapproved of Mubarak frequently lamented that when regimes are about to fall they often resort to violence in order to silence opposition. Table 3.2 below shows results in more details. Articles which took no stance or were neutral or supportive in their position toward Mubarak were listed under the "supportive/neutral" category.

Table 3.2. Stance toward Mubarak

Press System	No (%)	Yes (%)	Total (%)
National Press	26 (100)	0 (0)	26 (100)
Independent Press	15 (78.95)	4 (21.05)	19 (100)
Party Press	6 (66.67)	3 (33.33)	9 (100)
Total:	47 (87.04)	7 (12.96)	54 (100)

As we have stated above, the national press disapproved of the Nazif government but not of President Mubarak, with many of its journalists urging him to dissolve it and appoint a new one; hence, the national press was in many ways a propaganda voice of the president. Many of its journalists said they supported youth and their right to express their opinion but called on them to remain calm and not to "vandalize." Yesterday's events were not a "revolution or an uprising," wrote Alaa Mohamed in the national paper *Al-Gomhuria*,

> but legitimate rights and a natural reaction against a government characterized with carelessness and disengagement with the public and the surrounding reality. It cared about economic figures but overlooked their effect on citizens and low-income individuals.

> How many times have we cautioned the government of Dr. Nazif not to turn its heads away, of not caring and listening to people's complaints who no longer can stand it because of its behavior and disregard of what is printed in the press or shown on satellite television stations?[112]

Mohamed blamed the Nazif government for not shouldering the responsibility and depending primarily on President Mubarak to resolve its problems.

Journalists at the national press laboriously tried to defend what they described as the "president's decision" to dispatch military forces on the ground. Citing articles from the Egyptian constitution which empower the president to do so at times of crises to protect the nation, Anwar El-Hawari of *Al-Ahram Al-Masae* criticized the Friday protests because of what he labeled as acts of "provocation and intimidation" that later turned them into "protests of destruction, burglary, and animosity," leaving the president with no choice but to order the military to go down on the streets in order to maintain security for the Egyptian people. And the president did that well and on a timely manner. El-Hawari further extolled Mubarak for promising to change his government and possibly reshuffle Parliament in the future.[113] Mohamed Ali Ibrahim, editor in chief of *Al-Gomhuria*, said "Egypt and its President respect counter opinion," and that has been unveiled when protests began in the country in the summer of 2007. He alleged, "Egypt has never seen freedom of expression except under President Mubarak's rule," and he criticized Washington and Paris for trying to "intervene" in the internal affairs of his country even though both states had embraced violence to deal with the protests that erupted in them recently.[114]

In a piece written as a letter addressed to President Mubarak, *Al-Ahram* commentator Abdel Azim Darwish spoke of how Egyptians trust Mubarak and know that "at his hands alone there lies the solution" for their problems. "All Egyptians love you and believe in you," added Darwish. Our youth feel a sense of "despair," and they went out on the street to directly express their "suffering" to you.[115] The chief editor of the national paper *Akhbar El-Yom*, Mumtaz El-Kot, applauded what he described as Mubarak's contemporary era of freedom and democracy, arguing:

> We all have mixed feelings of happiness and despair. Happiness for we are living in the reality of a new age of freedom, democracy, and broad diversity of opinion. This is in all measures one of the overlooked achievements and victories which have been accomplished under the rule of President Mubarak—a President whose first decision after assuming office was not only to order the release of all political detainees but also to meet and engage in constructive dialogue with them about the future of Egypt.

El-Kot asked his readers to "recognize" that all the youth that participated in the latest protests were aged between fifteen and twenty five; they have been "born and raised in the atmosphere of freedom" which Mubarak has installed.[116]

An *Al-Masry Al-Youm* article which criticized Mubarak was titled "The Road to Qasr El-Qobba [the presidential palace]." In it, Amin posed the questions: "Is President Mubarak searching for a scapegoat? Will it be Prime Minister Ahmed Nazif or the interior minister?"[117] Protesters went out on the street to show their refusal of the state of poverty and unemployment under which they live, noted Ahmed Hassan El-Sharqawi in *El-Dostour*, but the complaints of these "poor citizens" did not draw the attention of the president and the political leadership, making them wonder if he truly cares about them. El-Sharqawi said he found the statements of Nazif and El-Sherif "unconvincing." It was a "grave mistake" from the government and the presidential consultants to intentionally disseminate news about the president's meetings and contacts with Arab and foreign leaders as if the country's internal affairs were going well. This shows "lack of political vision" on part of these presidential consultants.[118]

Many Egyptians citizens, noted *Al-Shorouk Al-Jadeed*, have become aware that most of their problems are connected to the fact that the head of their state has not been changed for thirty years.[119] Injustice and class division have driven Egyptians to revolt and break their fear, stressed Abbas. "They have nothing left to fear about and cry that the pharaohs' patience has limits. They declared that from now on there would be no negotiations with those who steal their homeland, detest its progress, and drive it backward. There would be no settlement with a regime that sold its laborers and their companies and factories to foreigners."[120]

There were, however, those commentaries in the independent press which embraced a somewhat neutral viewpoint by being neither critical nor supportive of Mubarak. El-Erian wished that the president learned that his consultants and ministers deceived him and did not truthfully convey to him the feelings of the public. "I wish the president learns from the last speech of his former presidential colleague Ben Ali [Zine el-Abiden Ben Ali of Tunisia] in which he frankly declared that his consultants, ministers, and the select a few around him had deceived him and did not tell him the truth about the feelings and aspirations of his people."[121] Ahmed El-Sawy of *Al-Masry Al-Youm* asked Mubarak, whom he described as the "father" of Egyptians, to respond to the demands of his people who own nothing but their voice to express their views about their "legitimate dream of having a nation in which they live in dignity and freedom, a homeland wide enough to embrace all its citizens." El-Sawy called on Mubarak to "come back to us; we know you are not Zine el-Abiden ben Ali."[122] Citing how the events of September 11 have changed Bush and America, *Al-Masry Al-Youm* columnist Soliman Gowda stressed that after the January 25 protests Egyptians want a Mubarak who is different from the Mubarak before January 25, just as we saw a Gamal Abdel Nasser and an Anwar Sadat who were different after the protests of 1968 and 1977 respectively.[123]

As in the state and independent press, criticism of government in the partisan press was fierce. Oppression is not a means to end the uprising of anger which is sweeping the country, commented Wagdi Zeineddin. On the contrary, it further inflames it. This is the fault that the government has fallen in because it has overlooked the political solution. Zeineddin said he sympathizes with the interior ministry and blamed the Nazif government (which he described as the "culprit") for pushing for the use of force against protesters rather than engaging in dialogue with them. He cried that Nazif should "go to hell" and demanded the resignation of his government.[124] Abbas El-Tarabilli, a former editor of *Al-wafd*, argued that during the protests he searched for the government and the NDP but he found neither. They have both failed in their first direct "test with the public." They both, together with their representatives in Parliament, should quit, added El-Tarabili whose column was titled: "A Government Whose People Never Liked It."[125]

In another article, the party paper wondered, "Why the president has not taken action until now? What is he waiting for?"[126] The popular columnist Nabil

Zaki wrote that the nation was facing a government which failed in making people patriotic and abolishing illiteracy. He called for raising the minimum wage.
He further reproached government for inflating the electricity and water bills
over the last a few years and empowering "businessmen to embezzle Egypt's
wealth by granting them state land for a few coins to build on it their palaces,
villas, and tourist villages. And, regrettably, officials of the ruling NDP party continue to speak of poverty as a natural destiny." These wealthy men, added Zaki,
also bought seats in Parliament.[127]

None of the members of the NDP ever expected the day to come when they
would see the incidents that are "sweeping" Egypt today, wrote Mohamed Mustapha Sherdi, a member of the editorial board of the party paper. "Government
studies and reports released by the interior ministry deceived us all by propagating that things are going well in Egypt with the exception of a few problems
that can be solved. This was all lies." He stressed that this is the time that they
should listen to the demands of the protesters which can be summarized in the
sign some of them carried and which read: "People Want the Downfall of the
Regime."[128] Members of the regime must realize that it is time for them to leave
Egypt, and that there will be no country granting them sanctuary but Saudi Arabia, noted Arebi.[129]

The Themes

The Egyptian media's discourse debate on the Friday of Anger clashes have
centered on the following five main frames, or themes:

Egyptian Youth

The debate in the national press on this theme focused on that the country's
youth have the freedom to demonstrate, but some journalists accused them of
instigating the clashes by committing acts of vandalism and forcing the security
police to intervene to stop them. "Egyptian youth" should not try to disrupt the
norms of our daily lives, cautioned *Al-Ahram*.[130] Responding to the demands of
our youth must not be viewed as a sign of "weakness" or "submission," wrote
Samir Ragab in *Al-Gomhuria*. It was ill-advised from Prime Minister Nazif to say,
however, that there were no jobs available in government. It would be "wise"
to secure for these youth two million jobs in the state sector, added Ragab. He
concluded that Egyptians want a government that does not every now and then
engage its security police in confrontation with those whom it is entrusted to
protect.[131]

The protests have come to "unveil the birth of a new power that cannot be
undermined—the power of youth," wrote El-Kot.[132] Citing the rising number of

youth in many parts of the world, Ali El-Deen Hilal, a senior member of the NDP and a former minister of youth, called in an op-ed in *Akhbar El-Yom* on institutions in every society to try to understand the rising diversity of youth and their desire for "self-assertion" and independence in behavior, a move which could at times form a rebellion against all forms of power in society.[133] Naglaa Zakri of *Al-Ahram* rejects the argument that the youth protests began with "political demands," because they are "essentially of pure economic backgrounds." She added that most of these youth do not belong to political parties, charging the latter of overlooking the power of the earlier. These youth have not been bred on politics and constitute sixty percent of unemployment in Egypt, she wrote. All they want is "a job, a house, a wife, and children."[134]

In an attempt to calm down the youth uprising, the well-established *Al-Ahram* columnist Annes Mansour told the "youth of Egypt" that their message—which they delivered from their homes, offices, buses, mosques, and churches—has been received and the state is "reading it and searching for a solution, and it must find one" that insures for you better standards of living.[135] Abdullah Hassan, chief editor of the country's Middle East News Agency (MENA), said that although he supports the right of youth to demonstrate for better standards of living, their clashes with police have severely hurt the Egyptian stock market. He proclaimed that Mubarak's political and economic policies "have greatly contributed to the reduction of the effects of the world economic crisis on the Egyptian economy." These policies, Hassan stressed in his piece in *Akhbar El-Yom*, have tried to reach low-income individuals.[136]

Support of youth and their demands was strong in both the independent and partisan press. *Al-Shorouk Al-Jadeed* observed that people of all walks of life, particularly youth, participated in the protests in a noble and peaceful manner.[137] The ones who conducted the protests, emphasized *El-Dostour*, were youth—a "new generation" of Egyptians.[138] Government's false promises, wrote Salama Ahmed Salama, chief editor of *Al-Shorouk Al-Jadeed*, "did not receive any response from the generation of youth, university students, and activists who know more than what a political party and a political leadership do. It is a generation which gets its information, knowledge, and political culture from the Internet, Facebook, Twitter, and depends on a wide network of sources for information."[139] Issa affirmed that the enthusiasm of these youth for politics forms an "important asset to the political and constitutional reform move."[140] Nafah, on the other hand, called on youth to stand united in face of those who try to divide them and abort their revolution. He further elaborated that what we are witnessing is "a revolution by all the Egyptian people and not the creation of one political party, movement, or individual; hence, we should all shoulder its responsibility."[141] Issa furthermore blamed government officials for not embracing political reform and for taking "one step forward and another backward" in their policies over the past five years without realizing the hole they are throwing themselves and their country in. Then they saw this young, digital, and apolitical generation suddenly coming out at them in thousands.[142]

Praise of the role of youth in constructing and initiating the protests was also strong in the partisan press. The protests are the product of youth who belong to no political party, observed Zaki of *Alwafd*.[143] The people who went out to demonstrate on January 25 all love Egypt, commented El-Tarabili, and youth exhibited such love for their motherland by shouting loudly for a better Egypt.[144] Their Friday of Anger is turning into "days of anger," and the government is not watching.[145] Egyptian youth's view of themselves and the regime has also changed," said Shafiq. They, like most Egyptians, have been "humiliated by poverty, hunger, high prices, and corruption."[146] The current regime has left us no choice; it has employed all means of violence against our youth who are suffering unemployment, poverty, and mistreatment by police, contended Arebi.[147] We need to seek quick solutions for the social, political, and economic problems of a "society in which more than 60 percent are youth aged under thirty five," a society in which the education they receive is poor and does not qualify them for a "market full of contradictions, a market engulfed in nepotism and bribery," wrote Amina El-Naqqash, a managing editor of a weekly party paper.[148]

The Tunisian Effect

When the Tunisian revolution took place some wondered: What about Egypt? Can something similar happen in the Arab world's most heavily populated country? In all, the national press fiercely denied any effect of the Tunisian revolution on the breakout of Egyptian protests; while many commentaries in the independent and partisan press embraced the opposite view. In a piece in *Al-Ahram*, Makram Mohamed Ahmed, chairman of the country's Syndicate of Journalists, argued that those who "conspire" against Egypt falsely believe that what took place in Tunisia can be repeated in Egypt despite the disparity between the two cases. They planted themselves among the demonstrators and carried red flags in an attempt to push the "wave of angry youth to clash with security men." They foolishly hoped that the security police fires at them, repeating what happened in the "sister state of Tunisia," added Ahmed who is known for his staunch support of Mubarak and is believed to be the one who writes the presidential speeches.[149] We welcome our children going out on the street in peaceful demonstrations, remarked columnist Sabri Ghoneim in *Akhbar El-Yom*. But for some of them to set fire on the streets and "violate the law is a tragedy because we are not in Lebanon, Tunisia, or Gaza. . . . We are in Egypt."[150]

The independent press criticized the Mubarak regime for underestimating the influence of the Tunisian revolution on Egyptians. It is "silly" from some to argue that "Egypt is not Tunisia," wrote Heikel.[151] The demand of protesters for political reform was buttressed "by what they derived from the Tunisian spectacle," asserted Issa.[152] The lesson from Tunisia was "fresh," and government officials misunderstood how strong the determination of protesters was, argued *Al-Masry Al-Youm*.[153] There was no action taken at first for fear of the Tunisian scenario taking place in Egypt, yet the government implemented the same Tunisian state of affair by granting the security police a "carte blanche" to do as they wish, wrote Mohamed Mosallam. Those government officials (who disseminated false statements) were not worried about Egypt's safety but about their own seats.[154] Amin criticized the lack of action on part of the "political leadership," but he said it was foolish from some to predict that the regime would surrender in the same manner Ben Ali did.[155] For fear of it spreading in their countries, wrote Ibrahim of AUC, Arab rulers had tried to ignore the Tunisian revolution but they later found that they had no choice but to admit its occurrence after Cairo's statement on it. He further derided how the Libyan leader was calling on Tunisians to be patient and wait for three years until presidential elections and then vote on whether or not they wanted Ben Ali. The sociology professor cunningly hinted that there is the possibility of an uprising also exploding in Libya.[156] There was only one mention of the Tunisia revolution in the partisan press, in which a position was made on whether or not it had an influence on the outbreak of Egyptian protests. According to El-Naqqash's op-ed in *Alwafd*, the protests in Egypt came to contradict with government officials' statements which downplayed the effect of the Tunisian revolution and made a mockery of it.[157]

The Conspiracy Theory

The Mubarak regime, including his then-newly appointed Vice President Omar Suleiman, claimed that "foreign elements" were behind the protests. And the national press propagated that message, often referring to outside forces as trying to instigate insurrection. For example, the state-owned media reported at the time of an Afghani being arrested for looting in the Egyptian capital. On page four, *Al-Ahram Al-Masae* carried the large headline: "Friday of Anger Hands Power to the Thieves and the Army Is in the Street to Restore Security."[158] Some pointed to how Iran had been describing what took place in Tunisia and Egypt as an "Islamic awakening."[159] Prior to the eruption of the January 25 protests, the Minister of Interior Habib El-Adli also declared that foreign hands were behind the 2010 New Year's Eve suicide bombing of the Two Saints Church (or Al-Qiddissin Church in Arabic) in Alexandria, with fingers pointing at a Palestinian militant group in Gaza.

Al-Ahram columnist Darwish noted that from noon to 6:00 p.m. on January 28 the behavior of our youth was civilized and well-mannered; they did not vandalize and riot police stood peacefully to protect them—to protect their "sons, brothers, sisters, and possibly neighbors gathered at a wedding or a funeral ceremony." That scene sadly changed after the "elements of darkness crept in among them" in order to spread chaos.[160] But we as Egyptians, wrote Maged Nawar in *Al-Gomhuria*, have always managed to emerge "unified from attempts to incite racial division among our people, and we have always done it in a civilized manner because we are the land of civilizations."[161] Those who conspire against Egypt will not win, observed *Al-Ahram Al-Masae*, and Egypt will stand strong in spite of "yesterday's acts of damage and destruction of public and private buildings." These acts have saddened every Egyptian, but our nation will emerge from this crisis as brave and determined as ever to continue building better future.[162]

Hassan of MENA also claimed that there are "elements lurking" for opportunities to harm our homeland. He stressed that the protests were not running "randomly but the outcome of arranged plans aimed at destabilizing security and stability in Egypt."[163] Yes, there are outsiders who try to intervene in Egypt's internal affairs, stressed *Al-Ahram Al-Masae*. "Egypt will remain a lighting minaret in its Arab-Muslim-African sphere, carrying its message and increasing its giving with unrelenting trust, steadfastness, and determination."[164] Similarly, a column in *Al-Gomhuria* described Egypt as the "minaret" of its neighboring states.[165] In an op-ed in *Al-Ahram*, seventy-year-old journalist Mofeed Fawzy, a former chief editor of the popular state-owned arts magazine *Sabah El-Kheir*[166] cited how Egyptian culture and mass media have helped his generation develop a passion for their homeland and encouraged them to stand united in face of those who "conspire" against Egypt.[167] Like Fawzy, Ahmed characterized the Friday of Anger events as a "conspiracy" organized by a small number of people who were able to "deceive a few thousands of our youth." The chairman of the Syndicate of Journalists called for dealing with that conspiracy with an "iron feast" and to "reconsider the freedom of expression" they are granted because most of them abuse it at a time the country is facing terrorist threats and outside attempts to export "creative chaos" to our streets.[168] The investigations by the country's general persecutor will undoubtedly "unveil the truth about the childish conspiracy whose perpetrators have thought it will hit stability in Egypt," observed El-Kot.[169] Others alleged that Israel would be the sole winner from "political instability" in the Arab world. Lamenting the "regretful developments" in Tunisia and the Arab Maghreb, a column in *Al-Ahram* (which did not mention Egypt's protests) claimed that the main "profiteer" from behind all this is Israel, because Tel Aviv can now achieve its long awaited "dream" of "eradicating the Palestinian cause and building a Jewish state with Jerusalem as its capital." Mahmoud

El-Menawy asked: "How did these outsiders come to us? Who opened the door for them?"[170] We must not allow those hidden among the protesters to ignite division and weaken the spirit of unity in our country, cried *Akhbar El-Yom*.[171]

Independent newspapers rejected the conspiracy theory altogether. For example, Hazem El-Beblawi argued in *Al-Shorouk Al-Jadeed* that we must admit that we are facing a "big problem," and hence it would be foolish to speak of a conspiracy, [or say] that the protests are the product of hooligans or people infiltrating the protesters. He advised officials to open an honest dialogue with all "political currents and embrace political reform—at its forefront are the abolishment of the emergency law, granting political parties freedom to be established, amending the constitution, preparing for new and clean presidential elections, and ferociously fighting corruption."[172] They also want an assurance that Mubarak's son, Gamal, will not run for office, argued another piece in *Al-Shrouk Al-Jadeed*.[173] Egyptians, in the opinion of Abbas, have gotten tired of the "same old symphony" that reiterates that the protests are stirred up by people popped among the protesters; that there are "outside fingers" involved. This is a lie because those who participated in the demonstrations are "very Egyptian" folks who have gotten tired of oppressive governing, he added. It is time for change; after all, change is the norm of life.[174] There was no viewpoint expressed on the conspiracy theory theme in *Alwafd*.

Whom to Blame? Political Parties (Muslim Brotherhood)

The national press, unlike the independent and partisan press, pointed out that political parties, particularly the banned Muslim Brotherhood, are angered by the results of the 2010 elections of the People's Assembly in which the NDP won a sweeping victory in what many described as a forged election. A number of political parties withdrew from the second round of the elections. The first round of the parliamentary elections was held late in November of 2010 and the second one was held early in December of the same year. Described by international human rights groups as the most rigged elections in the country's history,[175] four hundred forty four ordinary seats were contested of the total five hundred eighteen seats of Parliament, of which the NDP won four hundred and twenty seats. Of the seventy four seats left, sixty four are reserved for women and the president appoints the remaining ten members.

Journalists of the national press often injected the phrase "political parties and forces" in their criticism of what they called "those behind the protests." For instance, El-Kot argued that "some members" of political parties have tried to use the demonstrations and the police-protesters clashes to their benefit.[176] A column in *Al-Ahram* accused "political groups and parties on the periphery of trying to settle standing issues with the ruling [NDP] party."[177] In the opinion of

Hilal, Egypt has recently seen a few demonstrations but this time the number of protesters was extremely high. Yet, he added, we must distinguish, nevertheless, between the acts of youth and the attempts by "some political parties and forces" to use them to their benefit and to fulfill their private agendas.[178] Ghoneim also blamed "political parties," which pulled out from the second round of the 2010 elections, for encouraging youth to spread damage and chaos to settle issues.[179] Ibrahim of *Al-Gomhuria* cautioned that the cost of freedom should not be the "blood of Egyptians which is too precious to allow some to use for achieving their political goals or revenging for lack of representation of legitimate parties or banned groups in Parliament."[180]

It is important to stress here that when journalists at the national press spoke of political "forces" or "banned" groups trying to benefit from the protests, they were cunningly and equivocally referring to the Muslim Brotherhood. Others were more forthright in their criticism of the banned Islamist political party. For instance the chairman of the Syndicate of Journalists, Ahmed, observed that the banned Muslim Brotherhood party is watching the political street closely, weighing events and measuring how it can benefit from the breakout of violent clashes between protesters and the security police.[181]

The independent press did not tackle the political parties theme, yet much was debated in it on the Muslim Brotherhood. Some idiotically spoke of a "minority being shoved in among the protesters, of a few thousands from the Muslim Brotherhood who do not represent the whole Egyptian people," commented Mosallam in *Al-Masry Al-Youm*.[182] Azouz emphasized that although the Muslim Brotherhood's participation in the protests was "symbolic," those in power falsely claimed that it was behind the Friday of Anger protests and cautioned that a change in regime would mean the endangering of U.S. interests. This, added Azouz, was the same tool they employed in the past in "convincing the U.S. administration that a free and fair election would bring the Islamists to power," particularly after the Muslim brotherhood won eighty eight seats of the total four hundred fifty four seats in the People's Assembly in the 2005 elections. Thus, the White House kept silent about a rigged 2010 elections in which only one member of the banned Muslim Brotherhood party was "allowed" in Parliament.[183]

Similarly, Salama accentuated: "It is not correct what the ministry of interior stated—and the ruling party promoted—that the number of protesters doubled after the Muslim Brotherhood joined them. The public protests in Egypt resembled those in Tunisia in that there were no religious or pro-political party mottos. Both groups joined later but did not influence the general atmosphere of the protesters."[184] El-Erian stressed that the "Muslim Brotherhood has been on the level of responsibility" in their participation in the protests, which he characterized as "a legitimate right." But, he added, the ministry of interior's accusation was an "escapade from facing the clear reality that protesters were motivated by a desire to move people out of a severe crisis which is the product of the NDP's corrupt politics." He labeled the 2005 parliamentary election as "semi-free" and the 2010 ones as a "forged" one.[185]

The partisan press blamed the NDP and the role it played in "forging" the 2010 elections. No wise man, commented one piece in *Alwafd*, can accept the outcome of the 2010 parliamentary elections.[186] Placing the blame on the Muslim Brotherhood is a scapegoat and an attempt to protect the NDP which has become a "center of power" for those who have the wealth. Egypt has become a nation of two groups—of haves and have-nots—and political Islam caters to the poor, and that is why we are seeing a reinvigoration of the Muslim Brotherhood.[187]

Police or Protesters

The national press showed no criticism of police's tackling of the protests and the violence it employed to disperse them. El-Kot praised the security forces for handling the situation, but he did not make any reference to the number of causalities that took place as a result.[188] The chairman of the Syndicate of Journalists stated that clashes did not erupt until after 4:00 p.m., and that showed a great degree of "civilized behavior" on part of the security police and the protesters.[189] The chief editor of MENA described the behavior of the security forces as well-mannered and professional and decried the acts of destruction and attacks on public and private properties by protesters, whom he described their acts as premeditated. This, added Hassan, pushed security forces to intervene.[190]

Commentaries in the independent press vehemently denounced police ruthlessness toward the protesters. In a column titled "How Old Is Anger?" Salama wrote:

> The day of anger has turned into days of utter suppression. The security forces did not carry what the interior minister had said, that there would be no obstruction of protests as long as they do not violate the law or jeopardize public properties. But the police quickly resorted to the use of power and threw teargas bombs, obstructed mass telecommunications vehicles, and used open violence to attack protesters and arrest hundreds of them in a desperate attempt to silence a nation regaining its freedom and divulging its demands for the first time in an extraordinary courage.

Salama added that people around the globe have realized that "political oppression" is much deeper in Egypt than they have thought. They realized that it is but a "volcano of anger" that has suddenly erupted. This is a fact that we must admit.[191] The party paper *Alwafd* did not tackle this theme.

Arab Satellite Stations & Al-Jazeera

As is often the case when crises erupt in Egypt, the country's national press launched a fierce campaign against popular pan-Arab satellite stations, particularly Al-Jazeera, for what it called blowing the issue out of proportion. Nawar of *Al-Gomhuria* cautioned that Egypt is "in danger," not because of the "peaceful demonstrations of its youth and people" but because of the audacious attempts of the media of some countries to harm Egypt." He added, "When I follow some satellite television stations I realize there are those who want to see the downfall of Egypt. He argued that the world has witnessed a number of demonstrations recently and cited the 2010 one against the French government orchestrated by Africans and Arabs living there. Yet, added Nawar, the Western media never gave them as much focus in coverage as they did with the Egyptian protests. "Egypt is in danger because we have become the next target after Iraq."[192]

The chief editor of MENA charged the independent Egyptian and Arab media of exaggerating the incident.[193] Likewise, the chairman of the Syndicate of Journalists accused these "immature media" of pushing those youth and spreading "gossip" in public opinion. He lamented, "The main goal of the press is sensationalism of the news and increasing circulation figures. The satellite television programs are managed by a number of new stars who construct of themselves court judges putting everyone on trial without having the experience and knowledge that can enable them to deal with facts objectively."[194] In a way, said *Al-Ahram*, the Egyptian press "intentionally or unintentionally" contributed to the widening of the gap between those in government and the public; alas, journalists ignited the confrontations.[195] El-Kot charged Al-Jazeera of inciting schism among Arabs and accelerating the momentum of "creative chaos" in the region.[196] Egypt needs to "define who its enemies and friends are," observed Fikri Kamoun in a piece *Al-Gomhuria*. Al-Jazeera's coverage of the events lacked "honesty" and was meant to "stir" them up. It echoed nothing but the voice of the "CIA and Mossad," and "I challenge its correspondents in Israel or the United States to do the same when covering their hypocritical stand toward builders of settlements on Palestinian land."[197]

The independent press rejected the claim that pan-Arab satellite stations fueled the protests in Egypt. Certainly there would be those who claim that satellite television stations tried to exaggerate the events of the Friday of Anger in order to motivate people to go out on the street, wrote Heikel.[198] In the "Media of Nakba," Hatim Gamal Eddin of *Al-Shorouk Al-Jadeed* mourned that the state broadcast media since Egypt's defeat in the 1967 War with Israel can be characterized as *nakba* (Arabic for "defeat") media, in which state television and radio stations at times of crises feed the public with propaganda in order to protect government. Eddin mockingly wrote: These "free" media stations stood as watchers from their giant Cairo-based broadcast and television building (known as "Maspero") during the Friday of Anger and did not offer the protesters the coverage they deserve. "As if those protesters, who were only meters away from Maspero, were not of interest to state television, and instead allowed the events in Lebanon to make the headlines." He cited how the state television station Al-Masria, in search of an enemy to put the blame on, pointed finger at Al-Jazeera merely because the Qatari station broadcast a "life picture of the protests."[199] There was no mention of this theme in *Alwafd*.

Summary

After the Friday of Anger clashes, Mubarak's rule looked more precarious than ever before. On the evening of that day, there were reports of looting and a number of police cars and stations set on fire, together with prisons being opened and its inmates escaping. That resulted in a state of chaos spreading across the country, which pushed people to form vigilance groups. This state of chaos that Egyptians experienced in the two days that followed the Friday of Anger is documented in the next chapter, Chapter 4, which is titled "Chaos of a Revolution: Police Withdrawal and the Vigilantes." I lived that experience myself and spent two nights with neighbors on the streets protecting our vicinity.

The sudden eruption of fighting on Tahrir Square between revolutionaries and pro-Mubarak demonstrators shocked the eyes of the world and cost the Mubarak regime its legitimacy. I went out on the noon of Saturday January 29 to buy as many daily newspapers as possible since we had no Internet access for two days. I also wanted to speak with ordinary citizens on the street and get a feeling of the pulse of the Egyptian society after the horrific experience of the day before. On the destruction that was inflicted and fire set on a number of buildings, a young man in his early twenties denied that Egyptian protesters were the ones that did it, "as some officials claim," asserting that criminals had been released from prison by government to "plant fears" in the Egyptian society and offer the Mubarak regime full authority to do whatever it wishes to silence "our revolution." As I was standing at a supermarket in a middle-class area I asked a lady in her late forties about her views on what happened, and she immediately shouted at me: "We are Egyptians and none of us would destroy buildings. These criminals are planted in by those who hate Egypt and want to destroy us." In way back to my residence, one car driver told the man sitting next to him, "With Allah's will, we are capable of protecting our country."

The official government statements made on the Friday of Anger did not respond to the message of pro-democracy protesters—who were demanding relief from decades of emergency rule, economic stagnation, and social inequality—and that further infuriated them as the coming chapters will reveal. Reports estimated the number of protesters (among whom were film stars, politicians, and factory workers) to be over 300,000 on that day. That number increased on the day after, leading to Tahrir Square being shut down to traffic.[200] The clashes on Tahrir resulted in the death and injuries of many.

The independent press and partisan press tried to be objective in their covering of the Friday of Anger protests. They did not rule out that the Tunisian revolution had inspired Egyptians to demonstrate and call for political and social changes in the Land of the Nile. The independent press was critical of the claim by the national press that Al-Jazeera and other independent Arab satellite stations were provoking the protests. Only the national press propagated the conspiracy theory. Its journalists often quoted Egyptians speaking of foreign forces being involved in igniting the violence and looting. But many of the ordinary Egyptians I chatted with stressed (in rage) that no Egyptian would break into his own museum to steal and damage his or her own treasures. But why was the partisan press more critical of Mubarak than the independent press? Why did it speak more of a revolution? The answer to these questions lies in the fact that the partisan press, as I have mentioned above, is known as the opposition press. And examining articles from the paper of the liberal New Wafd Party, we see a perfect example of that. It is also possible that the "forged" 2010 parliamentary elections, which diminished the opposition Party's hope to increase its seats in Parliament,[201] played a role in mounting its criticism of Mubarak and opting for a change in regime.

As I have noted in the introduction of this book, Egyptians are known for their humor, including political jokes. Here is one such gem for this chapter. Mohamed Amin El-Masry, a journalist at *Al-Ahram*, tells the following story: On a bitter cold winter evening, a child hears the expression "political corruption" and asks his father what it means. Finding it difficult to explain to his child, the father tried to use symbolic expressions to draw his son's attention away from it. So, he says to him, "I earn the money we need to take care of the house, and therefore I am 'capitalism.' Your mother manages the house and hence we call her the 'government.' You are on a lower rung and spend the money; hence, you are the 'public.' Your baby brother is our hope, and thus we call him the 'future.' Our servant earns her living from us, so she is the 'working class.' " The child went on thinking about what his father had said, hoping perhaps he could understand something. Then came the night and he could not sleep because of the cries of his baby brother. He jumped from his bed in worry and went to check his brother, whom he found wet in his diapers. He went to inform his mother and found her deep asleep, but he wondered why his father was not sleeping next to her. While searching for his father to change his baby brother's clothes, he heard whispers and giggling in the servant's room. He peeped in and saw his father with the servant, holding her in his arms. On the next day, the child told his father: "Dad, I have learned what political corruption means." The father wondered how his son could learn the meaning in such a short time, so he asked him: "What did you learn then, son?" The child answered, "When capitalism plays with the working class while government is deep asleep, and the public becomes worried but is completely ignored, and the future sinks in dirt, then we have political corruption." The father was dazzled by his son's intelligence and how well he had grasped the true meaning of political corruption.[202]

CHAPTER 4. CHAOS OF A REVOLUTION: POLICE WITHDRAWAL AND THE VIGILANTES

In the a few days that followed the eruption of the Egyptian revolution on January 25, 2011, a state of chaos swept Egypt, with a looting drive hitting major cities. The police had withdrawn from the streets on the evening of January 28, known as the Friday of Anger. There were numerous questions on people's minds at the time, most prominent of which was: Why did the police abandon their job and leave the citizens vulnerable to violence and the streets to vandalism? The worst day of looting and threat to people's security was Saturday January 29—the day that followed the Friday of Anger. Chapter 4 is an attempt to record people's feelings and reactions to the state of disorder that engulfed the country as mirrored in media coverage in the two days that followed. Although the army had increased its presence since it was dispatched on the streets on the evening of Friday January 28, protesters defied the curfew (which was imposed from that day on from 6:00 p.m. to 7:00 a.m.) and kept pouring into Tahrir Square and major squares across the country in the days that followed. The military exercised restraint and did not fire live ammunition at protesters.

Public anger was also soaring among Egyptians who were seeing their nation's capital set aflame. The scale of the unrest was massive; indeed the country was passing through a very difficult moment. Fear soared among Egyptians who were concerned about protecting their families, properties, and the future of their nation. Protests and images of soldiers on the streets rocked the nation and forced tourists and diplomats to leave the country. It was a moment that no one had ever anticipated, and it happened in a flash. People in cars reported being stopped and robbed of their money and belongings.[203] On the evening of that day, my uncle, together with his son, went to pick his daughter from the airport; she was coming from Saudi Arabia. On their way back they were stopped by "criminals" but managed to escape, with their car receiving slight damage. The headquarters of the then-ruling National Democratic Party (NDP), which is located nearby Tahrir Square—in Abdel-Moneim Riad Square—was burned.[204] Similar events, including attacks on police stations and government entities, were reported in other major Egyptian cities. Alas, all I can remember is hearing people speak of looting sprees, attacks, raids on houses, plundering, and lack of safety on the streets. This left Egyptians wondering who was behind it all. This is when I knew that the Hosni Mubarak regime had lost its credibility in the eyes of Egyptians and that he would have to step down.

Police Withdrawal

On January 28, we heard that the police had collapsed and disappeared from police stations in Cairo and major cities across the country (at the time Egypt was formed of 29 governorates) after police attacked peaceful demonstrations with rubber and live bullets and tear gas bombs, and protesters fought back; the police crushed some of them with unmarked cars on the Friday of Anger. Questions have emerged as to why there were no police officers on the streets beginning the following day, Saturday January 29. Why did most police stations shut down? A piece on the cover page of the January 31 issue of Egypt's English language daily newspaper *The Egyptian Gazette* invited readers to go online and fill out a poll that asked them whether the sudden disappearance of the police from Cairo streets was (a) deliberate or (b) due to exhaustion. I personally asked the same question of many of the people whom I met during that time. Most of them said it was "deliberate" and aimed at frightening people to get them to accept the "Al Mubarak" rule. A lawyer in his mid-twenties whom I met on a train coming from Alexandria to Cairo described to me the fear he and his neighbors felt due to the lack of security. He spoke of seeing police officers chasing around in cars in their neighborhood in Cairo shooting bullets in the air, and that made him stay in his flat holding members of his family in his arms. When he and his neighbors took the courage to go down to ask the police why they were doing this, he said one of them replied: "We're doing this just to frighten the looters." He swore that the police were shooting those bullets to frighten his neighborhood and coerce the youths of the working-class area not to go out in the streets and protest. Based on this young lawyer's story, one can conjecture that while the police disappeared in most parts of Cairo, they showed up in some other areas. It is possible that his story was an exceptional case, yet I think it worth telling.

The police, whose numbers total 750,000, were absent for three days; this was previously unthinkable. Protesters were unarmed and had nothing to defend themselves with but small stones which they collected by breaking up the street platforms in the square. I documented that myself when I went to visit the Square a week after Mubarak stepped down.

On Saturday, January 29, there were reports that prisoners were being released from major jails and detention centers—such as Wadi Natroun, Qanater, Abu Zabal, Fayyoum—and some police stations were looted and burned. On that day, looters were seen in my hometown city of Benha, located 35 miles north of Cairo. Neighborhoods across the city formed networks of vigilantes, and we all—doctors, lawyers, engineers, university lecturers, shop owners, college students, among others—had to hold sticks and spend a couple of nights in the streets to protect property. We clashed with some looters; I saw a couple of them myself. They were both on motorcycles and one had what some called a "criminal face"; the other was well-built and had the look of "national security forces" staff, in some people's opinion. When one of them was caught, the other ran away and abandoned the motorcycle. A neighbor who serves as a lawyer said that both these motorcycles (which carried no plates and were in bad shape, with large numbers and words written in white on their black seats) were kept in a police-maintained isolated area on the side of the Nile River because they are often "stolen" or carry no identification of ownership. The question that came to on my mind then was how they had got them, and where were the police. It seemed to me at the time that their aim was not just to loot but to frighten people. I took the risk and walked late that night to take a close look at the police station in our neighborhood; I found it deserted. That was Saturday. On Sunday, we realized that similar events were taking place in many other cities. And we knew all about it, not through the Egyptian media but via the pan-Arab satellite stations. In my case, I got most of the news via the BBC, CNN, and Al-Jazeera English, mainly because I trusted their coverage—particularly their accuracy and objectivity, which at times the Arabic-language, Arab-owned satellite stations lack.

The human-rights violations by the police and the acts of vandalism and thuggery that took place angered Egyptians to such an extent that when a police officer was seen in the days that followed, many people felt uneasy. It was reported that police stations were set fire in a number of cities, with some 99 police stations said to have been attacked across the country, particularly in Cairo, Suez, Alexandria, Ismailia, and Mansura. Prison and jails were also attacked. But many Egyptians continue until this very day to believe that police released prisoners under an order from Minister of Interior Habib El-Adli to frighten protesters and spread chaos across the country. It was said that up to 12,000 prisoners were released (that number later increased), some of whom were considered a threat to the country's security. It was also reported that some of the prisoners who had only a few months left before their official release refused to leave, and that prison staff shot them dead. A woman who appeared on the privately-owned Dream2 television station spoke of how her imprisoned son—who was only weeks away from being released—was shot by prison guards because he was reluctant to leave or go on the street to "commit acts of vandalism." Popular journalist and long anti-Mubarak activist Ibrahim Issa was also on the TV program and alleged that police released prisoners to spread chaos and frighten people, and to weaken the protesters' impact.[205]

Similarly, claims were made by Egyptian intellectuals that Minister of Interior El-Adli was the one who ordered his police forces to abandon their jobs and release prisoners. Yehia El-Gaml, a law professor, spoke in an interview with the independent Al-Hayat television station of a possible "conspiracy," that releasing prisoners and sending central security forces out on the streets was aimed at intimidating people into ending the protests and accept the Mubarak rule. He called for an immediate investigation.[206] Others said that there was a clash between Mubarak and El-Adli because the latter did not want the army put to do what he felt was more properly his ministry's task, and thus he released prisoners and ordered his officers to abandon their posts in revenge. There was also the rumor that El-Adli refused a Mubarak order to shoot on protesters and resigned, and that Mubarak was the perpetrator.

And these rumors have kept on flying in the skies of the Land of the Nile. Some people have even alleged that the bomb blast at the Two Saints Church (or Al-Qiddissin Church, in Arabic) in Alexandria on New Year's Eve was the work of security police, who had *carte blanche* to commit whichever atrocity it wished against demonstrators (whom it often refers to as members of the then banned Muslim Brotherhood). In a speech on January 23, El-Adli claimed that the blast, which left twenty-three killed and ninety wounded, was the work of an al Qaeda-like group in Gaza. Mubarak later took to the stage and praised police for the "identification of the perpetrators," and this, he added, "comforted the hearts of all Egyptians." Yet there was still, and despite Mubarak's statement, a sense of uncertainty among Coptic Christians as to who the true criminal was. (As this book went to print, the issue of police withdrawal remains under investigation, with no clear answers offered to the public of who was the true culprit.)

Findings

According to Ibrahim Nafie, former board chair of the giant Cairo-based Al-Ahram Publishing Group, the night of Sunday January 30 was horrific—one in which police disappeared, security was lost, and prison cells opened for criminals to loot and vandalize. I, like most Egyptians, never thought I would live to witness "a night such as that one" in a country "whose ancestors had lived in a stable state for thousands of years," as Nafie added.[207] We have had enough of "destruction and vandalism," cried the head of the Egyptian Syndicate of Journalists Makram Mohamed Ahmed, who called on protesters to abide by the law and remain indoors during curfew time. We have had enough of "collective suicide," he said. He praised Omar Suleiman as a man "capable" of executing the duty of a vice president.[208] A piece in the party paper *Alwafd* also commended Mubarak for appointing Suleiman as vice president and Ahmed Shafiq as prime minister.[209] Likewise, a commentary in *Al-Ahrar*, another party newspaper, praised Shafiq and chronicled what it called his "history of courage."[210]

However, Mustafa Bakri, chief editor of the independent *El-Osboa* paper, pointed out that the appointment of a vice president came too late. Hence, people expected Mubarak to declare his resignation from office during the speech he delivered on the evening of January 28.[211] The independent paper *Al-Masry Al-Youm* wrote that the speech offered us nothing but more of the same rhetoric, in which Mubarak only declared he was dissolving the government. He overlooked that it is not just the "government" but also the "administration" which is behind the state of sorrow which Egypt is in today. The article spoke of how Mubarak when he came to office was a modest man who claimed he did not intend to hold power for many years, but that changed as time went by. The article stressed that the only way out for Mubarak is to declare that he will not run for another term.[212]

As anticipated, the criticism that came at Mubarak emerged solely from the independent and partisan Egyptian press. In a piece written as a letter addressed to President Mubarak, Bakri stressed that the thousands of people who went out in protest were supported by eighty million Egyptians. He admonished the regime of Mubarak, describing it as an emblem of "corruption and despotism" that has thrived on the back of the poor over the past three decades. Due to its failing policies, six million Egyptians are now suffering psychiatric diseases and twenty million are complaining of deep depression. Bakri added that Mubarak's "police state" has widely violated human rights.[213] They want us to "either accept Hosni Mubarak and his regime or live in chaos and with criminal gangs," declared the independent paper *Al-Shorouk Al-Jadeed*.[214] In his *Al-Masry Al-Youm* commentary, El-Gaml asked Mubarak to dissolve the recently-elected Parliament, abolish emergency law, state that his son Gamal would not "inherit" the presidency, elect a committee to write a new constitution, and declare that he would not run for another term in office. El-Gaml added, "Mr. President: You are the longest standing ruler in the country since Mohamed Ali, the founder of modern Egypt."[215] He chided, "the consultants and decision-makers close to you have deceived you by giving the wrong advice at the wrong time.[216] *Al-Shorouk Al-Jadeed* asked some of Mubarak's closest associates—members of the armed forces such Vice President Suleiman, Prime Minister Shafiq, and Field Marshal Hussein Tantawi—to call on him to step down, dissolve Parliament, hold new elections, and write a new constitution.[217]

The Vigilantes

Egyptians battled to cope with police absence while hordes of hooligans spread across the nation and reach even to the treasures of the Egyptian Museum. To build a sense of unity among a disillusioned Egyptian public, the Egyptian broadcast media—both national and private—spoke about and showed images of ordinary Egyptians holding hands and circling together with tanks to protect the Egyptian Museum, which holds precious monuments that date back five thousand years ago. A number of people spoke with tears in their eyes of how they would do all they could to safeguard these treasures which, as they observed, belong not only to Egyptians but to the whole of humanity. Some of the streets of Benha were a scorched mess of broken bricks, glass, and pieces of woods. I saw the city's main police station ablaze, and there was not a single policeman on the street.

People in my city, as in many other cities, had to fend for themselves because army units were mostly stationed on main streets and crossroads. Egyptians of all ages had to take matters into our own hands and form networks of vigilantes to protect our neighborhoods, and again the youth in our neighborhood and across the country deserve praise for exerting so much effort to keep peace and order; they carried the heavy burden. Many of them spent whole nights on the streets, wielding sticks and knives and putting up barricades to protect their properties and themselves. They sat at roadblocks, at times using stone blocks, empty barrels, and pieces of trees. In some places, they asked people to park their cars sideways to block vehicles from driving in our neighborhood. With courage, wrote *El-Osboa*, the youth of Egypt—from tiny villages to big cities—broke the "barriers of fear" to protect Egypt from gangs of criminals and rescue it from chaos. "This is a situation unseen before in Egypt's modern history."[218] And, yes, I saw some of them battling it out with looters. But when the army started spreading in the streets, some sense of relief was seen on people's faces; Egyptians hold a deep sense of trust and respect for their country's military forces.

The pace of events had taken Egyptians by surprise; I saw some of them, particularly children and the elderly, sitting in bewilderment, trying to decipher what was going on. Until January 31, I saw no police officers or police cars in our neighborhood; only a couple of army vehicles showed up to insure peace. I saw young men appointing themselves traffic wards; others forming human shields to protect places of national importance. At noon of that day, I witnessed a scene that will always remain in my mind. Four of our neighborhood's kids (aged between eight and ten) were holding small sticks in their hands and imitating what we had been doing the night before. They even tried to pull down one of the barricades which we put on the street's platform during the daytime and which we used at night to stop traffic. They must have been eagerly watching what we were doing from their balconies. A couple of them were shouting: "We will protect our communities." In fact, I never heard folks in our neighborhood say that, but they were copying also what some imams and priests were repeating by microphone from mosques and churches in an endeavor to raise the spirit of unity against looting in their communities.

Release of Prisoners

The military estimated that 24,000 prisoners were released from prisons across the country between January 25 and February 11. They were "ordered to escape"—that is what some of them later said. It was reported that 11,000 of them were captured prior to the end of February. In articles published in the Egyptian press on January 31, journalists and political commentators denounced the state of chaos from January 26 to 30. The independent and party press called it a "silly satire" mainly aimed at frightening people into accepting the status quo by ending the protests and accepting the rule of Mubarak. "The country's security apparatus is an enemy of the people," commented *Al-Masry Al-Youm*.[219] In "President Wants the Downfall of People," *Al-Shorouk Al-Jadeed* columnist Wael Quandil, known for his political satire, lamented that the "only way out to remain in power for a person who has occupied office for thirty years is to exterminate the eighty million Egyptians. . . . Mubarak has heard and seen some of them cry, "People Want to Bring Down the Regime," but he is not listening, and there seems to be no hope but for the people to leave and let him relish being in power." Quandil disdainfully added:

> You, who stick to ruling people who do not want you, go ahead then and bomb the thousands of angry citizens in Cairo and Egyptian governorates with Napalm and germ weapons. Go ahead and exterminate us or detain us, wipe us from the face of this earth so that Egypt remains only for you to play with as you wish. You have put its people in a state in which death has become better for them than life under your "intelligent" leadership.

Quandil further claimed that some police officers were seen taking part in spreading this state of fear in the country (which included shortage of bread, food, and petrol) in order to force citizens to accept that security is more important than political reform and change of leadership.[220]

Many wondered not only why all this was happening but how it could have happened. A piece in *Al-Shorouk Al-Jadeed* put it this way: "Let's assume policemen could not find their officers to ask them what to do. Let's suppose that Habib El-Edli was not a conspirator but failed in his duty, with his forces being unable to counter the disorder. Why did not Hosni Mubarak then intervene and quickly issue instructions to contain the situation and stop the looting?"[221] Likewise, *Al-Gomhuria* asked: "How did these thieves control the Egyptian street? Has the number of criminals truly reached that level? What benefit would they gain from invading and stealing from hospitals and setting fire to public institutions?" The state-owned paper further wondered who had released the prisoners from jail.[222]

In "Rebuilding the State," Mohamed Mosallam of *Al-Masry Al-Youm* stressed that we "must rebuild the country's institutions on the basis of justice, competence, and accountability so that they do not collapse another time." He demanded that El-Adli be tried for using "live ammunition" against protesters.[223] Alaa El-Ghatrifi drew a parallel between those who spread chaos and destruction and the acts committed by the priests of the god Amun of ancient Egypt, who were angered by the pharaoh Ikhnaton's abandoning of polytheism and promoting monotheism,[224] which meant weakening their position and hurting of their business. "The looting and vandalism came from them [pro-Mubarak], and not us," stipulated El-Ghatrifi. "We are now 'breathing freedom'; we were never born to be 'slaves.'"[225]

Safwat Kabel, an academic, does not doubt that there are pro-Mubarak puppets trying to widen the state of fear among people via vandalism and looting to coerce us to lament the "good old days" of Mubarak's rule. Certainly, argued Kabel, there have been looting and vandalism in many parts of Egypt over the past a few days but the state television has placed it in a much bigger scale.[226] It seems as if the decision of police withdrawal was taken in order to "release gangs from prison to loot" so as to "frighten people and tarnish the reputation of protesters in these critical moments in the lives of Egyptians," asserted Salama Ahmed Salama, chief editor of *Al-Shorouk Al-Jadeed*.[227] These "criminals," said *Al-Gomhuria*, have hurt the main principles of the protests and tarnished the picture of the Egyptian society in front of the whole world.[228]

Portrayal of Armed Forces

As I stated earlier, the army was out on the streets of Cairo early in the evening of January 28, when the police inexplicably disappeared. A day later, government television stations broadcast a statement by the armed forces that imposed the curfew and cautioned that looters would be punished. Praise for the role the armed forces played during the protests was reiterated in all forms of the Egyptian media. For example, *Al-Gomhuria* extolled the army for maintaining the security of Egypt.[229] The armed forces have always been the "shield" that protects Egypt against all dangers, said *Al-Shorouk Al-Jadeed*.[230] In the opinion of *Alwafd*, all Egyptians "value and respect" their military establishment as the one that protects them in "times of war and peace." But even so, we were told, we needed a "government of national salvation" that represented all citizens and that could be entrusted with the task of reforming the constitution, maintaining security, and dissolving a Parliament whose members have come to power through "fraud."[231]

Again, the Egyptian media offered positive coverage of the army (whose presence increased in the days that followed the Friday of Anger). Egypt had lived through "four days of a nightmare," wrote *Al-Ahram*, and unless the President had dispatched the army things could have gotten worse.[232] Yet the breakdown in law and order, or what many characterized as a "counter revolution," and which we will touch on below, went on nonetheless in the Land of the Nile.

Summary

From the time violence broke out on Friday January 28, Egyptians were living in a nation at risk, and thus they had to form citizen groups to see to local security. According to distinguished *Alwafd* journalist Abbas El-Tarabilli, vigilance groups (or "vigilantes") are nothing new; Egyptians have employed them throughout history when "facing danger from outside invaders or internal chaos."[233] In the days that followed January 28, there were demonstrations everywhere by unions and religious-dominated groups and ordinary citizens as well to protest the lack of security, looting and vandalism, fear of violence breaking out on the borders with Israel, and on top of all that the issue of the conflict over Nile water with other Nile Basin countries.[234] All I can remember of the evenings of Friday and Saturday December 28 and 29 is people asking: How long will this state of chaos go on? Weeks, months? What if the police leave us like this until we breathe our last breath? When a new interior minister was appointed in the transitional government after the revolution, a new motto—"Police in Service of Its Citizens"—was instituted, superseding the previous one which advocated, "Police and Citizens in Service of Their Homeland."

But in order for a true civil state to be established, Egyptian intellectuals at that time demanded the following:

- End of what renowned *Alwafd* columnist Nabil Zaki called the "police state."[235]

- Establishment of an independent body to monitor police conduct.

- Appointment of an interior minister with a background in politics and not from the police.

- Abolishment of the central security forces, which operated under the interior ministry (and whose number is estimated to be more than double of the armed forces).

- Production of a better sense of professionalism among police officers by reforming their training system and curricula, and providing them with improved technology tools.

In conclusion, it is also worth citing how Washington's strong ties with Egypt were characterized in the news. In his televised speech from the White House on February 1, President Barack Obama praised the "sense of community in the streets" that Egyptians had shown. He added that that sense of truth and courage could "be seen in the mothers and fathers embracing soldiers. And it [could] be seen in the Egyptians who linked arms to protect the national museum—a new generation protecting the treasures of antiquity; a human chain connecting a great and ancient civilization to the promise of a new day." Obama stated, "To the people of Egypt, particularly the young people of Egypt, I want to be clear: We hear your voices. I have an unyielding belief that you will determine your own destiny and seize the promise of a better future for your children and your grandchildren. And I say that as someone who is committed to a partnership between the United States and Egypt." The private and partisan press voiced no criticism of the United States; however, the state media at times denounced Washington and the U.S. media for their "unbalanced stance" toward Egypt. For example, Abdelmoneim Said, board chair of Al-Ahram Publishing Group, criticized U.S. television stations for blowing the protests out of proportion by repeating coverage.[236]

Chapter 5. Black Wednesday: The Battle of the Camel

Tuesday, February 1, 2010, was called as a "day of determination," with protesters calling for one million people to gather in Tahrir (Arabic for "Liberation") Square. Anti-government demonstrations were huge despite the government reshuffle in the preceding two days. In the speech he delivered late on that evening, President Hosni Mubarak appointed for the first time a vice president but he indicated no intention to leave office, insisting that he would stay until the elections (scheduled for September) to oversee constitutional reform during the transitional period. He appealed to Egyptians to remember his "accomplishments" and his record as a war veteran. But protesters denounced his message, called for his immediate removal, and vowed to go on demonstrating. Chants echoed in Tahrir Square, against a backdrop of anti-Mubarak signs, with one proclaiming: "Out Mubarak: You're a Client of America." Some of the signs were funny: one said "Get Out!" written in reverse Arabic letters, and beneath it the explanation: "Maybe he'll get the message when he's turned upside down." Another man was sleeping in a tent, with a banner inscribed: "Get out! I miss my wife (married 20 days ago)."

After Mubarak's interview with ABC TV[237] on February 3, in which he said he was "fed up" of ruling Egypt, a young man at Tahrir Square came up with a sign that read: "Why are *you* fed up, Mr. President? Has anyone insulted you, hit you, given you electric shocks at a police station; are you tired of a state hospital in which a son of yours has died of negligence? Are you unable to pay for private lessons for your children; are you out of work and sitting unemployed at a coffee shop? Can't you find money to buy a flat so your son can marry and move out? Why are *you* fed up, Mr. President?"

Unlike the "Friday of Anger," this million-person march was peaceful and no clashes broke out. Protesters carried placards calling for political reform, release of political prisoners, and an end to emergency law. Popular Egyptian figures such as Hollywood actor Omar El-Sharif and Nobel Prize winners Mohamed ElBaradei and Ahmed Zewail (both are Egyptian nationals)[238] attended the protests. In an interview with the BBC from Tahrir on that day, El-Sharif wished that Mubarak would step down, but he accused the Egyptian President of being "stubborn." In an interview with Egypt's privately-owned Dream2 television station, also held on February 1, Zewail praised the "Egyptian youth" who marched for change without any "political or ideological" background. He, like ElBaradei and El-Sharif, called on Mubarak to step down.[239]

Following Mubarak's speech—the second of three televised speeches he delivered to the nation before he stepped down—some protesters left Tahrir Square, believing that their demands were being met, or, rather, that they should now give him a chance and wait and see what would come out. The majority of Egyptians were not satisfied, however, and jeers such as "mesh meshyeen" ("we are not leaving") and "erhal, erhal" ("Step down, Step down") filled the air.

On the next day, February 2, violent clashes erupted between pro- and anti-government groups; this became what was described as "Black Wednesday" or the "Battle of the Camel." Mubarak supporters—some called them state-sponsored thugs ("baltaguiya")—entered the Square at around 1:00 p.m. riding camels and horses and attacked protesters with whips, sticks, stones, and knives. In the evening, gunshots and Molotov cocktails rained down on protesters from the rooftops of what were later said to be the Mogamma (the biggest government employment building), the American University in Cairo, and the Cairo Museum. The hours-long, Egyptian-against-Egyptian battle left many injured and a number of fatalities. Protesters showed Arab journalists identification cards which they had found and claimed belonged to the secret police. All this made protesters more insistent in their call for Mubarak's removal from office. Some of those anti-Mubarak protesters enchanted: Tahrir hatta tahrir ("Tahrir until liberation"). The return salvo from pro-Mubarak supporters was: "He will not leave; it is you who should leave."

Chapter 5 examines media materials (commentaries from newspapers and television broadcast) from the day that followed the Battle of the Camel—Thursday, February 3. Broadcast materials aired on February 2 are also included.

Findings

Opposing viewpoints concerning the clashes of the Battle of the Camel were apparent in coverage of the state media on one side and the partisan and independent media on the other side. Criticism of protesters mainly came from the state media. "What do the protesters want?" asked the state paper *Al-Akhbar*. "All we see is their craving to spread chaos in the country and try to turn it into another Iran."[240] Many of the independent papers denounced what they described as the "dreadful scene" of pro-government men entering Tahrir on camel- and horse-back and attacking protesters with sticks, stones, and knives. The independent paper *Al-Shorouk Al-Jadeed* called for the trial of Mubarak's men who orchestrated the Battle of the Camel. "The devilish mind that designed the plan to save Mubarak's face in the manner witnessed yesterday in the Egyptian capital should be tried for mass extermination and igniting a civil war."[241]

An editorial in the party paper *Al-Ahali* called on Egypt to join hands with its youth to break the "barrier of fear" and push the country forward because the "countdown for the Mubarak regime has begun."[242] While the state paper *Al-Gomhuria* recognized that a revolution was taking place, it cautioned that "chaos was spreading in Egypt from Sinai to Aswan." The paper recommended that the youth revolution has achieved its goals and protesters should go back home and allow life to get back to normal. The paper then challenged some of the protesters' claims: "I call on the young people to ask themselves who distributed to each one of them a bag of food, bottles of water, an apple and fifty pounds. Can any party in Egypt afford to spend fifty million pounds daily—if the number of protesters is one million, as they claim? Who is paying for this?" The youth that took part in the protests were not those that received money. They are different individuals who try to gain from a youth revolution led by good young people who desire reform and change.[243]

"I didn't ask anyone at Tahrir to express my views," said an *Al-Akhbar* columnist. "Enough chaos and gambling with the future of this nation; what is taking place supersedes demands for change. It is an attempt to trample on constitutional legitimacy."[244] Egypt will stand "strong" despite all its enemies, stressed an Al-Azhar University professor, and it will remain a "minaret" of science and a hub of civilizations.[245]

Most of the commentaries in the semi-official state-owned *Al-Ahram* newspaper focused on the destruction caused during the week of protests. Who should carry the financial burden, wondered one of its editorials, which went on to ask President Mubarak to place it on the shoulders of businessmen who had accumulated huge amounts of wealth over the past a few years.[246] Another *Al-Ahram* piece proclaimed that Vice President Suleiman had been entrusted with the task of initiating dialogue with protesters, and said they must realize that dialogue is the way out from this ongoing confrontation.[247]

Al-Gomhuria columnist Mohsein Mohamed lamented, "Egypt has lost a lot in a week of evil and crimes. They did not just attack the present and the future but also the past because they tried to rob the Egyptian Museum at Tahrir." He called for a rapid embrace and implementation of democracy in Egypt so that these protests would not be repeated.[248]

Should Mubarak Go or Should He Stay?

Disapproval of Mubarak was repeated mostly in the privately-owned (independent) media and the partisan press, with some stressing that his speech came too late and that he failed to apologize to the families who lost loved ones in the protests. Commentators furthermore criticized the Egyptian President for not responding to the demands of demonstrators—namely dissolving parliament, reforming the constitution, and publically stating that he did not intend to pass the presidency to his forty-four-year-old son Gamal. The party paper *Alwafd* said that Mubarak's declaration that he would not run for office raised questions and bewilderment. "Had he intended to remain for another six years after ruling already for thirty years?" Why did not he declare that his son would not run for the presidency? The party paper further mourned, "Prior to Mubarak's rule, Egyptians hated to leave their homeland. But under his leadership they have become the fastest migratory birds among nations of the world."[249] Other commentators were more pointed in their criticism and demanded that he step down immediately.

A column in *Al-Shorouk Al-Jadeed* pointed out:

> I liked President Mubarak during the early years of his leadership, a period in which he offered Egyptians great hope—hope which was perhaps honest, too. But many years have passed, more than ... any person in power can handle.... things have gotten worse to a degree that makes any person who sincerely admires the President or his humaneness must recommend that he quickly relinquishes power.[250]

Gamal Younis of *Alwafd* admonished Mubarak for delaying before addressing his people—and for forming a new government and an administration of "senior citizens." Younis reminded readers that when Mubarak first assumed the presidency after Sadat's assassination, he promised he would not rule for more than two terms, but once he had his "grip on things" he refused to amend the Constitution so that "he remain[ed] in office for life."[251] The independent paper *Al-Masry Al-Youm* suggested that the men who surrounded Mubarak deceived him because they made him believe that all Egyptians supported the National

Democratic Party (NDP), and that it had smashed the opposition in a "fair" election in 2010.[252]

Many commentators in the independent and partisan press described Mubarak as a stubborn man: former editor-in-chief of *Al-Ahram* Mohamed Hasseinein Heikel said he holds a "doctorate in stubbornness." In a piece in *Al-Masry Al-Youm*, Heikel, who also served as an advisor to President Gamal Abdel Nasser and is known today as the Arab world's most distinguished journalist and author, cautioned that Mubarak had placed everyone in a crisis by clinging to his office. But, he added, the million-people marches brought him down despite his stubbornness.[253]

Alwafd wondered from where Mubarak's "stubbornness and arrogance" come from. "Is it because of staying too long in power or is it because of Egypt's pharaonic heritage that turns a ruler from a human being into a god ruling on earth? Or is it because of the heritage of the July 23 [1952] Revolution when Gamal Abdel Nasser established Egypt's political reality from the top of a tank?"[254] Mubarak's decisions during the protests were nothing but an "attempt" to abort the dream of democratic change in Egypt, proclaimed *Al-Shorouk Al-Jadeed*.[255] El-Shafai Basheer, a legal expert, decried those decisions and described Mubarak as an "obstinate man who has killed three hundred Egyptians" without explaining why. He condemned Mubarak for dispatching his "national army" to the arena and sending military planes to fly over the "heads of protesters" at Tahrir. He further accused the "devils" of the NDP of manufacturing a constitution to "suit" him and his son, Gamal. Basheer sardonically wrote, "What more ... do you want, you longstanding and obstinate man? You have had your chance from October 1981 to January 2011—that is a total of three hundred sixty months and more than ten thousand days—and all you have brought us to is last week's sea of blood and the killing of three hundred citizens by the bullets of your tyrant police hordes." He called on Mubarak to step down immediately (even if on the pretext of medical conditions and based on articles 82, 83, 84 of the Constitution) and to appoint two civilian leaders, besides his military one, Field Marshal Mohamed Tantawi, to form a presidential council to guide the nation during the transitional period and based on article 139 of the Constitution. Basheer's piece was published in the independent paper *El-Dostour* and titled "You the Longstanding Obstinate."[256]

The acclaimed commentator Fahmi Howeidi vehemently denounced Mubarak's speech for remarking on the destruction that took place during the protests but overlooking the causes behind people's anger, adding that Mubarak had changed "individuals and procedures but not policies." He stipulated that it was "good" that Mubarak had declared that he would not run for another term, but that he should have also stated that the emergency law would be abolished and Gamal would not run for the presidency.[257]

Ekram Lamai, a professor of comparative religions, spoke of how the NDP and the Mubarak administration have become unable to communicate with Egypt's growing generation of youth. Drawing on religious verses from the Bible and the French Revolution, Lamai argued that Egypt's ruling regime could surprisingly be characterized as dictatorial, royal, and democratic all at once. Dictatorial because its focus was on establishing "security via fear," and royal because it insisted on being "glorified" while remaining disconnected from the public; and democratic because it "allows for elections and press freedom."[258] The paper also said that before Mubarak's speech "we held hope that Egypt was a step away from ... freedom," but "we were wrong because his words came as a great disappointment.[259] They came to confirm that a dictatorial regime never changes. "This regime must be changed."[260] The President should declare that he will not run for a second term and lay out a time frame for reforming the Constitution in a manner that allows for "free competition," wrote Amina El-Naqkash, editor of *Al-Ahali*.[261] Under Mubarak, noted the popular political analyst Amr El-Shobaki, Egyptians have lived in an age of "oppression and humiliation," and this youth revolution "will put an end to the pharaonic heritage which has governed much of our social and political relations." This regime is experiencing political failure but also "an ethical, social and economic one as well in a manner unseen before." He praised the "January 25 Revolution" as one of the greatest revolutions carried out by civilians, reflecting the peaceful and friendly nature of the Egyptian people. "Yes, Egypt has changed; it has been born again."[262] Mr. President, said *Alwafd*, it is time for you to leave.[263]

Gamil Matar, director of the Arab Center for Development and Future Studies, believes the Egyptian media played a "disrespectful role" when they selected "unclean personalities from among Egyptian businessmen and promoted them as successful models for youth to follow their footsteps. Under Mubarak, he lamented,

> [W]e lived a very long and sad period in which a sense of pessimism about Egypt's future prevailed. It was hard or impossible for Egyptian youth to dream and for new ingredients capable of constructing a new society to emerge from among them, simply because all they were hearing daily from the police machines and the state media were stories and investigations portraying them as trivial at best and criminal or divergent in most cases.[264]

Others observed that Mubarak is "not our father," and we are "not living on his own land; we are living on the land of Egypt."[265] His regime has stripped people of their rights, making them feel like strangers on their own lands, wrote Camelia Shukri in *Alwafd*. It has spread unprecedented corruption, with its members distributing to themselves massive expanses of state lands.[266] But we should also blame ourselves, for we have gotten the regime used to not listening to our wishes.[267] *Al-Masry Al-Youm* columnist Mohamed Amin conjectured that Mubarak would declare his resignation on February 4,[268] and suggested the best person to replace Mubarak was ElBaradei because he is an "honest" man who is known to the West and has a "liberal" mind that speaks the language of "globalization."[269]

Other independent and partisan papers spoke in favor of Mubarak or avoided criticizing him altogether. For instance, Galal Abdel Aal of the party paper *Al-Ahrar* stipulated that he supports "change and reform but not destruction." President Mubarak, added Aal, said he will stay through his term and we should give him a chance. "We are a nation that does not respect its symbols. This man has accomplished a lot for Egypt."[270] There were other claims. He opts to leave it in a safe and stable condition, and we should give him a chance because he defended "Egyptian soil" in the 1973 War with Israel, said *Al-Masry Al-Youm*.[271] He is a great military leader—the brain that orchestrated the big air force hit in that War—and his holding to power today unveils not only his courage but also his "patriotism, sincerity, and love for this nation."[272] Mubarak was, according to writer Selim Azouz, against his wife Susanne's arrangement to pass the presidency to Gamal. Azouz, who took part in the protests, said that all he and the protesters wanted was to see Egypt move from a "police state" to a "law-abiding state." He proclaimed, "Our revolution has succeeded, and the evidence are Mubarak's decision not to run for the presidency, the constitutional amendments that will be implemented and the appointment of Omar Suleiman as vice president."[273] Mohamed El-Shafey of *El-Dostour* stressed that Mubarak's speech has achieved seventy five percent of the demands of youth and political forces because it has put an end to Gamal's ambitions to "inherit" the presidency and raised hope for constitutional reform and that Mubarak will remain in office only for a few months. El-Shafey predicted that the People's Assembly would be dissolved because of the rigged elections that brought its members to power. He cautioned, however, that an immediate dissolution of Parliament and forcing Mubarak to step down could result in "tempestuous political chaos."[274]

Likewise, *Alwafd*'s distinguished columnist Abbas El-Tarabilli called for calm and cautioned of a conspiracy, arguing that Mubarak had to some extent responded to protesters' demands. He accused "some impudent media" of trying to provoke division among Egyptians. "We do not want to see protesters standing against protesters, forcing the army to intervene and a tragedy to occur."[275]

In the view of an *Al-Masry Al-Youm* writer, "Egyptians are faced today with two choices": either to force Mubarak to step down and allow a state of chaos spread in the nation or to let him finish his term for the sake of our country's stability. "I support the second choice because the President also has an 'honest' vice president currently working side by side with him." The independent paper writer further cautioned: If Mubarak steps down now, the police will not come out on the street and will let the protesters face violence from those who wish to destabilize Egypt.[276]

"Egypt has tough days ahead" before it truly sees a new dawn, observed Cairo University Political Science Professor Hassan Nafaa in a piece titled "Crucial Days in Egypt's History," "but I am absolutely certain that the Egyptian people whose 'ingenuity' sparked this big revolution are capable of protecting its path" until it reaches its goals. Only a Mubarak decision declaring his resignation can open the door for "solutions suitable for establishing a true democratic system."[277]

Most of the support for Mubarak came from the state media, with many citing the pro-Mubarak marches that went out on the streets a day earlier, on February 2. The editor of the state-paper *Al-Ahram Al-Masae* wrote, "The support that the Egyptian people exhibited yesterday for President Mubarak—the leader who has led Egypt from defeat to victory—shows that there is no place for advocates of destruction and division" among us.[278] State media commentaries stressed that protesters at Tahrir do not represent the whole Egyptian population, but avoided admitting that there were demonstrations in other major Egyptian cities. President Mubarak, observed *Al-Gomhuria*, holds his post "in the name of 85 million Egyptians, and to protect them he must continue his duty until the end of his term."[279] Mohamed Abdel Moneim, a columnist at *Al-Akhbar*, spoke of how the "majority" of Egyptians and leaders of opposition parties continue to back President Mubarak and oppose the "youth of Tahrir Square."[280] The protests of Tahrir should have ended by now because Mubarak's speech has received "positive response" from the public, said *Al-Akhbar* columnist Galal Dowider. What took place invites "sadness" and "fear" about Egypt's future.[281]

Many in the state media focused on Mubarak's "highly respected" military background and the "pivotal" role he played in winning the 1973 War.[282] Mohamed Ali Ibrahim, chief editor of *Al-Gomhuria*, praised Mubarak for the victory Egypt achieved in that War, regaining of Taba, cancelling half of Egypt's debt, and insuring that no foreign military forces be stationed on Egyptian soil.[283] Gameel George described him as the "hero of war and peace," a man who "has raised Egypt's name around the globe." He added that we cannot deny that there exists corruption in Egypt under Mubarak but watchdog governmental institutions are working hard to fight it.[284] What more do we need from Mubarak after he has already declared that he will not run for the presidency, proclaimed Sabri Ghoneim of *Al-Akhbar*. He criticized Arab satellite stations for launching a "poisonous attack" on Egyptians and stressed that Mubarak will remain until his term ends.[285] Since January 25 Egypt has been witnessing the "biggest earthquake for democracy" in its history, wrote political analyst Hisham El-Sherif who praised Mubarak's leadership. He pondered,

If we have entered a new stage for democracy, do we then have the education, knowledge and freedom to practice it? We must insure of the existence of educational institutions that teach democracy, practice democracy
and produces leaders for democracy. The leaders of the twenty first century and of the information age are the leaders of January 25. Similar to the
revolutions and battles which we are proud of—such as the 1919 and 1952
revolutions, building of the High Dam and the October 6 War—history
will also record Egypt's safe passage from war to peace and that President
Hosni Mubarak is a man who has protected homeland and rebuilt modern
Egypt.[286]

In "Before and After February 1," Ibrahim of *Al-Gomhuria* agrees that "if January 25 is a historic event for the Egyptian people so too is February 1 for all Egyptian presidents." He added that Mubarak is the first president to respond to the
demands of the youth of Tahrir, most important of which are reforming articles
76 and 77 of the Constitution and the declaration that he will not run for another
presidential term.[287] Ibrahim stressed that the appointment of Suleiman as vice
president puts an end to Gamal's aspiration to succeed his father. Furthermore,
the abolishment of the emergency law can easily be implemented by the country's next president. "Mubarak is not an angel or a prophet, and his regime has
its mistakes like any other regime." But making him step down at these "crucial circumstances" is not the right method for correcting these mistakes.[288] The
Egyptian President is not against democracy and his latest speech has proved
that.[289] Youth should end their protests, wrote *Al-Ahram* columnist Salah Montasser. Mubarak has called for reforming articles 76 and 77, making it easier for
individuals to run for office and restrict the time a president stays in power. It is
"unacceptable" from some to say that Mubarak's statements were mainly meant
to "calm things down," and that they will not leave Tahrir Square. It is time to get
back to work and let life come to normal in our homeland, added Montasser.[290]
Mubarak's speech has fulfilled "almost all" of the demands of these youth who
have led this movement for change and registered a new page in Egypt's history,
proclaimed *Al-Akhbar*.[291]

Editorials in the state papers went to the extent of frightening Egyptians
about the future of Egypt if Mubarak is forced to step down. A fall of the
Mubarak regime, of state "legitimacy," would mean the "beginning of the episode
of the collapse" of Egypt, cautioned Ibrahim Nafie, former chairman of the giant,
Cairo-based Al-Ahram publishing group.[292] In "The Worst Has Yet to Come," an
Al-Gomhuria editorial holds fears that the end of the road can mean not just the
end of Mubarak's rule but of the whole of Egypt. It cautioned, "We fear that the
worst has yet to come. We fear of days in which there will be shortage of bread,
higher food prices, and a lack of security prevailing." The editorial added in a
manner as to frighten protesters, "We do not want Egypt to slowly turn into

another Lebanon filled with militias."[293] The chairperson of Egypt's Syndicate of Journalists, Makram Mohamed Ahmed, emphasized that Mubarak has declared that he will not run for another term. He deserves an "honorary and civilized exit" from the presidential office because what the man has offered Egypt "surpasses hundred times the mistakes of his regime and men." Ahmed, who many claim is the one who wrote the speeches of Mubarak, continued:

Mubarak has committed no sin to denounce him in such a manner which resembles treachery, vileness and disloyalty. He fought greatly to regain land and dignity, has widely opened the doors for expression and managed to establish an infrastructure for all development projects to be created on. He has established stability for the nation, and that has helped in making Egypt an attractive home for investment capable of achieving a seven percent economic growth. He has protected his country's soil, never accepted foreign troops to be stationed on it or threw his homeland in uncalculated adventures. Moreover, he has worked to achieve an honorable and comprehensive peace that secures the best for Egypt.[294]

The destruction and lack of law and order that spread in Egypt over the past a few days has raised Egyptians' anger, wrote Morad Ezz El-Arab, a columnist at *Al-Ahram Al-Masae*. He alleged that "foreign forces" are trying to make Egypt experience the chaos that Arabs "have witnessed in Iraq, Lebanon, Tunisia, among other states," claiming that ElBaradei was involved in that.[295] Novelist and writer Youssef El-Qeid mockingly wrote: "They all have appeared suddenly. ElBaradei introduced a program to the U.S. Ambassador to Egypt Margaret Scobey on how Egypt would be governed and Ahmed Zewail arrived on a plane stressing to us that he is 'one of Obama's fifty consultants.' And Farouk El-Baz [an Egyptian American scientist] spoke from his palace in Dubai, saying things about Egypt which he never said before."[296] Ibrahim Ali El-Essari, an Egyptian and a nuclear scientist who worked with ElBaradei at the International Atomic Energy Agency, praised Mubarak's leadership and criticized ElBaradei's support of acts of "disturbances and civil disobedience" in Egypt. El-Essari spoke highly of ElBaradei's work at the IAEA, but claimed that he never presented a proposal in support of Egypt's call for a nuclear-free Middle East or on Israel to be subjected to inspection by the Agency.[297] "Whether we agree or disagree with Hosni Mubarak, he is the son of Egypt and a man who has fought to protect it and complete the battle for establishing peace" in the region.[298] Let history judge Mubarak, said *Al-Akhbar*, and let us unite now to protect our country from chaos because there is a power out there that does not want good for Egypt. "They want to destroy Egypt from the inside because they have failed to destroy it via outside wars and conspiracies."[299] The decisions that Mubarak has taken "does not come out of fear of protesters at Tahrir or amount to a submission to American pressure," concluded Samir Ragab of *Al-Gomhuria*.[300] The Egyptian President has taken them "to save the people of his nation from igniting the flames of division while at the same time responding to the wishes of protesters."[301] Mr. Mubarak: You are not alone because we all stand by you and we all respect you. "Allah will grant you victory."[302]

The "Ugly Policeman"

Criticism of the police and the minister of interior was mammoth in Egypt's diverse independent and partisan press, with many wondering how such failure of the security system could take place.[303] Habib El-Adli was the "head of a militia and not a minister of interior," cried *El-Dostour.*[304] He is responsible for the death of ordinary civilians and policemen, and he must be put on trial.[305] Nafaa praised the protesters and vehemently denounced police "brutality."[306] In "Why Did You Kill Your People?" *Al-Masry Al-Youm* columnist Balal Fadl condemned Mubarak's lack of action toward police violence and for ordering the shooting of protesters. "If it was not you who ordered, who did it then?" Mr. Mubarak, he added, if "you say you did not know, this will be even worse and you do not deserve to be president."[307] Wafiq El-Gheitani, a member of the New Wafd Party, reprimanded Mubarak and his government, particularly the minister of interior. The January 25 Revolution, he wrote,

> was, and still is, a peaceful revolution by wise and educated youth who respect the law and fear for their country and its capabilities. But the police, which is led by the traitor Habib El-Adli, dealt with them violently, pounding them with sticks, tear-gas bombs and rubber bullets in random manner that resulted in the death and injury of many. Failing in his confrontation with the courageous Egyptian youth—heroes of the revolution of change—El-Adli and his entourage withdrew from the streets, preferring to sit at home and wear the pajama instead.[308]

In "We'll Not Be Slaved Again," *Al-Masry Al-Youm* columnist Ahmed El-Sawy praised the Egyptians who went out to demonstrate on the streets, forcing the Mubarak regime to take decisions that it would have not made had it not been for the spirit of revolution that spread in the nation. He commended the police for changing its motto from the "ugly" one of "Police and Citizens in Service of their Homeland" to the reasonable one of "Police in Service of Citizens."[309] *Al-Ahali* ruminated over how the central security forces that are equipped with all tools to counter rebellion could not crush the protests.[310] No matter how strong the police forces become, they cannot overcome the will of the Egyptian people, wrote Ahmed Yousef Ahmed, a Cairo University professor of political science and director of the Institute of Arab Research and Studies. "If the 1973 War has led to the demise of the theory of [invincible] Israeli defense, the January 2011 uprising must be viewed as the beginning of the end of the theory of achieving political security by force alone." He called for a judicial investigation of police withdrawal to be held immediately.[311] Why spend so much money on the police if they cannot protect our citizens?[312]

The state media was not as critical of the police as the independent media and the partisan press, though denigration of El-Adli was audible. Anees Mansur, the famed columnist from *Al-Ahram*, admonished the police forces and called their withdrawal from the streets a "betrayal" of trust between them and the public. This act of "shame' will be added to the "great history of the police," he said.[313] In an op-ed in *Al-Gomhuria*, Azza Ahmed Heikal described the sense of fear she and her neighborhood experienced because of police withdrawal. "Young and old stood on the sideways of streets holding sticks, knives and guns to protect their homes." We want change and reform, but we do not want chaos.[314] The protests exhausted the security forces, resulting in the loss of control and in a number of police stations being burned and prisoners escaping with some arms at their hands, noted *Al-Akhbar*. The goal was to cause disturbance and spread chaos in the nation.[315] We need to know who is responsible for the release of prisoners from jail; we must know and bring those responsible to justice.[316] The act of police absence and release of prisoners was intentional and preplanned to spread fear among people. "It has reached the level of grand treachery."[317] We need an immediate instigation of who is behind the withdrawal of police from streets so the souls of martyrs rest in peace, including those of police officers who lost their lives defending their country.[318]

Portrayal of the Army

There was little or no criticism of the way the army had handled the protests with commentators at the country's three press systems describing it as positive at times and neutral at others. The Egyptian army handled the Tahrir protests in a noble, non-violent manner, said Awatif Abdel Rahman, a mass communications professor at Cairo University, in an interview with the privately-owned ONTV station.[319] Although we cannot call on the army to coerce Mubarak to hand his resignation, wrote *El-Dostour*, we can ask it to "protect Egypt and not make its economy fall years behind."[320] The army will continue to embrace this neutral position, proclaimed *Al-Masry Al-Youm*.[321] El-Qeid posited, "I wish from the great army of Egypt to exit this unacceptable neutral stance and form a barrier between supporters and denouncers of Mubarak. Every human being has the right to protest and express his or her viewpoint but there is a difference between freedom of opinion and chaos."[322] The army and police should unite for we have never seen such a "schism" between the two in the history of this nation.[323]

Fear of America

In a direct response to Mubarak's speech, U.S. President Barack Obama said on February 1 that he supports a change of regime in Egypt, and that an orderly-transition to a new government "must begin now." Obama commended Egypt's peaceful protests, characterizing them as "inspiration to people around the world." He praised Egyptian youth's role in the revolution. "To the people of Egypt, particularly the young people of Egypt, I want to be clear," continued Obama. "We hear your voices." While an article in *Alwafd* praised President Obama and officials at his administration for the "decisive statements they have made in support of the Egyptian people,"[324] reference to America in the Egyptian media was predominantly negative, with many fearing U.S. intervention in their country's internal affairs. Matar alleged that the Mubarak regime has established a strong security apparatus in Egypt under the pretext of "countering terrorism and maintaining peace with Israel and an alliance with the United States."[325] Mubarak's call for a change of the two constitutional articles possibly came following "an advice from America," proclaimed *Al-Masry Al-Youm*.[326]

Fear of America and Saudi Wahabism meddling in Egypt's internal affairs was reported on in the Egyptian press. During the Egyptian revolution and the protests that took place in many parts of the Arab world, I heard people claiming that America is "manufacturing presidents" for the Arab world and will sell them to the Arabs after the Arab Spring brings down bureaucratic leaders. So, America might be getting one ready for Egypt. "What took place in Egypt during the last eight days is certainly a big and stunning national battle despite all the pain that accompanied it," wrote foreign affairs expert Rafaat Said Ahmed in *El-Dostour*. He cautioned of American/Israeli and Wahabi cells in Egypt trying to "steal" the revolution and benefit financially from it. He called on Egyptian youth—particularly those at Tahrir Square—to head to the U.S. embassy (which is located a few meters away from Tahrir) and denounce America's "criminal role not just in Iraq, Palestine, Lebanon, Afghanistan but also in Egypt during the past forty years of Sadat and Mubarak's rule."[327] Howeidy observed that by joining the "camp" of American politics Egypt under Mubarak was "humiliated" as it was coerced to join the siege on Gaza "in defense of the security of Israel while ignoring its own."[328]

Anyone who follows how the United States has dealt with the situation on the Egyptian street during the past week can say that Washington exercised a sort of "teenage diplomacy," wrote Essam Kamel, editor in chief of *Al-Ahrar*. Washington began by stating that Mubarak solved many of the region's problems and contributed tremendously to world peace. It then changed tone of its statements by saying that it sees the government in Egypt as stable. After that

Washington turned around and said that President Mubarak must respond to the demands of his people, added Kamel. Such change in statements was made, to the amazement of many, within a "week period and not months or years!"[329] El-Shafey cautioned that those who call for an immediate resignation of Mubarak are following the policy of "America and Israel," though we cannot deny that Egyptian protesters' call stems from a "patriotic and sincere" passion for a better Egypt. "But as usual the Americans have employed the situation to serve their benefit and dealt with Egypt as an American protectorate or a small country living under U.S. occupation, as we have seen in many of U.S. officials' statements." El-Shafey further denounced Obama as a "dirty occupier" who wants to dictate who should stay in power and who should not.[330]

Criticism of the U.S. government's reaction to Mubarak's second speech was high in the state media. America must not intervene in Egypt's internal affairs, said an *Al-Ahram* column.[331] Moneim admonished Washington for not reporting on the large number of protests that went on the streets in support of Mubarak as if there were only anti-Mubarak demonstrations in the country. It was a "mockery from President Obama to come out with these misleading reports that televisions channels such as the BBC and Al-Jazeera, among others, aired. His statements entirely contradict facts on the ground," wrote Moneim. "The U.S. President should have waited more, even for an hour, and double-checked that his information is from accurate and neutral sources."[332] Ibrahim of *Al-Gomhuria* claimed, like El-Qeid, that an "American official" unveiled on February 1 that Scobey had a telephone conversation with ElBaradei seeking his opinion on the shape and structure of a post-Mubarak Egypt. Ibrahim sarcastically wrote, "Who assigned America with the task of exploring Egypt's future after Mubarak? Have Egyptians become without a will or voice? Do these Egyptians at Tahrir represent the whole of Egypt?" Ibrahim denounced the United States (along with other nations) for trying to "divide" the Middle East and spread the "creative chaos which it has succeeded in installing in Lebanon, Iraq, Palestine, and Sudan. So why not try it in Egypt?"[333] When Condoleezza Rice spoke of creative chaos we thought those were merely words but it turned out that the matter was more serious, emphasized El-Qeid.[334]

Summary

During the revolution, Al-Jazeera TV station repeatedly broadcast an Arabic song by the late Egyptian singer Om Kalthoum—the Arab world's most popular singer—in which she says: "If God destines Egypt to death, the East will never raise its head thereafter." The implication of the song is that Egypt stands at the center of the world, belonging to the Near East and serving as a connection between the East and the West. Thus if it falls, the whole East will be affected. During the first week of the revolution, protesters went out on the streets with two main demands: firing the interior minister and dissolving parliament. But that did change in the week that followed, particularly after the Battle of the Camel. Following Mubarak's second speech, we began to see both the independent and partisan press speak of the need not just for regime change but for an immediate departure of Mubarak from office. While the state media were shouting "people want regime to stay," the independent media and the partisan press were crying "people want regime change." This war of words began from the time the revolution erupted and got ugly at times, with each media system trying to air its own story. On February 1, for example, the privately-owned Mehwar television station's talk-show "48 Sa'a" (Arabic for "48 Hours"), presented by Hanaa El-Simary and Sayed Ali, hosted a female activist whose identity was concealed and who claimed she was paid and trained in America by the "Jews" to depose the Mubarak regime and instigate chaos in Egypt. The print media later reported that the "activist" was a Cairene journalist who never left the country and fabricated the story. Many public viewers later accused the news channel of trying to inject the idea into viewers' minds that there was a foreign hand involved in the revolution.

At times one also felt confused by the way the independent and party press covered the revolution. While some writers said they support the revolution and a total change of regime, they spoke highly of Suleiman and Prime Minister Shafiq and described them as capable men. But the state media continued to back the Egyptian President, who showed no sign of intending to step down,[335] while they did criticize members of his administration and the ruling party. On February 5, the six members group of the NDP's executive office decided to resign. The group included Gamal Mubarak, chairman of the party's influential Policies Committee, and Safwat El-Sherif, who held the post of secretary-general of the party for nine years. The remaining four includes Moufid Shehab, the party's assistant secretary-general for parliamentary affairs; Zakaria Azmi, assistant secretary-general for membership affairs; Alieddin Hilal, secretary for media affairs; and Ahmed Ezz, secretary for organizational affairs. But it was not until February 22 when the newly appointed government of Shafiq assigned a fact-finding committee to investigate the events of the Battle of the Camel. In an interview with BBC Arabic television station a week before Mubarak's downfall, Shafiq also denied that pro-Mubarak protesters were paid.[336]

It is also worth mentioning that in early March revolutionaries, many of them were youths, invaded the buildings of the State Security Intelligence Agency (SSIA) which was in many ways a state within a state about which government knew nothing except that which the interior minister—who is directly responsible to the president—permitted. The youths claimed to have found many documents burned. A small number of other documents were collected by protesters who posted some of them online and sent copies to Egyptian journalists.

Chapter 6. Friday of Departure

Friday, February 4, 2011, was meant to be the "Friday of Departure," a day aimed at forcing President Hosni Mubarak to leave office. Protesters at Tahrir Square chanted: "We will not leave, he will leave." But they were disappointed for it was not until the Friday that followed, February 11, that the Egyptian president stepped down. The protests continued despite negotiation attempts such as the one held on February 6 between the protesters and the newly-appointed Vice President Omar Suleiman who promised that his government would embrace wide reform. Social activities for entertaining protesters at Tahrir Square blossomed during the last week of the revolution, with demonstrators shouting the slogans: "Revolution, revolution until victory" and "No to tyranny and oppression" and "We are the revolutionaries of Tahrir." A day before the toppling of Mubarak in a peaceful popular uprising, the renowned Egyptian singer Medht Saleh went and sang for protesters at Tahrir and they sang along with him. Poet Hisham El-Gekh spent days there reciting poetry for protesters that the Egyptian media later identified him as the "poet of the revolution." During those days we also began to see the military shouldering wider security duties such as guarding government buildings and the Egyptian Museum. On the other side, once Mubarak was ousted the state media and supporters of Mubarak started to speak less of foreign states trying to intervene in Egypt's internal affairs, this is despite the Obama Administration's earlier approval of Suleiman to be suited for running the post-Mubarak transitional period—to be the transitional president. In this chapter of the book I am going to talk about the euphoria and deep feeling of jubilation that spread in the Land of Nile when Egyptians heard of the news of Mubarak's departure.

The Last Speech

Mubarak began his final televised speech on Thursday February 10 at 10:45 p.m. in which he stressed that he would delegate some of his presidential powers to Suleiman whose cabinet would employ a long list of reform steps. This meant that Mubarak would remain in power to serve as the country's head of state. He said he "will not run for the next presidential elections." He further stated, "I have told you my determination that I will hold steadfast to continue to take on my responsibility to protect the constitution and the rights of people until power is transferred to whomever the people choose during September, the upcoming September, and free and impartial elections that will be safeguarded by the freedom – the call for freedom." Mubarak called for a national dialogue between all factions, and that he would pursue constitutional reform. He continued, "During the victory in 1973, my happiest days were when I lifted the Egyptian flag over Sinai. I have faced death several times when I was a pilot. I also faced it in Addis Ababa, Ethiopia, and elsewhere. I did not submit nor yield to foreign dictations or others. I have kept the peace. I worked towards the Egyptian stability and security. I have worked to the revival in Egypt and the prosperity."[337] Unlike in his second speech, Mubarak did not speak much of fear that Egypt would lose law and order if he was pushed out of office. The public, which was expecting Mubarak to declare his resignation, was angered by the speech and anti-Mubarak chants filled the air. "Erhal! Erhal!" ("Leave!" or "Get Out!") was one of them. Protesters in many parts of Egypt called for his immediate resignation, downfall of his cabinet, dissolution of parliament, and the establishment of a national government. Rumors were spreading that Mubarak had fled to an Arab Gulf state or was ousted by the army and held in prison. But protesters were disappointed and infuriated when they found out that he was still in power, with about a thousand of them marching to the giant state television building (known as Maspero), which remained strongly loyal to Mubarak during the eighteen days of demonstrations and in the a few days that followed his toppling despite the slight change in tone that was visible in the state-owned print media. But the army managed to protect Maspero with tanks and barbed wire. Other protesters headed to the presidential palace.

While the state media praised Mubarak's speech, the independent and partisan media were mostly critical of it. In the speech, observed the independent newspaper *Al-Masry Al-Youm*, Mubarak seemed as if he was talking to himself, with his main focus being on what he achieved in sixty years.[338] Mubarak tried to appear as the "hero" of the Arabs, pointed out the independent paper *El-Dostour*.[339] Those who wrote the Mubarak speech misunderstood the mind of Egyptian youth, an "SMS generation" that communicates and trades words in seconds.[340] When I and my friends listened to the speech we realized that we are in front of an "old and insane man both mentally and psychologically," wrote Mohamed El-Gheity in the party newspaper *Alwafd*. He compared Mubarak to Romania's Nicolae Ceausescu in his manner of "despotism and arrogance."[341] "Mr. President," noted Ahmed El-Sawy in *Al-Masry Al-Youm*, "it saddens to hear what you have done to my people over 30 years and never thought of departing from office. Early in your presidency you said you would only spend two terms in office but you did not; you have stayed forever." El-Sawy denounced Mubarak for speaking as if he was the only one who fought for Egypt, forgetting that there were great men fighting alongside with him. Alas, he continued, government corruption under Mubarak's rule was widespread. "Mr. President: He who creates corruption cannot create freedom."[342]

Downfall of Mubarak

On Friday February 11, Suleiman appeared at 6:00 p.m. on state television to declare Mubarak's resignation and that the Supreme Council of the Armed Forces (SCAF)—chaired by the supreme commander of the army Field Marshal Hussein Tantawi—would be entrusted with the task of ruling the country. Once it was announced that Mubarak was stepping down, protesters clapped and cheered. Celebrations were heard all over Egypt, with people in my home city Benha, a suburb of Cairo, dancing in joy. But there were also a sense of cautious optimism on the faces of some of them, as if they were asking: Will Egypt make it? Picture-heavy articles filled Egyptian newspapers—with front pages carrying large pictures of protesters celebrating at Tahrir—giving Mubarak's downfall a high degree of salience. So, how did Egypt's three different press systems cover the major event and what difference was there?

Independent Press

In a way, mainstream independent Egyptian newspapers, such as *Al-Masry Al-Youm*, *El-Dostour*, and *Al-Shorouk Al-Jadeed*, did a fair job in their coverage of Mubarak's downfall. Their journalists spoke of Mubarak's "demise" and "ouster" and not of Mubarak's "resignation" as the state press often observed. It is worth mentioning that privately-owned satellite stations came under restrictions under the Mubarak regime but most of them did a somewhat fine work in their coverage of the revolution, though they remained cautions and did not utterly declare that Mubarak should be removed from office. And, yes, there were also those at independent television stations who tried to lure protesters to leave Tahrir Square and end their demonstrations. For example, Al-Hayat TV station's Amr Adeeb's talk-show "Mubashir Maa Amr Adeeb" ("Live with Amr Adeeb"), with co-presenter Rola Kharsa, consistently called on protesters to end their demonstrations and go home and "rebuild" their country. But when it was clear that there would be a change of regime, Adeeb supported the protests; he even went to Tahrir to back the anti-Mubarak protesters. The popular Dream TV station talk-show "Al-A'shera Ma'san" ("Ten Evening") by Mona El-Shazly hosted three members of the SCAF and Wael El-Abrashi, chief editor of the independent paper *Sout Elomma*, right after the toppling of Mubarak. El-Shazly was also the first to host Wael Ghonim, a Google executive and a Facebook activist, after his release from a twelve-day detention by police officers of the Mubarak regime. Al-Hayat, which is owned by the head of the New Wafd Party, El-Sayed El-Badawi, was also the first TV station to interview the then-newly appointed Prime Minister Ahmed Shafiq.

On the day that followed Mubarak's downfall, independent newspapers carried screaming headlines on their cover pages in celebration of the event. *El-Dostour* filled it with a photo of Mubarak and on top of it written the words: "Down at Last." Below it is the subhead: "Army Assumes Power." *Al-Masry Al-Youm* ran at the top of its cover page small photos of about a dozen of youth who died during the revolution. Below them is written the blaring main headline: "If I Die Do Not Cry Mother: I Died for My Country to Live." There was a big photo of the protesters celebrating at Tahrir below that headline. At the top of it is written: "The People Wanted and Toppled the Regime." The independent paper *Al-Shorouk Al-Jadeed* likewise carried a large photo of the protesters with the following words at the very top of the page, above the paper's flag: "The People Have Won." Below it is the subhead: "The Revolution Overthrew Mubarak and SCAF Assumes Power." Below the photo in each of those two papers are written a few paragraphs. *Al-Masry Al-Youm*, for example, commented: "There is a major difference between revolutions carried out by people and revolutions undertaken by armies. The latter, even if embraced by the public, could be labelled as military coup d'état or an officers' action." It cautioned that the path to democracy will be a long one, and that the January 25 Revolution "did not end with Mubarak's departure; it has in fact just begun and protecting its achievements has become the responsibility of both its brave, patriotic army and the public." *El-Dostour*, on the other hand, wrote: "In a historic scene that history will remember, the will of the Egyptian people has triumphed and forced President Mubarak to step down in one of the most marvellous revolutionary battles in modern history, in an act that cost three hundred martyrs from the nation's finest youth and hundreds of injuries under the cruelty of a despotic and tyrant regime that did not respond to people's pain and dealt arrogantly and disdainfully with their fair demands."

On the evening of Mubarak's departure, Egyptians felt a sense of honor and freedom that their goal was achieved. On that evening, proclaimed *Al-Masry Al-Youm*, the "birth of Egyptians that had begun on January 25 was completed." Tahrir Square is not just a symbol of the Egyptian revolution but of all Egyptians.[343] Mohamed Hasseinein Heikel, the Arab world's most distinguished journalist and political analyst, expressed in an interview with El-Shazly his great happiness about Mubarak's demise, describing it as a "historic" moment. It is a moment filled with both hope and concern. He further stressed that what took place is not a "military coup" but a "true revolution." Heikel, who served as an advisor to President Gamal Abdel Nasser, spoke of how Mubarak in 1982 told him that if he got fed up with running Egypt he would hand it to the military and leave.[344] Writing in *El-Dostour* a couple of days following the toppling of the Mubarak regime, columnist Rafaat Said Ahmed called Mubarak a "puppet" of Washington and Tel Aviv and denounced him as "one of the most important hands for the CIA in the world."[345] *Al-Shorouk Al-Jadeed* celebrated, "This is a time for happiness. This is a time for honor, dignity and pride. This is a time in which every individual that took part in the revolution or supported it should feel he is a precious human being."[346] *Al-Masry Al-Youm* wondered, however, whether Egyptians will remain united when they face disagreement in post-revolution Egypt. Will we stand united at Tahrir Square to protect what we have achieved?[347] A commentary in the same paper congratulated Egyptians for they now can say they have a "former president," because only death was able to remove a president from office in the past.[348] Congratulations to the Egyptian people, declared Cairo University's Political Science Professor Hassan Nafaa who characterized the revolution as a "miracle." He called on Egyptians to remain vigilant and protect their revolution from "evil" hands that will try to "steal its fruits."[349] But the youth of the revolution know this well, emphasized *El-Dostour*, they fully "realize that many plan to steal, exploit or turn their revolution off its right path."[350]

These ruminations over the possible rise of a counter revolution or rather fear that power remains at the hands of pro-Mubarak men have continued in the independent press. Mubarak thought that a nation is like an apartment that he could rent with a contract granting him the right to stay in it for ever, Alaa El-Ghartriffi sardonically wrote in *Al-Masry Al-Youm*, and thus he damaged the "Egyptian personality" over the past thirty years. He cited how after the collapse of socialist Romania (which according to the journalist has now become a democracy), the men of the former regime remained in control of the country's wealth, cautioning that Egyptians might encounter the same scenario in their country.[351] *El-Dostour*'s Ahmed likewise contemplates whether or not Mubarak's resignation could be considered a new beginning of a new political system or just "a replacement of his soft grip with a solid military one?" He argued that from what we see so far we can say that Mubarak's downfall is not enough and that there is a need for an "immediate ending to the state of emergency law, releasing of all political prisoners, revoking the current constitution, dissolving the People's Assembly and local councils, and establishing a transitional ruling presidential council of five members of whom one is a military figure and the remaining four are civilians." He also stressed the need for the liberty to establish political parties and abolish military courts. Egypt, he cautioned, is entering a new stage, a new political scene in which it will be hard for one to "predict" events. His editorial was titled, "Is It the End of the Revolution or a New Beginning?"[352]

Amro Hamzawy, an Egyptian who headed research at the Carnegie Foundation in Beirut before settling in Egypt and engaging in the country's media and politics, wondered how the transitional period would look like and whether Egyptians would see the implementation of a new constitution soon. He called for the quick establishment of a transitional government of "technocrats and independent experts."[353] To insure a safe future for Egypt, "we must put aside the idea of revenge because it is destructive," cautioned one political commentator. A future for us means that our revolution must not turn into defeat.[354] Other Egyptians, including some legal staff, demanded that Mubarak be put on trial immediately. The "tyrant Mubarak" is finally out; he has "gone to hell," wrote Morsi El-Sheikh, a member of Egypt's legal system, stressing that the former president and his followers should be "put on trial."[355] The people of Tahrir' have brought down the state of tyranny, said *Al-Masry Al-Youm*,[356] and praise goes to Mohamed ElBaradei and Ahmed Zewail for the strong support they have exhibited for this revolution.[357] Congratulation to the "respectable Egyptian people" who have made the world raise its head in applause of their great revolution, said *El-Dostour*. "The pharaoh who almost told his people 'I am your god' has been deposed by God in a way that he can never come back." He has gone like Zine el-Abdine Ben Ali did.[358] An end to the pharaohs' age means that our country can now join the "camp of common nations."[359]

Commentaries at the independent press were supportive of the position and rule played by the military forces and SCAF. An *Al-Masry Al-Youm* commentary praised the army for intervening or else under the Constitution the head of the People's Assembly would have had to assume the presidency for sixty days until a new president was elected, posing a "great constitutional puzzle" and making us feel that we achieved nothing. The paper criticized those who demanded that the transitional period in which the army holds power should be of no more than six months, simply because the process necessitates a period of at least a year after which the army would hand over power to the presidential council to form a transitional government followed by electing a committee to put together a new constitution.[360] Despite the police state's disruption of means of telecommunication and satellite stations that broadcast the truth, posited *El-Dostour*, the Egyptian youth, the Egyptian people, have achieved "an enormous revolution," and this could not have been accomplished without the support of the armed forced.[361] The "sun of freedom and democracy" has risen on Egypt after almost thirty years of absence, proclaimed Salama Ahmed Salama, chief editor of *Al-Shorouk Al-Jadeed*. He added

Hence we can say that Egypt is about to hub on the train of developed nations and to accomplish what it was not able to achieve during those three decades. It is clear that the youth's determination was not confined only to the downfall of President Mubarak but also to the obliteration of the unilateral rule, one party system, emergency laws, counterfeiting of elections, squandering of the country's wealth for the benefit of a few corrupt businessmen, and the use of Parliament as a tool for granting authority to the regime.[362]

In "Departed at Last," Selim Azouz of *El-Dostour* emphasized that he never thought that Mubarak would leave office and wrote in celebration: "With never-ending efforts [from protesters], President Mubarak has departed at last. He said I am staying here but destiny refused and said you stay there." Borrowing a verse from a poem by the great Tunisian poet Abu Qassim Al-Shabi, Azouz wrote, "'If people one day want to live, destiny then will have to obey.'"[363] Writer and researcher Samir Mourkos noted that the greatest achievement of the revolution is the return of the middle class with all its strata. He denounced Egypt's politics of open market economy and privatization which, in his opinion, severely hurt the middle class whose condition deteriorated under Mubarak.[364] Egypt under the rule of Mubarak was divided into two groups, wrote Amr El-Shobaki of the Cairo-based Al-Ahram Center for Political and Strategic Studies in a commentary in *Al-Masry Al-Youm*. One benefited from it and concealed its "crimes," while the other rejected not only its politics but also its values of coercing people to submit to Mubarak's "republic of fear which was established on separating social classes, instituting fear among politicians, distancing Christians from Muslims and separating women from men."[365] *Al-Shorouk Al-Jadeed* observed, "How great and wonderful these moments feel, and how beautiful it is that you read these words after Egyptians have gained the rights to determine their own destiny."[366]

Some have called the January Revolution the "revolution of roses," or the "youth revolution," said one commentator, but I prefer to call it the "word revolution" because a word is the "secret of existence and the source of knowledge."[367] At last Egypt has revolted and deposed its repressive regime, observed an economics professor at Al-Azhar University. We must pay tribute to the youth of the revolution—a revolution which has awakened Egyptians from their deep sleep and exploded the anger that was inside them for many years.[368] If these youth do not get what the revolution has promised them, they will return back to Tahrir Square. If Egyptians ever face injustice again in the future they must not remain silent but take a civilized action and go to Tahrir.[369] Restricting religious freedom and violating international charters were a main reason for the eruption of this revolution.[370] We no longer want a government in which one person (one party) controls its three branches—the presidential, parliamentary and judiciary ones—wrote Ibrahim El-Sayeh in *El-Dostour*. We do not want "new tyrants" or

one president whom one hypocrite tells him that Egypt was not born until his birth and another telling him that fetuses in their mothers' tummy support him and a third informing him that he was sent from God and that he is His shadow on earth. Or a fourth hypocrite telling him that he was cited in the Quran, Bible and Torah, and pronounce him as the chosen leader to save Egypt and the world from poverty, ignorance, wars, earthquakes and volcanoes.

El-Sayeh further accentuated that Egyptians should now move from a presidential representative system of government to a parliamentarian one with a new constitution written.[371]

Al-Masry Al-Youm pointed out: There is a deep sudden change in the "chemistry" of politics these days, with those who sided with the Mubarak regime in the past (what you can call the pro-Mubarak puppets) now turning on it and becoming anti-Mubarak.[372] A piece in *Al-Shorouk Al-Jadeed* likewise portrayed those individuals as "liars" and "chameleons" that color their skins according to the atmosphere they live in. It declared, "You clowns should show some shame; we need to breathe some clean air so stop polluting the atmosphere."[373] These ugly individuals have changed their "skins and colors" after Mubarak's fall, and they no longer support that his son, Gamal, inherit the presidency, noted *Al-Masry Al-Youm*. They no longer criticize the youth protesting at Tahrir Square but highly praise them—what a mockery? The independent paper further cited in disdain how on February 3 the lead headline on the cover page of the state paper *Al-Ahram* read "Millions Go Out in Support of Mubarak," and how after his demise the state paper's cover page carried the main headline: "People Toppled the Regime." This shows the state media's great degree of "hypocrisy."[374]

Partisan Press

Egypt's three main opposition parties—New Wafd Party, National Progressive Unionist Party, and the Arab Nasserist Party—and their newspapers welcomed what they characterized as Mubarak's resignation. In its official statement issued on February 12, the New Wafd Party, which publishes *Alwafd* newspaper, called for formation of a presidential council (to deal with temporary presidential matters), immediate dissolution of both the Shura (Consultative) Council and People's Assembly, and rewriting of five articles in the Constitution. The main headline on *Alwafd*'s cover page read, "The End: People's Resolve Wins and Mubarak Falls." At the bottom of the page it stated: "People's resolve wins and the January 25 Revolution succeeds in bringing down Hosni Mubarak after 18 days from the day the revolution began. Happiness and celebrations dominated all the streets and squares of Egypt in celebration of this giant public revolution."[375] The party paper *Al-Ahrar*, published by Al-Ahrar Party, proclaimed on its cover page, "Viva the Revolution: The Regime Has Fallen."[376]

Egyptian youth have done it and brought respect to every Egyptian, observed the renowned *Alwafd* columnist Mustapha Sherdi who proclaimed that he is writing his words in the "first day of freedom" for Egypt. Today, he added, is the "first day of Egypt's modern history—a history which we will all write." Like the 1952 revolution, which brought back freedom to Egypt from foreign rule, the January 25 Revolution has liberated Egypt from Mubarak's oppressive reign.[377] Essam Kamel, chief editor of *Al-Ahrar*, stipulated: "At last the President stepped down to open a new door for a hopeful future for Egypt, its people, history and regional and international role. Mubarak resigned to open a door that had been closed for thirty years, bringing with it a chain of surprises." Kamel cautioned that Mubarak left behind him an Egypt that entirely needs to be rebuilt,[378] because the revolution meant not only the end of Mubarak's rule but also the need to write a new constitution and form a new People's Assembly and Shura Council.[379] Similarly, another *Al-Ahrar* editorial writer spoke of the "mixed feelings" that he sensed when he heard of Mubarak's resignation and how tears fell from his eyes. He wondered if they were tears of "happiness" for the departure of a man who occupied office for thirty years or tears of "fear of the open freedom which we may breathe," and for which the Egyptian people are not prepared for.[380] *Alwafd* warned that there will be some who will try to "steal" the revolution.[381]

The Egyptian people have offered the world a lesson on how an "effective, social revolution—a peaceful revolution in the true meaning of the word—can take place."[382] Praise goes to Egyptian youth, the hero of this revolution, who have initiated a new political scene in the country suitable for economic and political reform and establishing social justice, observed Helmi Salem who heads Al-Ahrar Party. You have brought to us "a new world of freedom and sacrifice" and "history will record that. It will record that you have succeeded in generating a new and honorable face to Egypt filled with hope and giving." Calling on youth to fully cooperate with the army to insure security for Egypt, Salem added: "I declare as president of one of the country's oldest political parties my complete solidarity with your legitimate demands that aim toward bringing about total renaissance to Egypt, and I call on all political and intellectual leaders to back these demands. Hope can be established through a new constitution and clean and multiple presidential and parliamentary elections that insure fair and honorable competition for all."[383]

In a loud voice, the youth of the revolution have declared the "downfall of the tyrannical Mubarak regime," proclaimed Ismail Ibrahim in *Al-Ahrar*. I do not know how the media personnel who had continually propagated that Gamal Mubarak should inherit the presidency and introduced him as the "savior" of Egypt and overlooked "all his crimes" against this country will face it now that the whole of Egypt know that they are liars and hypocrites.[384] It is time to cleanse Egypt from the ugly and hypocritical face of these individuals whom the regime has installed in the media to guard its interests, announced an *Alwafd* column which was titled "Cleansing Egypt's Face."[385] Sherdi said it is time now to clean the state media, which belong to the public, from its staff and officials whose main task has been to defend government and the NDP. "They practiced that not out of fear but out of hope to gain more profit and promotions and hold their seats."[386]

A piece in *Alwafd* called on Egyptians to pursue political reform while keeping in mind that the Turkish model may be the best one for them to embrace.[387] The Mubarak regime was living in isolation from the "pulse" of the Egyptian street, proclaimed Gameel Georgi, who holds a doctorate in political science, in an op-ed in *Al-Ahrar*. Our revolution has come to ascertain that Arabs have the capacity and will to embrace democracy, and that those in the West who once claimed that we do not were wrong.[388] Likewise *Alwafd* emphasized that Egyptians should no longer believe those who tell them that they are "not qualified for democracy" because Egypt has a long experience with democracy. And we thank God that the army has taken rule and promised that it will not take a decision which Egyptians do not approve of, and we certainly will not accept but a peaceful and democratic life.[389] The new regime should put in place a long-term strategy in order for us to build a homeland that dispels all forms of submission, corruption, and bribery, observed Kamel of *Al-Ahrar*. He cautioned that not every "white revolution" has succeeded because some of them "have brought their people backward, particularly when considering that our geographic surrounding will endeavor to tarnish our revolution in a way or another so that it does not become a disturbing model for it and its rulers."[390] It is worth noting here that Kamel sees no mistakes in Egyptians honoring Mubarak and accepting what he characterized as an apology from the president. We must show some passion to the hero of war and peace; after all the man did admit in his last speech that the regime had made mistakes and apologized for the corruption that took place under his rule.[391]

State Press

While the cover pages of state newspapers recognized Mubarak's departure, they were less jubilant than those of the independent and partisan media. State papers were filled with large pictures and headlines—though they were less screaming. *Al-Ahram*'s page was led with the headline: "People Toppled the Regime." Below it are the two subheads: "SCAF Takes Charge of Country's Affairs" and "Revolution Forced Mubarak to Leave." The state paper *Akhbar El-Yom* proclaimed, "Mubarak Has Departed." The state paper *Al-Gomhuria* observed, "The January 25 Revolution Has Won" and "Mubarak Steps Down and Army Rules." In an editorial on its cover page, the paper wondered whether the story which the British daily *The Guardian* published claiming that the wealth of Mubarak and his family exceeds seventy billion dollars is true.[392] "Whether this number is true, exaggerated or is a lie, the popularity of the President (which was founded principally on him supporting the poor and people of low wages and those deprived of social justice) has been damaged even if that number is not correct." The state paper *Al-Ahram Al-Masae*, an evening version of *Al-Ahram*, carried on its cover page only the three words: "A New Age." At the back page of *Akhbar El-Yom*, the paper's Chief Editor Mumtaz El-Kot mourned Mubarak's departure. Mubarak, he wrote, has departed from his post today, leaving to us a history of which we should be proud of.[393]

Little did the state media say about what the independent and partisan press characterized as Mubarak's autocratic rule; columnists at state papers focused instead on what Egypt could face and how that might "make matters worse."[394] In the "Last Pharaoh," *Al-Ahram* columnist Mohamed Sabrien believes that the revolution came to liberate us from the "republic of fear," but he asked: "What kind of Egypt do we want?" We do not want an "Uncle Sam's Egypt," a religious state, an "Egyptstan" or a Somalia.[395]

International relations expert Said El-Lawandi also wonders if post-revolution Egypt will be a democracy or an "autocracy governed by a military class."[396] We must now focus on fulfilling the demands of the revolution, wrote the notable *Al-Gomhuria* columnist Samir Ragab, and dissolving the People's Assembly and the Consultative Council and putting together a new constitution are a good beginning.[397] "We must define quickly to where we are going and what kind of Egypt do we want," cautioned Morsi Attallah, a former chairman of the giant Al-Ahram Publishing Group.[398]

State papers praised Mubarak as a great military leader but characterized him as a naïve politician. They strongly denounced the NDP but not its leader:

Mubarak. They spoke of stolen wealth and bribery of members of the NDP and how they forged the 2010 People's Assembly elections[399] but without touching on whether the Al Mubarak had accumulated mass fortunes as claimed by some in the independent media. A number of them spoke of the pharaohs that ruled Egypt but without referring to Mubarak's reign as pharaonic or oppressive.[400] Mubarak was a "great military leader" but a "naïve politician," said *Al-Ahram*. He was surrounded by hypocrites.[401] These same hypocrites who promoted Mubarak's rule are now "advocates for a military rule" and have been cuddling up to the SCAF which is aware of their double standards, wrote popular political commentator Nabil Zaki in the state paper *Al-Akhbar*. Our military leaders have stressed in all their statements that they will abide by the revolution's legitimate demands for securing a civil state and democratic rule.[402] Ibrahim Saada, an *Al-Akhbar* columnist, praised what he described as Mubarak's endeavors to fulfill the demands of protesters. Mubarak "does not risk or venture with his country's safety and the security of Egyptians," and that is why he rushed to resign from power.[403] My "applause and appreciation go to the former President Hosni Mubarak, the hero of war and peace," wrote Ibrahim Nafie, a former chairman of Al-Ahram Publishing Group.[404] While numerous articles commended the army's role during the revolution and the partnership it formed with youth, little was said in the state press about the need to write a new constitution. Journalists at the state press spoke instead of the "unforgettable days,"[405] of a fulfilled "dream" that makes an Egyptian "raise his or her head up high."[406] Mubarak's departure is a lesson for any upcoming president that if he does not meet the demands of his people he will meet the same fate, said *Al-Ahram*.[407] None of us expected his regime to fall that quickly; in eighteen days only youth forced him to step down and hand power to the SCAF, stressed *Al-Akhbar*. It would have been wise from him to have asked Egyptians to forgive him for his "faults" and then resign. Certainly his son's "gang of businessmen of thieves" was of no help.[408]

In the days that followed Mubarak's ouster, the state media began to somewhat change its attitude in coverage, from being exclusively pro-Mubarak to offering a somewhat balanced coverage of the events. We saw members of the banned Muslim Brotherhood, which was established in 1928 and outlawed since 1954, appear on state television—something that rarely took place prior to the revolution. For the first time in history, Egyptians can now say they have a former president, noted *Al-Akhbar*. Mubarak spent thirty years in office—the longest period ever an Egyptian president had held—and survived with six American presidents, from Jimmy Carter to Ronald Reagan, from George Bush to Bill Clinton, from George W. Bush Jr. to Barack Obama. Indeed Tahrir Square has written a new chapter for Egypt.[409] Under the "dictatorial rule" of the past regime, observed *Al-Gomhuria*, the level of corruption in Egypt reached its highest.

The state paper criticized Mubarak's wife, Susanne, for misusing power in order to secure the presidency for her son, Gamal. It further blamed Mubarak for not listening to the advice of many individuals and handed power earlier that way he would have saved the "blood of our youth."[410] It is now four days since Mubarak's resignation, wrote *Al-Ahram* columnist Mohamed El-Sadany, and I still cannot believe that the Facebook youth's revolution has succeeded in defeating the "biggest police regime," bringing down the NDP, ending Gamal Mubarak's hereditary project, and chasing members of the corrupt regime. Mubarak, he added, is after all a "victim of the devilish group that surrounded him" and lured him not to leave office, violating the promises he had made early in his presidency that he would not stay more than two terms. "Deposing those who corrupted Mubarak's rule is not enough; these persons must be put on fair trials and hung in public squares," added El-Sadany.[411] But we must also admit that most of us, Egyptians, did contribute in the corruption process by our submission, by bowing our heads and contributing to the ugly world of offering bribes and other wrongdoings wherever we went to get work done.[412]

No articles in the state papers demanded that Mubarak immediately stand trial although they were critical of members of his government as we have documented above. Some of them asked that the country's general persecutor bring those who tried to spread chaos, "burn Egypt," and steal its treasures to stand trial; while others offered their "salute and gratitude to President Mubarak— the son of the brave military forces."[413] There were those commentators who when speaking of "Mubarak's achievements" blended them with a bit of criticism which was often placed at the end of their pieces. Listen to this one at *Al-Gomhuria*: We cannot forget that Mubarak was the leader of the air forces that brought our victory in the 1973 War, and that he was the one who regained Taba back to us. Under his rule "many of Egypt's debts were reduced or lifted off our shoulders. He is the builder of modern Egypt—a man who saved the blood of Egyptians by not throwing them in many anticipated wars. He is the one who stood solid against the establishment of any foreign military bases on Egyptian soil and completed the path toward peace after the departure of the leader of war and peace Anwar Sadat." Mubarak's fault was in chairing the NDP and placing his trust in a group of businessmen, resulting in the "outlawed marriage between power and money" and widespread corruption.[414]

Many of the board chairmen of state publishing houses and chief editors of state publications had tried to rescue themselves from public criticism that strengthened after the toppling of Mubarak as many Egyptians were demanding that they be removed from their posts. For example, Abdelmoneim Said, chairman of Al-Ahram Publishing Group, wrote a lengthy article in Al-Ahram on February 14 in which he articulated that Vice President Omar Suleiman invited board chairs and chief editors of state and independent papers to the presidential palace on February 8 and asked them to propose ways for getting out of the "crisis" (the word "revolution," according to Said, was not yet installed at the lingo). He stressed that he told Suleiman and those who attended that the solution is for Egypt to immediately embrace "freedom, law, and development."[415] But one also must admit that in analyzing state papers we witnessed some of its journalists, though a few in number, criticizing state television channels and newspapers' coverage during Mubarak's rule, characterizing them as a voice of government and a propaganda tool of the regime. "Corruption breeds corruption," and state television and newspapers contributed in the process of political corruption by caring not about people's suffering but glorifying the "ruling god" who blesses them with his gifts, *Al-Ahram* accentuated. They contributed to Egypt's loss of its regional and international position. "Instead of Egypt leading the Arab world toward a true democracy, they were teaching Arabs how to endorse the god in power."[416] But all Arabs, said *Al-Akhbar*, "know that their advancement comes with the renaissance of Egypt and by enabling them to regain Arab identity and role on the world stage." They fully realize the strategic importance of Egypt.[417]

Journalists at the state media glorified what they depicted as Egypt's white and peaceful revolution but they cautioned about the future, at times even making comparison between it and other revolutions in Africa which did not bring positive results in the long term. According to *Al-Ahram* columnist Attiah Aessawy, the "popular uprisings" that resulted in regime change in Africa—with the exception of that of Sudan in 1986 and Egypt and Tunisia in 2011—were the product of military coups that later resulted in civic, ethnic, and religious conflicts and wide violations of human rights, hurting a state's social and economic stance despite regime change.[418] In Egypt, the regime and its institutions have fallen not just after thirty years of undemocratic rule but from an autocratic rule that stretches back to the year 1953, noted political analyst Abdel Moety Ahmed. And it was all done peacefully. Yes, the Egyptian revolution has succeeded but this is not the "end of the road," and one fears of division taking place.[419] *Al-Ahram* cautioned: "The January 25 Revolution must be the beginning of the road for reform and development for Egypt in various fields. Or else it can turn into destructive chaos, and not creative chaos."[420] Now I can dream of a true democratic Egypt like all countries of the free world because we are not less than them in anything.[421] We want a state founded on the principles of citizenship and the rights of Egyptians to live freely, said *Al-Akhbar*. "Egyptians were not deceived by the claim that democracy and human rights are merely ideas 'imported from the West,' nor were they ever convinced that 'outside danger' can be a justification for imposing dictatorship."[422] We want a free and democratic Egypt in which there is a new constitution, social justice and respect for human rights, fairer elections, a free press system, and an end to emergency law.[423] Cairo's air after January 25 has, undoubtedly, a new and special smell; it is the "air of freedom and the smell of democracy," said *Al-Ahram Al-Masae*. The responsibility of securing a better future for the country does not only lie on the shoulder of the SCAF but on all of us.[424] Egypt's youth should stay united;[425] they should form a party for themselves.[426]

In conclusion, one must admit that when analyzing commentaries of the state press they often felt like old news in comparison to those in the independent press. On April 15, however, and after offering two months of "balanced" coverage and granting a voice to the Egyptian people and their revolution, the editors of *Al-Ahram* stated in a short piece on their paper's cover page: We have come back to our readers and they have come back to us. The newly-appointed editors of the one-hundred-thirty-five-year-old paper asked readers for "forgiveness" for their paper's pro-Mubarak coverage during the revolution. *Sabah El-Kheir* magazine promised to be on the reader's side because "when a journalist becomes an enemy to the truth you can then say goodbye to this world." It mourned that the worst that the Mubarak regime committed was corrupting state institutions, including the press. "The inverted pyramid relationship between the journalist and the state and the reader must be overhauled and not allow the state to be at the top."[427] Other renowned state television hosts who abandoned or were forced to leave their shows during Mubarak's rule returned back. Popular talk-show host Mahmoud Saad of Al-Masriya returned back on February 12 to his "Masr El-Naharda" ("Egypt Today") show after being forced to take an "unpaid leave" for declaring, on the day the revolution erupted, that Mubarak should resign. (Saad later quit his post, possibly because he anticipated that major changes were to come at state television; he joined a private television channel instead.)

Abdel-Latif El-Minawy, who chairs the news department at state television, appeared on Masr El-Naharda on February 17, conveying a sense of regret and guilt for submitting to the government's demands in covering the revolution. He stated that they had been asked not to exclusively cover (or rather kill the story) of the clashes at Tahrir Square on Black Wednesday—the day during which the Battle of the Camel took place and which Chapter 5 of this book tackled in more detail. In the major reshuffle that took place at the state television in the weeks that followed the revolution, El-Minawy was replaced.

Revolution Without Leadership

The secret that captured the attention of the world about the Egyptian revolution was how it could have erupted when it had no leader. Just as elsewhere, all Egyptian revolutions (or revolts)—from 1772 to 1952—had had a leader, a

symbol which they idolized and glorified in their struggle for freedom and justice. The Ottoman Empire's occupation of Egypt in 1517, which made the Turks
in Egypt rich but impoverished Egyptians, ignited the spirit of revolution in the
entire Arab world.

According to the leftist Egyptian intellectual Salama Moussa and author of
the 1954 Arabic-language magnum opus *The Book of Revolutions*, Egypt has gone
through four revolutions. The first revolution is represented by Omar Makram,
an Egyptian who was educated at Egypt's Al-Azhar, a religious institution established in the tenth century. Born in southern Egypt in 1750, Makram first
revolted against the Turkish ruler and later against Mohamed Ali Pasha (1805-
1848) who Ottomans appointed as governor of Egypt and whom Egyptians first
accepted because he promised to rule fairly but they later rejected him for what
they called his harsh reign. When Mohamed Ali imposed taxes on Egyptians
they shouted in anger that they want "Omar Makram"—who served then as a
religious consultant at a governmental institution—to stand against the unjust
rule of the governor of Egypt. But Mohamed Ali never listened and tried to force
Makram to accept and endorse his decision but the latter refused. Mohamed Ali
then fired him from his post and expelled him to the city of Duyat—an Egyptian
town located on the Mediterranean—for almost a decade. Makram returned to
Cairo but was later expelled to another small Egyptian city, Tanta, where he died
a few months later in 1833. In the opinion of Moussa, Makram's revolution was
guided more or less by religion; it was like the "dark ages." A nationalist conscious
did not, however, materialize in Egypt until the 1882 "Urabi Revolution," which
forms the second revolution and was led by Ahmed Urabi (1841–1911). Moussa
accused Khedive Tawfiq (who governed Egypt from 1879 to 1892) of betraying
Urabi and siding with the British and backing their occupation of Egypt. In the
years that followed, nationalist Egyptians, such as Mustapha Kamel and Ahmed
Lutfi El-Said, emerged on the political sphere and coined phrases such as "Egypt
for Egyptians."[428] We then witnessed the third revolution taking place in the
Land of the Nile. Known as the 1919 Revolution, it called for independence from
British rule and was led by Saad Zaghlul. But its hopes for establishing a form of
"nationalism" was never fulfilled, wrote historian Mohamed Shafiq Gharbal in
his Arabic-language 1957 masterwork *The Formation of Egypt Across Ages*.[429] The
Revolution of 1952 was a coup d'état against British rule and abolished the monarchy system and declared Egypt a Republic a year later. Led by Colonel Gamal
Abdel Nasser, it put an end to the rule of the dynasty of Mohamed Ali which
ruled Egypt for almost a century and half. On this Moussa expressed: "For fifteen
years, until 1952, Farouk was the head of the society in which we lived. It was a
corrupt society, as is the norm when the head of a body grows more corrupt than

the body itself." He added that Farouk inherited such corruption from his father, Fouad, who was bent on corrupting Egyptian society.[430]

Some Egyptian thinkers made a comparison between the 1919 Revolution and the 2011 Revolution. In a commentary in *Alwafd* titled "Our Revolution and the 1919 Revolution," Mohamed Abdel Qodoos wrote: "In March 1919 a volcano of anger erupted in Egypt after the arrest of Saad Zaghlul and his companions, and this was the beginning of a great revolution that entirely changed the face of life in our country." He stressed that that was the first "revolt of the masses" in the whole world against British occupation after the end of World War I. He noted that the 1919 and 2011 revolutions carried things in common, the first of which is that the foundation on which both revolutions were established on was the ordinary middle class people with the masses joining later. The 1919 Revolution was against an outside occupier; the 2011 Revolution was against the autocratic regime of a ruler whom it succeeded in bringing down in eighteen days. The 1919 Revolution had a leader—Zaghlul and followed by Mustapha El-Nahaas. The 2011 Revolution was against the marriage of power and money and meant a "strong hit" at "corrupt capitalism" and demanded the establishment of social equality and political freedom. Qodoos added that it is a revolution by the "people downstairs" against the "new pashas"[431] and the uncontrolled open market economy.[432]

While media personnel spoke positively of how the January 25 Revolution had no leaders; others tried to raise a sense of fear of that. This revolution has no leader and all Egyptians are its leaders, proclaimed Makram Mohamed Ahmed, head of Egypt's Syndicate of Journalists, in his *Al-Ahram* column.[433] Today I say with all honor, and with my head high, that "I am Egyptian," wrote Osama Heikal, chief editor of *Alwafd*. "This revolution had no leader; it belongs to all Egyptians" and sets an unforgettable lesson for any upcoming leader. He or she should realize that Egyptians are patient people but they do not accept tyranny. This revolution "has unveiled to us, Egyptians, our country's destiny and place."[434] Columnist Ahmed of *El-Dostour* cautioned of the "militarization of the revolution," and that Egyptians can suddenly find that it is "being stolen from them and instead of having one Hosni Mubarak we discover that after waiting that long we have five or six Hosni Mubaraks from the military and those who yearn for power and wealth currently riding the revolution bandwagon." He urged for the formation of a leadership of ten persons that represents all of the country's political currents.[435] El-Shobaki emphasized that the 2011 Revolution's key characteristic was that it did not revenge on the symbols of the former regime in a "haphazard manner" as took place in Iran, for example, and it did not set up a revolutionary court outside its founded one but abided by the decisions of the established legal and constitutional institutions to put on trial those "symbols of tyranny and corruption." He fiercely criticized an Egyptian who told him that we should adopt similar techniques used by Russian and French revolutionaries (like the guillotines) to deal with corrupt leaders caught. El-Shobaki asked his readers to denounce such thinking and not to engage too much in "political maneuvers" but focus instead on how to create democracy and progress in a peaceful manner parallel to what Turkey, Brazil, and Malaysia did. He cautioned that the road ahead would be a long one, however.[436]

When writing on the January 25 Revolution, some writers at the independent press made reference to the French Revolution, not as a model to abide by in persecution but rather as a symbol of how social division between classes in Egypt was rapidly widening and heading to a level that could resemble that of France in the eighteenth century. In 1789, the middle-class in France revolted against the king and the elitists in responding to the demands of people which included ending monopoly on agricultural land and distributing them evenly. It demanded that elitists and priests not be exempted from paying taxes, stressing that the government should serve the ordinary citizen. Although it was not a "white revolution," the French Revolution has had the most powerful effect on the world sphere with its slogans still being taught in textbooks. At the time the French Revolution took place, wrote Kamel Abdel Fattaah in *El-Dostour*, France's population was 26 million; 1 million of whom formed the aristocratic class—the kings and his royals, nobles, and religious figures—while the remaining 25 million constituted the "third class" that owned nothing and lived in extreme poverty.[437] Dina Abdel Fattaah of *Al-Masry Al-Youm* wrote:

> Although I reject corruption in all its kinds, shapes, and forms and feel the breeze of freedom which the January 25 Revolution has granted us all, I have started to feel that we are living at the same time in a stage similar to that of the guillotine one that took place following the French Revolution which erupted in the late eighteenth century, and in which Paris and other French cities were filled with and turned into arenas of executions in which guillotines are placed to cut off heads of enemies of the Revolution in public.[438]

Shifting Image of the United States

Once the demise of Mubarak was declared, there was little criticism of America in Egypt's state media. During the revolution the state media had frequently evaded denouncing him and his family by claiming that there was a plot against Egypt, with articles often pointing at the United States and Israel. *Al-Gomhuria* columnist Mohamed Gabullah described the fear he felt when he "read and heard" of U.S. warships sailing close from Egyptian shores and of maneuvers on his country's borders with Israel. (These were rumors made in the Egyptian media and for which the author of this book found no proof.) He called on the SCAF and any upcoming transitional government to "utterly reject U.S. aid" because Washington employs it as a tool to exercise pressure on Egypt and Egyptians who benefit little from it.[439] Other journalists wrote of the end of what they characterized as America's influence on the Arabs. According to Salwa Habib, an expert on U.S. foreign policy, America may one day find itself without friends in our region despite the democratic reform that the Arab world is edging toward and for which Washington has been promoting in public and secret. That was clear in how in Tahrir Square there was no symbols or signs against the United States or burning of its flags. "America's presence was completely absent at the Square," added Habib in her *Al-Ahram* article. Events in Egypt seem to have "surprised and confused" Washington. "Who did expect Egypt to have all that influence on America's politics and interests?" The position and image of America that often used the "aid card" to place pressure on Egypt has weakened, not just in Egypt but in all countries of the region. Habib mockingly cried: Is there any country in the Arab world today that listens to America?[440]

In his interview with Dream TV, Heikel claimed that America did not get upset by the regime change in Egypt but got rather upset by the way it was changed. He pointed out that Washington welcomes such change but is "fearful" of the revolution itself.[441] There were also writers at the partisan and independent press who emphasized that political unrest taking place in the Arab world mainly serves the interests of America and Israel and their dream of changing the Middle East map. "Since the invasion of Iraq and the September 11 events the United States and other Western states have begun redrawing the map of the Middle to serve Israel's interest and its dream of widening its geographic map," wrote Georgi. After all, this is Condoleezza Rice's dream of a Greater Middle East.[442] We do not want an "Americanization" of our revolution, asserted Ahmed of *El-Dostour*, nor do we want our ties with the United States to remain as they were under Mubarak: submissive to Washington despite the "crimes" it commits against us and the Arab world.[443] Other writers and political experts touched on Washington's fear of the rise of Islamist governments in the Arab world. Certainly, wrote Alaa Abdel Azeem of the Arab Organization for Human Rights, Egypt is a vital alley for America in the region and U.S. policy necessitates that its peace treaty with Israel be maintained, and thus if the Muslim Brotherhood gain power in Parliament that will be the "biggest nightmare" for America and Israel, let alone the possibility of the rise of a nationalist movement that will call for Cairo's detachment from U.S. policy in the Middle East. Such nightmare will resemble in a way how a free and democratic election brought Hamas to power in Palestine and caused trouble for U.S. endeavors to strike a peace deal between Palestinians and Israelis on U.S. terms.[444] The January 25 Revolution was, nevertheless, and as Ibrahim of *Al-Gomhuria* put it, the first massive political protest in which there was no burning of the American or Israeli flag.[445] No outside foreign power has played a role in producing this revolution but Egyptian youth themselves,[446] and we expect it to be an ideal role model for the world nations to follow, including Obama's America, concluded *Al-Shorouk Al-Jadeed*.[447]

Post-Mubarak Media: A Futuristic Look

Many at the time of Mubarak's downfall wondered how would journalists at the state media "manufacture" their coverage which was entirely founded on defending the government and being a mouthpiece of the regime. Most state TV channels at times reduced the number of protesters at Tahrir Square, which reached a million, to only one thousand by placing their cameras only on one corner of the Square. Hence criticism of the state media in the partisan press and the independent media got fierce and even satirical at times. For example, the much-admired broadcast journalist and media critic Hamdi Qandeel described state media coverage of the revolution, particularly in its early days, as "media prostitution."[448] Others accused the state media of the Minister of Information Anas El-Fiqqi "not of defamation but of insanity."[449] An op-ed in *Alwafd* likened El-Fiqqi to Joseph Goebbels who served as the Reich Minister of Propaganda in Nazi Germany from 1933 to 1945.[450] *El-Dostour* stressed that chief editors of the state papers should stand trial because they are "corrupt" and "hypocrite;" they have misled their readers. It added, "It is a shame that the editors in chief of government papers underestimate the value and profundity of their readers, of Egyptians and their revolution." Many of them earn huge salaries without even having earned the basic journalistic qualifications needed to qualify for a job in the profession.[451]

What I found most odd as a researcher was that I did not read in the dozens of articles published in the state press in the a few days that followed Mubarak's toppling any which focused on his faults or loudly celebrated his departure. I must admit, however, that during the four years prior to the January 25 revolution there were signs of some freedom being granted to state newspapers (and to the state TV channel Nile News)[452] as it was normal to see criticism of top government officials—even of the prime minister—but not of Mubarak and his family. Though criticism of government was much fiercer at the independent press than at the state press, I only saw criticism of Mubarak once or twice in the independent press and I stated that in my 2010 book *The Egyptian Press and Coverage of Local and International Events*.[453] This partial freedom granted to the independent and the partisan press in the a few years before Mubarak's demise forced editors at the state press to embrace some independence and be more vocal in their criticism of government officials—becoming less of propaganda tools for government—so as to be able to compete with the independent media and the partisan press. But there were certain staunch government figures and members of the NDP which they never reported on negatively, such as Safwat El-Sherif, a leading figure in the NDP and head of the Shura Council. But issues of jail sentences against journalists of the independent press never ceased. Journalists who wrote stories too critical of certain powerful government figures, religious leaders, or of the president himself regularly faced libel and slander suits because of harsh press and publication laws and an emergency law that has been in operation since President Sadat's assassination in 1981.

After Mubarak's resignation, journalists at state-owned press establishments, such as those at Dar Al-Tahrir, which publishes the national *Al-Gomhuria* newspaper, engaged in constructive dialogues with protesters on how to fight corruption and insure Egypt's stability. In doing so, they practiced what one may call "citizen journalism." Campaigns were launched on Facebook calling on Egyptians to enhance their civic behavior by keeping streets clean and dressing in cloths that harmonizes with their society's social values. Citizens' writing, videos, and pictures of the revolution posted on blogs and social networking websites formed a perfect example of citizen journalism. Egyptian journalists at times depended on information from online activists, with emails and tweets and live blogs often cited. The work of these citizen journalists was essential for informing the world about what was taking place in the pharaohs' land and a supplement to that by the mainstream media.

The January 25 Revolution has "radically" changed the face of the Egyptian media, said Nabil Abdel Fattaah, head of Al-Ahram Center for Sociological and Historical Studies, in an interview with the state television station Al-Masria in March.[454] We began to see fierce criticism of government corruption and members of the former Mubarak regime being broadcast on state-owned television and reported in the national press. On February 14, an *Al-Ahram* editorial offered a brief apology to the Egyptian people for what it described as its support of the former "corrupt regime," and it promised to be a voice of the people from now on.[455] Similar apologies were issued by other state publications. At the time I was writing the book, there was a heated debate on how to restructure the state-owned media. And the whole of Egypt was watching cautiously how the state media were covering the transitional governments of Shafiq and Prime Minister Essam Sharaf which were established on February 21 and March 3 respectively. (The Sharaf government was also forced to resign on December 7.) I felt that that would be a difficult task—a major challenge for journalists of the state media who knew only how to glorify the ruling establishment. Can they practice the journalistic norm of objectivity, of covering the truth and nothing but the truth as those in the West opt to do? Allowing freedom in coverage will certainly be an asset to superior journalists who worked at the state media prior to Mubarak's demise such as Saad, Abdel Latif El-Menawi, Lamees El-Hadidi, and Amro Abdel Samea. A journalist at a state paper said he wished that the policy of his national paper would no longer be decided from outside the paper, advocating that Egypt in the future should attract the world's eyes by its political and media freedom.[456] We need a free media that reflect people's concerns and burdens, stressed *Al-Ahram*. The media, education, and an enlightened speech should be the "trio" that forms the passage toward development in the upcoming stage of Egypt's future.[457] Moamen Khalifa of *Al-Akhbar* called on the state media to stop being the "sweet" of the state. We no longer want that "god-to-servant" media relationship that flourished under the former regime. He added,

> We want honest media that express people's opinion and respect their readers and viewers. We want media that people like and do not adopt the view of the regime but freely and objectively criticize it. We want media that pursue a new path to win people's respect and truly serve as the Fourth State; we want media that affect change but do not change, media that handle the nation's problems and serve as watchdog on officials and embody the view of the public which they represent. We have gotten tired of those who idolize statues, of those who seek endings that are doomed to vanish and do not fear the God who created us all. We want media established by the public, and for the public; we want media that respect the blood of the martyrs who gave their lives to affect change.[458]

Late in February, emerging media groups that campaign against complicated policies and restrictions at the state media went on the streets in protest and chanted slogans such as "Minister of Information, Enough lying and tell people the truth" and "Minister of military media go back to them at the base."

We saw the rise of a number of independent and partisan television stations and newspapers in the post-revolution period, most prominent of which are Al-Nahar TV and *El-Youm El-Sabaa* newspaper. (Yet, most Egyptian intellectuals and distinguished political figures believe that none of these media are free from links or do not come under the influence of remnants of the Mubarak regime.[459]) This is the first time in my life I hear and see a television station that serves as the mouthpiece of a political party because Egypt never had television stations owned by political parties. In the days that followed Mubarak's fall, and as I mentioned earlier, I noticed journalists at the state media, particularly television, still having difficulty saying "Mubarak" without placing "president" before it, or to clearly and loudly state that Mubarak was ousted or forced out of office. It was as if those journalists were fearful still of punishment or not getting promoted by their chief editors or the minister of information as this was apparently the norm under which the press operated under the former regime. A number of them left state television and worked for private ones, many of which have been established after Mubarak's demise. Chief editors of state media who upheld their post until they were forced out late in March were also in confusion for they praised youth but did not bluntly and loudly criticize Mubarak to the extent that cartoonists in the independent and partisan press often made a mockery out of them. On February 13, for example, *Al-Masry Al-Youm* published a cartoon of three chief editors of state newspapers dressed in sailing attire with inflated rubber tires surrounding their waists. Two men, who apparently represent chief editors of independent and partisan papers or just two educated individuals, were standing on the side and dressed nicely. One of them said to the other: "These, my friend, are the chief editors of the state papers going to ride the wave." The implication is that the revolution has kicked them out of office.[460]

A year after Mubarak's fall, one can cautiously claim that Egyptian journalists today have wider press freedom and many of them are grapping it to devour. After four decades of restrictions, Egyptians now have the freedom to publish papers and establish television channels, but some journalists remain suspicion as was echoed in an interview which Al-Nahar TV station held with two journalists, a media expert, and a human rights activist in April 2012. According to media expert El-Sayed El-Ghadbane, Egypt's media scene, like many things in the country today, is in a state of confusion. The channels that were established after the revolution are owned by remnants from the Mubarak regime and money coming from suspected sources, claimed one Egyptian journalist. There is a threat to the media following the revolution because of the issue of media ownership, stressed another journalist. The country's mass media never stop denouncing one another.[461] There is also an urgent need to restrict the number of State Broadcast and Television Union media vehicles which reach twenty three TV channels and seventeen radio stations. The monthly salaries of Maspero staff—estimated to be 50,000 individuals—exceed 150 million Egyptian pounds ($25 million) and the government carries the burden of 55 million of the total bill.[462]

Conclusion

Military rule in Egypt instituted a state of submission, with people who are in lower positions professionally often saying *Tamam ya fandim* ("Yes, Sir") to their bosses or people in higher positions. Since the days of Ottoman rule, some Egyptians have been used to employing the word "pasha" in their lingo when glorifying someone. Ever since, many Egyptians, particularly the undereducated, have used it to show a sense of glory, if not submission, to someone—particularly police officers. A Facebook page posted on January 28 urged Egyptians to obliterate such a word from their vocabulary because we "live now in the age of freedom," an age in which an Egyptian should no longer be treated as a minion. One member posted a message saying: "The age of titles and pashadom has ended," and "we now need police officers who are trained on the ethics of dealing with citizens." Another supported the idea that an interior minister, unlike in the past, should be with a civilian background and not from the police. The third wrote: "A pharaoh does not create himself but is manufactured via the weakness of others."

A couple of days after Mubarak's ouster, and in response to demands of revolutionaries, the SCAF dissolved Parliament and suspended the Constitution and announced that it would remain in power for six months or until elections could be held, this is despite demands by many intellectuals and political analysts that a transitional government formed mainly of civilians should be established. SCAF's clinging to power has resulted in anti-military protests continuing in the Land of the Nile. Though Mubarak's downfall came as a surprise to many Egyptians, perhaps because it happened too quickly, there were many prominent Egyptian journalists and legal figures such as Qandeel, Ibrahim Issa, and Hisham El-Bastawisi and leftist journalists at the progressive weekly paper *Al-Ahali* and the Nasserite weekly party paper *Al-Arabi* who not only anticipated that it would happen but also promoted it in the social fabric of the Egyptian society. The toppling of Mubarak triggered a series of uprisings across the Arab world and was viewed as the most popular topic for tweets in 2011, according to a report by the micro-blogging site Twitter released on December 7, 2011. His ouster was a historic moment, a triumph of a nation over its mighty ruler. After all, that was the first time in five thousand years that Egypt found itself without a ruler. Perhaps this is the cause behind this sense of fear—fear about the future—which I continue to read on people's faces until I submitted this book to my publisher, as if they do not believe that the Mubarak regime was truly deposed. Others fear that *feloul* (remnants) of the Mubarak regime still maintain control over the politics of Egypt from behind the scene. But celebrations continue and most people are happy that Mubarak has gone, and they are exerting all efforts to document that in public. Immediately following the fall of Mubarak, a team of information technology experts from various Egyptian universities formed a web site (www.25jaagate.com) to document all the events of the January Revolution to benefit Egyptians and non-Egyptians alike. The revolution has also produce voices, including a rock-and-roll band named Digla, that call for the condemnation of oppression and shout against dictatorship.

There was a striking inconsistency in how Egypt's three different press systems covered the revolution. In the early stage of the revolution and until Mubarak's downfall, the state media exerted tremendous efforts to delegitimize the revolutionaries and reduce criticism of President Mubarak by drawing sources in their coverage from primarily officials or supporters of the regime in an attempt to frame protesters as members of the "counter revolution" and that among them are injected "hooligan," "looters," and "thugs." They gave a mirror opposite pattern of coverage in the independent and partisan press which was openly critical of the regime, though there was slight variation in coverage. Members of the state press wrote more articles than those at the independent and partisan press in support of the SCAF. *Al-Akhbar* journalist Yassir Rizk, who was later appointed as the chief editor of the state paper, stressed that the army, under Tantawi's leadership, has stated it aspires to hold no power and that it intends to hand it to civilian rule after the transitional period. We have "full trust" in the Egyptian military and SCAF, added Rizk in his piece which was titled "Egypt Regains its Spirit."[463]

Part of constructing the pharaoh mentality in Egypt is due to the way the state media had often glorified those in power. During the days of the revolution, the world—except for Egypt's state media—knew and fully accepted that the downfall of Mubarak was inevitable. In the weeks that followed the ouster of Mubarak, we saw a radical change in coverage of political events inside Egypt by the state media with journalists for the first time offering their readers and viewers a different picture and a somewhat balanced view of events. Some editors in chief and board chairpersons were forced to resign as they faced mounting opposition from their staff. For instance, Karam Gabr, board chairman of Rose El-Yossef Group, which publishes two weekly magazines and a daily paper, resigned during the three weeks that followed the toppling of Mubarak because of what one journalist there described as fear of being attacked by staff. The head of Egypt's Syndicate of Journalist, Ahmed, a staunch Mubarak supporter, also stepped down in late February. In the rocky, military-run transition period that followed Mubarak's fall, and despite the burgeoning of private media, Egyptians witnessed restrictions on media freedom under SCAF rule that I often heard people on the street say that the media under Mubarak enjoyed more freedom. During the rule of the military caretaker government, imprisonment and intimidation of journalists at the independent media were reported by Human Rights Watch, Reporters Without Borders, and Amnesty International. Online freedom of expression also comes under assault, with bloggers and netizens who voice criticism of the military being harassed and at times thrown in prison.[464] On the other side, the SCAF—as echoed in a statement made by Field Marshall Tantawi on May 17—called on "some" of the Egyptian media to be more responsible in their coverage.

In my opinion, the reason why the January 25 Revolution began is mainly because the majority of Egyptians found themselves living in poverty while those who hold power were living in lavish wealth and holding the power to decide the fate of the whole nation. True, Egyptians want democracy. But it is also true that the 2011 Revolution was more about "bread" than democracy. Hostility toward the widespread corruption that flourished during Mubarak's last decade of reign, particularly after the "forged" elections of 2010, was the ultimate cause of the gathering at Tahrir Square. Anger at the Mubarak regime was also because of its failure to embrace political reform and adopt policies toward establishing a fairer distribution of wealth, lack of a sound political vision, and the overlooking of the miasma that Egypt's youth were experiencing—particularly higher unemployment. Within this context, many referred to Nasser's "socialist rule." A piece written in the form of a letter by President Nasser's son, Abdel Hakim, and published in *Al-Masry Al-Youm* on February 13, spoke in praise of how members of the government of Nasser never accumulated wealth while governing.[465] This reference to Nasser's humble life has been going on since his death. The director of Nasser's office wrote in March 2009 on how the late Egyptian president died with nothing to own, not even a flat for himself or his family.[466] In a farewell piece in the October 1970 issue of *Sabah El-Kheir* magazine, the distinguished Egyptian journalist Salah Hafez lamented Nasser's death and praised his socialist ideologies. He wrote: "The man who turned the poorest farmers in Egypt into land owners has died without owning a house for himself." The man who ruled for eighteen years "made himself owned by his country; he did not make his country be owned by him." Hafez spoke of how Napoleon Bonaparte, Julius Caesar, Alexander the Great, and the pharaohs were great leaders but they served as elitists and not as servants to their people. "There is a wide difference between one who owns his people and one who is owned by the people," and Nasser gave himself and his life to his people, concluded Hafez.[467] Others also made similar comments about Sadat and how—despite his open market economy policies that widened the gap between the haves and have-nots—he and his family did not use their seats to amass capital.

I can well recall that when individuals went to offer their condolences to the parents who lost their loved ones in the January Revolution some mothers and fathers said: "We want no condolence; our condolence is the departure of Mubarak and the victory of the revolution." But Egyptian humor, which I have spoken of and cited in previous chapters, also spread among protesters at Tahrir who were celebrating Mubarak's demise. One sign called on the "shark fish in the Sharm El-Sheikh sea resort [where Mubarak moved to live following his ouster from his palace in Cairo] to get ready because Mubarak is there." Another one said, "Damn you, Sadat, for appointing Mubarak as your vice president." One of the many funny comments made on the streets and in the press was one saying that when Mubarak died, he ran into Nasser and Sadat and they asked him if the cause of his death was "poison" (many Egyptians believe that Nasser was poisoned) or being shot during a military parade (as was the case with Sadat). Mubarak replied to them that it was neither; it was via Facebook.

Another joke claimed that Mubarak is now on Facebook congratulating Egyptians for the downfall of their tyrant.

One can also argue that declaring that the SCAF will be in session indefinitely is tantamount to a military coup. With disregard to the counter-revolution and acts of violence that proliferated after the revolution, this was a significant fear that spread among Egyptians. A year after the toppling of Mubarak, I can say that it was *El-Dostour*'s columnist Ahmed, whose articles I quoted from above, who predicted many of the problems that Egypt is facing today, including the ugly military hold on power which has been continuing since Mubarak's departure and anticipated to end by late June 2012. In general, the protesters' demands in the weeks that followed Mubarak's demise focused on the following issues:

- Arresting and trying Mubarak and his sons Gamal and Alaa.

- Dissolving Parliament and the NDP and installing a new constitution

- Declaration by Vice President Omar Suleiman that he will not run for presidency.

- Abolishing the State Security Intelligence Agency (SSIA).

- Terminating the state of emergency (known among Egyptians as the "emergency law").

- Releasing all prisoners arrested since the revolution began.

- Ending the curfew that has been imposed with the revolution.

- Getting rid of university-police which is supported by the SSIA.

- Investigating officials accountable for hostility against demonstrators.

- Firing El-Fiqqi and stopping state-owned media from spreading propaganda.

- Compensating shop owners for losses incurred during curfew.

- Broadcasting all these demands on the state-owned television and radio.

Friday of Victory

I did not go to Tahrir Square on the "Friday of Departure" but on the day after, February 18, known among Egyptians as the "Friday of Victory." On the evening Mubarak stepped down, I went out on the streets of Benha and saw how some Egyptian men were sitting in coffee shops celebrating and enchanting "God bless Egypt." They were offering each other hot drinks. On the Friday of Victory, I went and spent half a day at Tahrir Square—arriving at 9:00 a.m. and leaving at 2:00 p.m., mainly to take notes of people's sentiment and reactions.

What was going on people's minds? The Friday of Victory was also an important day for many because the exiled popular Egyptian Muslim cleric Youssef El-Qaradawi who heads the International Union of Muslim Scholars was to lead the Friday prayer and deliver a speech from a podium at the Square. By early noon, there were hundreds of thousands of people present, both from Egypt's Coptic Christian and Muslim communities. The Egyptian media later reported that the Square area was packed with at least two million Egyptians. Whether it was two million or less is hard to tell, but I know that by noon the Square was so full of people that you could hardly move. It resembled Mecca during a pilgrimage—this time a pilgrimage by Muslims and Christians—to the extent that El-Qaradawi called on the latter to bow down with their Muslim brothers and sisters because all believers in God bow down to Him. The man who stood next to El-Qaradawi was an Egyptian Copt, George Isaac, a leader of the Kifaya opposition group which advocates for freedom and democracy. He was the one who managed the event on that day.

During that day, I saw people of all walks of life: rich and poor, Christians and Muslims, students of private and state universities, the highly educated and street venders selling all kinds of fast food, drinks, T-shirts, and flags. It was a true combination of the Egyptian society. I saw a sense of belonging and patriotism. I saw an impromptu memorial with photos and information about "martyrs of the revolution." I saw youth—boys and girls—cleaning streets and painting street platforms. There was truly a sense of social responsibility that resembled that which I had witnessed while living for over a decade and a half in America, Europe, and New Zealand. But there were also those who out of despair no longer wanted to see the name "Mubarak" hanging in public places. I saw on a few walls in the Square written words of humor that mocked the Mubarak regime and NDP. One major metropolitan underground train station, which is considered the center of Cairo, is named "Mubarak." In every underground train I took on that day, the name "Mubarak" of the station was scratched out and written on top of it El-Shohadaa "Martyrs." The station was later officially named El-Shohadaa.

El-Qaradawi, who lived in exile for years, called on Arab governments not to be stubborn and try to "stop history" but accept the will of their people. The huge public that was attending then clapped for him and shouted: "Come Mubarak and see El-Qaradawi is here." They further cried: "The people want to develop their country." El-Qaradawi, who resides in Qatar and often appeared on Al-Jazeera, commended Egyptian youth on their revolution and victory against "corruption" and "tyranny" and on the spirit of tolerance he has witnessed among the country's Christians and Muslims. He requested that the Square be named the "martyr square" of the January 25 Revolution. Alluding to Mubarak as a tyrant and a pharaoh, he said that a state which is founded on corruption and tyranny is a short-lived one; it is the one founded on justice that lasts forever. He asked Egyptians to exert their efforts toward advancing the state of their homeland, quoting from the Quran: "Indeed, Allah will not change the condition of a people until they change what is in themselves" (Surah 13: 11). He spoke of how Egypt was referred to in the Quran five times. He praised the Egyptian army and asked it to get rid of the government of the Mubarak regime and install a civilian one, a government composed of "honorable" Egyptians on whom he called to be "patient" because change will take time. He requested from the army to open its borders with Gaza and provide aid to Palestinians (on the following day the Rafah Crossing was opened).

In the weeks that followed, Mubarak and his two sons were held in jail on charges of being an accomplice with the former minister of interior Habib El-Adli in the killing of peaceful protesters and charges of corruption. Senior officials from the former regime, as well as leading business figures, were detained on charges of profiteering and the killing of pro-democracy protesters. They included four of Mubarak's longest-serving henchmen: former minister of the interior Habib El-Adli, former parliamentary speaker Fathi Sorour, former chairman of the Shura Council, the upper house of Egypt's parliament, Safwat El-Sherif, a leading figure in the NDP, and former Mubarak chief of staff Zakaria Azmi. Ahmed Nazif, Mubarak's prime minister, is also behind bars pending trial on a plethora of corruption charges. Two ministers from Nazif's government, minister of finance Youssef Boutros Ghali and minister of trade and industry Rachid Mohamed Rachid, fled the country and were sentenced in absentia. The weekly state-owned magazine *Akhabr Al-Hadadeth* ran on the cover paper of its March 2 issue photos of twenty of those officials with the headline: "Those Who Stole Egypt." Chapter 8 will focus on the trial of Mubarak, his sons, and members of his regime.

Since Mubarak's departure a state of chaos has also spread in the Land of Nile. Men of power of the former regime have continued to hold influence on the country's political process from behind the scene and doing everything they can to thwart the January Revolution and install what many have described as a "counter revolution." In a piece in *Al-Masry Al-Youm* on March 22, the distinguished writer and novelist Alaa El-Aswani addressed the many forces that could take part in the counter revolution, including the NDP and its failing members, security intelligence officers who withdrew from their posts to cause havoc on the street, governors and local council members, presidents of universities, deans of colleagues, head of media establishments—all of whom are approved by the security intelligence—and presidents of companies and factories. The plan by those running the counter revolution is to fulfill what Mubarak said before his resignation: chaos will spread and the country will fall to the Muslim Brotherhood. El-Aswani further claimed that 40,000 prisoners were released from prisons, armed and asked to "attack civilians." El-Aswani asked the general prospector why no investigations have been conducted yet with Mubarak and his family members.[468] "We must honestly admit that there are those who intend to delay the return of police to the street," wrote Abbas El-Tarabilli of *Al-Wafd*.[469]

PART TWO: THE AFTERMATH

CHAPTER 7. AMENDING THE CONSTITUTION

The ideal which the January 25, 2011, Revolution introduced was that "the people want to bring down the regime," and that does not just mean the ousting of President Hosni Mubarak and his government but the modification or abolishment of the Constitution of 1971 and replacing it with a "democratic" one that reduces the power of the executive branch and empowers people above all other branches. In dire need of reform at the time was articles 76 and 77 of the Constitution, which made it impossible for anyone other than a member of the ruling National Democratic Party (NDP) to run for the presidency. Worse still, the articles do not restrict the number of years a president can stay in office.

With Mubarak's downfall on February 11, many Egyptians stressed that amending the constitution—the supreme law of a state—was not enough because it was the brainchild of an "autocrat" and thus needed to be abolished. "We all want a new constitution" that "does not distinguish between a Muslim and a Christian," stressed Mohamed Mustapha, an activist of the anti-Mubarak Kifaya (Arabic for "Enough") Movement in a meeting held in the Egyptian city of Benha, a suburb of Cairo, on March 16.[470] Intellectuals and political experts, including distinguished journalists Mohamed Hasseinein Heikel and Salah Issa, spoke of a parliamentary representative system of government as more appropriate for their country. In an interview with the privately-owned Al-Hayat television station on March 28, presidential candidate Hisham El-Bastawisi, a judge who later ran for the presidency, also preferred a parliamentary system, one that is possibly modeled after the French system.[471] All this made me believe that Egypt was likely to embrace a parliamentary body of government, though it was too early to tell at the time I was writing these words.

The contemporary Egyptian Constitution does in many ways mirror the country's battle for independence from outside rule—from Ottoman reign to French and British occupations. Prior to Ottoman rule (1517–1805), Egypt passed through three main eras of governance: Mamluk era (1250–1517), Ayubi era (1171–1250), Fatimid era (969–1171). Their system of rule was mainly drawn from the principle of shura (consultation) embedded in the Quran.[472] Egypt's experience with a democratic constitution started in the late nineteenth century. Its first constitution, which aimed at restricting the power of the khedive, was the brainchild of the 1882 Urabi Revolution but was later abolished due to British occupation that began in the same year.[473] Mounting Egyptian resistance against the British resulted in a new constitution being introduced in 1923. Other constitutions were issued thereafter—in 1956 and 1964—due to the changing political atmosphere in the country and prior to the 1971 Constitution which remained in effect until President Mubarak stepped down.[474]

The 1923 Constitution

As was stated in chapter 6, the 1919 Revolution was ignited by Mustapha Kamel and led by Saad Zaghlul and carried the slogan of "total independence." It succeeded and the British succumbed to people's demands with King Fouad establishing a committee to form a constitution. The committee was not an elected one, and Zaghlul rejected it but King Fouad did not respond and a constitution that adopted a parliamentary system was formed in 1923 in which one article granted the king the right to dissolve the constitution at anytime.[475] The 1923 Constitution has continued to receive more criticism than praise, often being described as a step toward democracy and not the real democracy. While the Constitution of 1923 supported multi parties and the separation of state powers, wrote political analyst Raof Abbas Hamed, it produced a new political system that is "autocratic" in nature. It deprived "workers, farmers, and students" of their right to free expression and allowed British occupation to continue to have the upper hand over the country's affairs.[476] This, in the view of popular writer and author Alaa El-Aswani, resulted in the "corruption of political life and in parliament becoming a toy at the hand of the king." El-Aswani lamented how Zaghlul, as the nation's leader at the time, could have called on Egyptians to continue with their revolution until they reached the right path toward a "just and democratic constitution. It was a chance lost, one that resulted in Egypt not gaining its freedom."[477] Like El-Aswani, other analysts argued that the constitution of 1923 was a disappointment because of failure to "get rid of" British occupation and the continued intervention by the Egyptian royal palace in political life. The liberal Wafd Party, which was very popular among Egyptians at the time, was represented in government for only six years, noted Hisham Sadeq, a distinguished political analyst in his late seventies. In the latter years of royal rule, economic corruption and "division among classes" increased, bringing in to life the 1952 Revolution and the "historic leadership of Gamal Abdel Nasser," and a republic in which there is a fairer distribution of wealth and more connectedness to world, particularly among African and Asian nations—but without a democratic form of governing.[478]

The 1956 Constitution

The 1956 Constitution abolished Egypt's monarchy system and dismantled the political parties that flourished in Egypt under the constitution of 1923 whose articles (Article 14 and Article 15) guaranteed freedom of expression and of the press respectively.[479] The Constitution emphasized the "Arabness" of Egypt and the role it should play in uniting the Arabs as one nation. It stressed the need to insure social and economic justice and a fair distribution of wealth in a way that does not harm the country's good. It described Egypt as a "republic" that adopts the presidential system in which its president also assumes the role of the prime minister. The president holds the power to appoint and fire ministers as well as to dissolve the state's Assembly and revise an article or more of the constitution. In the commemoration held on January 16, 1956, to celebrate the launching of the constitution, President Nasser said: "The revolution has begun today; it is a revolution whose goal is to produce and build. This constitution amalgamates the whole nation."

A number of Egyptian intellectuals praised the 1956 Constitution and defined it as a new era of democracy for Egyptians. "The liberal democracy which Egypt knew prior to the 1952 Revolution was a fake democracy," proclaimed Hamed.[480] The most prominent feature of the 1952 Revolution, in the view of Ahmed El-Sherbini, was the "effort it exerted in the field of economic and political development," in insuring a fair distribution of arable land, securing water for land irrigation, and constructing the High Dam.[481] But while Nasser and his supporters described the 1956 Constitution as democratic and expressing the will of the Egyptian people, others criticized it for granting the president unlimited powers. "Perhaps the most danger in the articles of the constitution," argued political expert Ahmed Zakaria El-Shelq, is that it granted the president "colossal authorities" making him the "head of the state and the executive branch," as well as having the right to endorse or reject candidates for the legislative branch.[482]

The 1958 and 1964 Constitutions

The 1956 Constitution remained in effect until February 1958 when Egypt and Syria united, forming the United Arab Republic (UAR) with its capital in Cairo. The UAR revoked the 1956 Constitution and produced a quick constitution that bore a resemblance to the 1956 Constitution. In September 1961 Egypt's unity with Syria failed because of Damascus's withdrawal from the UAR. A year later, a provisional constitution was established which granted the president full authority. Elected at the time was a national congress to confirm a National Charter which stated Egypt's national policies. The National Charter was in no way a governing law but an attempt to guide the country and bring its policies closer to a socialist system. It continued to direct the political process until the 1964 Constitution was introduced and remained in effect for seven years. Embodying the principles of the National Charter, the 1964 Constitution somewhat corrected the freedom of expression deficiency of the 1956 Constitution and allowed for reference to freedom of expression and of the press. It continued, nonetheless, to accord the president sweeping powers, with the one-party policy that was implemented following the 1952 Revolution remaining in effect.

The 1971 Constitution

All of the four presidents who ruled Egypt since the 1952 Revolution that ended 2,300 years of foreign rule came from the military authority, and they were Mohamed Naguib (1953–54), Nasser (1954–70), Anwar Sadat (1970–81), and Mubarak (1981–2011). The constitution that was in application under Mubarak was issued in 1971 by the Sadat regime, and it was modified a number of times in the four decades that followed. Although it allows for some democratic practice, the 1971 Constitution, and the modifications made later to it, accords the president wide ranging powers, with only the president holding the authority to make amendments to the constitution. In 1976, a multi-party system was introduced in the North African state. Four years later, the Shura "Consultative" Council, or upper house of Parliament, and the power of the press were added to the 1971 Constitution, with Sadat making an amendment that allows a president to stay in power for an unstated length of time. Furthermore, he proclaimed (in Article 2) Sharia, or Islamic law, to be the foundation of the law of the state.[483] In 1988, Mubarak issued law 57 which grants the president the ultimate power to appoint the head of the General Accounting Office—the most powerful of two governmental bodies entrusted with monitoring fraud such as tax evasion.

In May 2005, and following a public referendum, Mubarak amended Article 76 of the Constitution, permitting for the first time for direct presidential election—for an electoral system based on multicandidate presidential election rather than the old yes-or-no referendum one. But, and to the regret of many, he deferred local council election until 2008 and lifted immunity from four established judges who criticized his regime. The changes to Article 76 also made it very difficult for a candidate outside the NDP to run for president. Mubarak won a fifth six-year term in office in September 2005 in an election tarnished by low voter turnout and charges of fraud. A constitutional reform was approved by Parliament in March 2007, and it included amendments to thirty four articles of the Constitution, one of which, Article 88, eliminated judiciary supervision on elections and entrusted an independent body instead with that duty. Of concern to the media, as I have personally seen when I spoke with reporters at the time, was the amendment to Article 179 that jeopardized individual freedom and the rights of journalists. The 2005 and 2007 amendments have, according to many legal experts, further strengthened a president's authority. Over a hundred members of the Parliament's four hundred fifty four boycotted the vote.

Constitutional changes—or "niceties" as often described by Egyptians—included that a president is elected for a six-year term and may succeed himself for an unlimited period of time. Mubarak, for example, was re-elected in 1987, 1993, 1999, and 2005. This has created a political system that is exceedingly centralized. State-recognized parties that hold a minimum of 3 percent of seats in Parliament and have been in operation for over five years can nominate a candidate for the presidency from their high-ranking leadership. Independent candidates can also run for election, but under restriction that two hundred and fifty members of Parliament approve them. A minimum of sixty five of the two hundred and fifty have to be members of the People's Assembly, twenty five of the Shura Council and ten members of local councils in at least fourteen governorates of the country's twenty seven governorates. Legal experts have often complained that these numbers are so high, and can only be gained if one belongs to the NDP. Easing the nomination requirements as stated in Article 76 has always been seen as essential for a fair presidential election. Article 93, which states that only Parliament can rule on the validity of its members, has also been criticized by law experts.

Hence, one can argue, and based on the views of members of the Egyptian judiciary system, that four articles (76, 77, 88, and 93) should be high on the agenda of amending the 1971 Constitution or when writing a new one altogether in the future, simply because the January 25 Revolution has abolished the 1971 one; it was after all an inadequate constitution.[484] Articles that are also prioritized for changes or abolishment altogether are 179 and 189 because of complaints that the earlier allows for civilians to be tried in military courts under a claim (by a president) of countering terrorism. Article 189 states that the president or one-third of the People's Assembly can propose amendments to the constitution. We must eliminate these bad articles which concern the power and authority of the president and make him or her "more powerful than any president in recorded history," wrote Saadeddin Ibrahim, a prominent sociologist at the American University in Cairo. The AUC professor named in particular articles 76, 77, and 88, as ones in dire need of amending.[485] "As long as the ghost of the 1971 Constitution remains, there will be no democracy," yelled Nabil Zaky, a member of an opposition party, in an interview with the privately-owned Al-Mehwar television station three days prior to the March 19 referendum which was sponsored by the country's ruling military government.[486]

The March 19 Referendum

Once Mubarak resigned on February 11, the Supreme Council of the Armed Forces (SCAF) dissolved Parliament, suspended the Constitution, and appointed a constitutional review committee of legal experts three days later to introduce new amendments to the Constitution in order to insure what it called free and fair legislative and presidential elections. (SCAF proposed that Articles 76, 77, 88, 93, 139, 148 and 189 be amended and Article 179 be removed.) On board of the referendum's committee, there was a leader of the Muslim Brotherhood, a Christian, and others belonging to different schools of thoughts. Chaired by distinguished judge and historian Tarek El-Beshri, the committee's authority was confined to amending articles related to elections while leaving the drafting of a complete new constitution until after members of Parliament and an Egyptian president had been elected. A council would then be elected and entrusted with that task of writing the permanent constitution. El-Beshri called it a "provisional constitution" that "will not last for more than a year" before a new one is written to replace it.[487] It was also agreed that in the transitional phase parliamentary elections would precede the presidential election.

The amended constitution was finalized on February 26, and a referendum was conducted on March 19 to see whether people accept or reject the amendments made to eleven articles in the constitution in what was described as the "first democratic experience" in the history of the seven-thousand-year-old North African state. But there was resentment by Egyptians of the amendments made, with some—particularly in major cities like Cairo and Alexandria—demanding a new constitution to be introduced once and for all without amendments first being introduced to the "defunct" one. The new amendments, which some of their opponents described as not going far enough in promoting democracy, primarily focused on limiting a president's rule to two four-year terms, fair presidential and parliamentary elections with wider judicial observations, and that a president must appoint a vice president within sixty days from assuming office. Furthermore, the minimum age of a president should be forty. Article 75 bans anyone married to a non-Egyptian from running for the presidency. It also prohibits anyone who has a non-Egyptian father or mother from being nominated. However, the most contentious amendment in the modified constitution revoked the unlimited power of the head of state to govern by emergency order only to replace it with a clause that allows the president to enforce a state of emergency for a period of up to six months before placing his decision to a public vote.

Although the new amendments wiped out despicable government policies that allowed for a president to be elected unopposed and to stay in power for an unlimited number of six-year terms, I saw disagreements among Egyptians on a number of issues once they were made. Some described the amendments as nothing more or less than the "suggestions" Mubarak promised he would make in the speeches he delivered prior to stepping down.[488] The referendum focused on points which Mubarak offered to tackle; there was nothing new, said political activist Mamdouh Hamza in an interview with the state-owned Nile News television station. "But we have to accept that move because we have no one else to bend on but the armed forces." The SCAF's choice of the committee that amended the constitution "was not good," added Hamza, and "the amendments took place in closed doors."[489] He stressed that a new constitution should have been written before elections are made to the People's Assembly and Parliament as a whole. "The first step toward democracy is a constitution and not the People's Assembly."[490]

In numerous media interviews, judicial experts, and prominent political figures wanted the constitution dissolved altogether, and I personally supported that since the success of the revolution meant in essence the collapse of the constitution. Presidential hopefuls Mohamed ElBaradei, former general director of the International Atomic Energy Agency, and Amr Moussa, chief of the Arab League, both declared their opposition to the referendum and later stressed that a new constitution should had been drafted before the parliamentary elections. There was also rejection of the referendum among youth and in major Egyptian metropolises. Yet following the announcement of the referendum results, the Coalition of the Youth of the Revolution, which took part in the demonstrations against the Mubarak regime, released a statement on Facebook asking its supporters to accept the referendum results.

The Muslim Brotherhood campaigned strongly in favor of the referendum. I even heard at the time that a few Muslim clerics called on people to accept the referendum because its content is *"halal"* religiously correct, and that it would be "un-Islamic" to reject it—a behavior that until this book went to print continues to frighten many secular Egyptians and Coptic Christians. Members of the Brotherhood, so it was reported, saw it better for them to accept the amendments and go to elections sooner than later because they were more organized at the time than other opposition parties, let alone those parties who were yet to be formed. The Grand Sheik of Al-Azhar, Ahmed El-Tayeb, said that any discussion of Article 2, which recognizes Islamic Sharia as the foundation of the law of the state, would be an invitation to religious dissension and could "burn" everything achieved. Writing in the independent paper *Al-Masry Al-Youm*, Samir Farid criticized President Sadat for adding Article 2 to the Constitution in 1971. He suggested that we add to it the following sentence: "The Constitution protects the rights of people of all religions to practice their faith and family matters within the rituals they accept." Farid claimed that Sadat possibly did that to gain the support of the Brotherhood in face of the leftist groups—socialists and communists of the Nasser era—that he was battling with at the time.[491]

Constitutional experts, such as Ibrahim Darwish and Tharwat Badawy, described the amendments as "unconstitutional" because the 2011 Revolution abolished the 1971 Constitution. Fahmi Howeidi, a popular columnist who often tackles Islamic issues, blamed the Egyptian media for blowing the issue out of proportion by quoting from the a few members of the Brotherhood who called on Muslims to accept the amendments and from the a few priests who asked the Coptic community to reject them. By doing so, he added, the media had exaggerated the "religious factor" in the voting process.[492] Whether you accepted or rejected the new amendments, wrote Hassan El-Mestkawy of the independent *Al-Shorouk Al-Jadeed* newspaper, we all agree that our "final goal is to construct a new constitution, restrict a president's powers, guarantee the rights of all citizens," and insure that parliament plays the role of a "watchdog."[493]

A day after the referendum was held, Democratic U.S. Senator John Kerry of Massachusetts landed in Cairo to hold talks with Prime Minister Essam Sharaf, Foreign Minister Nabil Al-Arabi, Moussa, and SCAF leaders. Kerry described the referendum as very moving. "I thought the referendum was very exciting. The numbers of people who voted, the excitement, the way they conducted themselves, there was a lot of energy," he said. "People voted for the first time in thirty years, not knowing what the outcome would be and I think it is a very good sign for the steps ahead, a very good sign." Likewise, U.S. Ambassador to Egypt Margaret Scobey saluted the turnout. "Egyptians yesterday took an important step towards realizing the aspirations of the January 25 Revolution. As we continue to assess reports about the voting, and regardless of the eventual outcome, the sight of Egyptians coming forward in unprecedented numbers to peacefully exercise their newly won freedoms is cause for great optimism, and will provide a foundation for further progress as Egyptians continue to build their democratic future," she said.

The Results

Most Egyptians had always been reluctant to cast their votes because they never trusted the results, and that is why voter turnout prior to the January 25 Revolution was very low; only between 10 to 27 percent of Egyptians went to the polls.[494] On March 19, the number of those who voted skyrocketed, reaching 41 percent—a miracle indeed. That, according to Abbas El-Tarabilli, a popular columnist at the party paper *Alwafd*, was the first time in half a century that such high number of Egyptians went to a poll. He prognosticated that a larger number of people—between 50 to 60 percent—would go to vote in the elections for Parliament scheduled in September. At that time we can then say that the Egyptian people "have succeeded and gained 'very good' in the world of democracy." We, concluded El-Tarabelli, are witnessing a "new renaissance" in a new century in Egypt. Let us advance toward a modern Egypt.[495]

The referendum results released on March 20 showed that the majority (77.3%) of the eighteen million people who voted of the forty five million eligible voters accepted the amendments made to the constitution. What I found most interesting about the referendum results was that most of those in the independent and partisan press—versus those in the state ones—said they voted with "no," or at least that is what I sensed. From talking with people on the street, highly educated individuals were more in favor of the "no" vote. People in high-class areas in Cairo tended to reject the amendments while those in low-class areas accepted them, so it was argued. The same can be said about inhabitants of urban areas vis-à-vis those in the countryside. Whether these assumptions are accurate or not is not known, what I know is that the referendum was another revolution because I personally never thought I would live to see all these constitutional changes taking place in the Land of the Nile, particularly that of confining a president's term in office.

After the referendum results were released, a top spokesman for the Muslim Brotherhood, Essam Al-Aryan, described the results as a "victory for the Egyptian people," something which he said would allow Egypt a new phase. Egypt's Pope Shenouda, head of the Orthodox Coptic church, called on Christians to respect the referendum results. The referendum results undoubtedly engaged Egyptians in fierce debates both in the print and online media. Following the release of its results, a group of youth placed an online poll asking whether or not they should continue their protests demanding that a new constitution be written straight away without waiting for the presidential and parliamentary elections. But the poll results showed that the majority of respondents accepted the amendments. Egyptians should respect the results, stressed Mohamed Hamd El-Sheriff in a commentary in the state-owned paper *Al-Ahram*. I congratulate my fellow citizens who said "yes' and those who said "no" in a new atmosphere away from the "age of despotism and tyranny." El-Sheriff said he anticipated that people would accept the new amendments because they wanted to see economic stability quickly established and knew that the amendments were just a step toward writing a new constitution. He called on "these minority" of Egyptians to "stop exchanging accusations" because that can provoke division.[496]

Salah Montassir, a columnist at *Al-Ahram*, theorized that if voters who said "no" had won, Egyptians would have been faced with many questions. They would have had to define whether the SCAF should continue running the nation's affairs and if so, until when? Would we elect a president without having a parliament first in place? Would we have had to elect a presidential council of three individuals, one from the military and two civilians? Who would elect the civilians? Montassir added that some said the army, but that would have meant electing a "military council with a civilian face." How would we have elected the council in charge of writing the permanent constitution: via election or appointment? He stressed that an answer to all these questions would have remained "hanging in the air." But saying "yes" meant that the SCAF would present a new constitutional declaration—a "provisional constitution"—whose articles "insure freedom and define the program of the next six months." Once a parliament is elected, its members will support the presidential candidates with their votes, added Montassir. The parliament would choose a committee of professionals and legal experts to draft a constitution in a period of not more than six months. The presidential election was most likely to be held prior to the end of the year.[497]

Like many of the columnists I read and analyzed their work outside the state-owned media, Khaled Edreis of *Alwafd* did not vote in favor of the referendum. He attributed the "large percentage of those who voted with 'yes' to the fact that they wanted to see stability returning quickly to their homeland; they were content with what had been achieved. They feared the future and desired a present with a secure and safe income." He emphasized that from now on all Egyptians know where Tahrir Square is.[498] I said "no," observed Ahmed El-Sawy in *Al-Masry Al-Youm*, because I believe we should give political parties a chance to "restructure and reform" themselves. There is the fear of the Muslim Brotherhood controlling parliament, added El-Sawy. "We desire to see lively and strong parties in operation before the elections because political parties are the heart of politics."[499]

Hassan Nafah, a political science professor at Cairo University, said that although he did not rule out that voters would accept the referendum he was "surprised" by the high percentage that the results had shown. He attributed that to three factors. The first is because of political Islam and those who currently promote it, employing as many avenues as possible to encourage people to accept the amendments. Secondly, there are still those "remnants" of the Mubarak regime and others who would benefit from making as little change as possible to the constitution and political process on the hope of coming back to power. They have no choice but to vote "yes"—be their interest is to regain places of power and wealth or just rescue whatever they can of what remains for them. Thirdly, there is still that "silent majority" which participated in the revolution but has now become fearful of its repercussions: lack of security, continued demonstrations, economic stagnation. Nafah added that it would be foolish to claim that Copts voted "no" and that the majority of Muslims voted "yes," or that those in support of the revolution voted "yes" and those who back the "counter revolution" voted with "no".[500]

Osama Heikel, managing editor of *Alwafd*, stressed that a revolution that emerged for the sole aim of political reform must have a new constitution implemented. He added that the referendum came quickly in an atmosphere "full of tension," one that is not "suitable for running a lively referendum."[501] I am all for a "new constitution" and not an amended one, proclaimed Aisha Rateb, a former minister of social affairs during the Sadat administration, in an interview with *Al-Ahram*.[502] Many of those who said "yes," according to Selim Azouz of the independent paper *El-Dostour* paper, were pushed to do so by a desire to see stability being quickly reinstalled at their country; while most of those who said "no" had no trust in a constitution constructed by a Muslim Brotherhood majority.[503] The Egyptian mind is conservative by nature, and most Egyptians said "yes" to settle the issue and "stop the ball from sliding on the snow," commented Moatzbellah Abdel Fattaah in *Al-Shourouk Al-Jadeed*. He criticized mosque imams and church priests who called on their people to vote "yes" and "no" respectively because that had hurt the voting process.[504]

Why Did I Vote "No"?

During the days prior to the referendum, I saw an entirely different Egyptian society—one that is not apolitical but rigorously engaged in political debates. I took my seventy-one-year-old mother in the morning of March 19 and went to vote on the referendum. I found voting centers filled with people, something that I never witnessed before. It was one of the happiest days in the lives of Egyptians, including my own mother, who for the first time in her life went out to vote. When I asked her why she never voted in the past, she said that election results since she could remember were "decided in advance." Also in the past, only those who had voting cards could go to the ballot box; while this was the first time where people could vote using their national identification cards. In the place we went to vote, I saw a lady in her late eighties, or possibly early nineties, being held by her two daughters because she could hardly walk with a smile dancing on her face. As I smiled back at her in front of the door of the voting center, she uttered the words: "Today is a feast."

Voting on the March 19 referendum was a new political experience for the Egyptian people. Outside the place where we voted, two intellectuals—presumably Ph.D. holders or physicians because they titled each other as "doctor"— engaged in a heated debate. One asked the other which side he took. He said he voted "yes" because he is worried about division and wanted the "country to move on." The other said he voted "no" because accepting the constitutional amendments would mean an acceptance of the NDP and the bits and pieces of the Mubarak regime. "We have waited for years and we can wait for a few more months to see our country better," he spoke in a loud voice. On the side of the street, one man said to another in amazement: "What is going on in our country? Are we living in the democracy of Great Britain?" Another said we are not just coming to vote; we are coming to "smell true democracy." These were people who apparently never voted in the past, because they argued that elections in Egypt were not the true measure for electing a candidate who is often selected in advance.

Why did I reject the amendments? I voted "no" for reasons that I wish to explain here to my fellow readers. The first of which is that I was not pleased with the low steps by which the committee that was selected to work on reforming the constitution moved, nor was I happy with the selection process either. It took them almost a month to make those a few constitutional amendments. I often told those around me: Why did not they just write a new constitution altogether? The whole process of writing a new constitution could have taken a month or two at the most, particularly when considering that Egypt has the finest and greatest legal minds in the Arab world. There is an abundance of distinguished constitutional experts at various Egyptian colleges of law. Furthermore, the amendments should have tried to limit the colossal powers that a president holds, even though I realize that the committee was mainly amending certain articles that deal with elections and not the entire constitution. I was relieved, however, to see the implementation of a short interim period of presidency because that does certainly limit a president's abuses. Staying in office for too long plants tyrannical machines in a regime, and one only needs to look at the Arab regimes over the past forty years to realize this.

Article 2 states that Sharia is the foundation of the law of the state, and that is fine since Islam is the religion of the majority in the country, but Egyptians need to also recognize in a more manifest manner (like other Muslim states such as Malaysia, Indonesia, and Turkey have done) their minority Coptic community which constitutes 10 percent of the country's population. It is important to stress here too that members of the Muslim Brotherhood should be allowed to play in the Egyptian political sphere as long as they respect the rights of all people and do not infringe on others' freedom. The world knows that at the roots of Islam is the respect of people of other faiths, hence I believe that we should highlight in Article 2 that the principles of Sharia do not deprive any believer from practicing his or her own religion freely.

A vicious constitution article that needs to be abolished altogether is Article 189, which states that the president or one-third of the People's Assembly can suggest amendments to the constitution. Also changes to Article 139 that deals with the appointment of a vice president should be considered, making the selection of a vice-president based rather on election in the same manner we do with a president. Other articles of vital need for change are 82, which permits the President to "delegate his powers to a vice president,"[505] and 84, which states:

In case of the vacancy of the presidential office or the permanent disability of the President of the Republic, the president of the People's Assembly shall temporarily assume the presidency; and, if at that time, the People's Assembly is dissolved, the president of the Supreme Constitutional Court shall take over the presidency, however, on condition that neither one shall nominate himself for the presidency. The People's Assembly shall then proclaim the vacancy of the office of president. The President of the Republic shall be chosen within a maximum period of sixty days from the day of the vacancy of the presidential office.

Summary

The state-owned media's coverage of the referendum was filled with inaccuracies. For example, *El-Massa* newspaper claimed that while ElBaradei went out to vote, he offered people sums of money to distribute on voters so as to encourage them to vote against the referendum. Such claim has been denounced as false by many in the independent and partisan press.[506] Furthermore, none of the work I have analyzed from Egypt's three media systems characterized the regimes that ruled Egypt since it became a republic as democratic. In their opinion, Egypt prior to the January 2011 Revolution went through two eras: Naguib-Nasser era and the Sadat-Mubarak era. The Naguib-Nasser period ended British occupation, implemented social justice and insured a fairer distribution of wealth but lacked democracy. In my view, Egypt has grown up exponentially since the 1952 Revolution which shunned the elitists and private-sector enterprise that flourished under kingdom rule and British occupation and guaranteed Egyptians jobs for life, a free health care system, free education, and strong social welfare systems. The proportion of youth in the population has been rapidly increasing ever since. The open-market economy of the Sadat-Mubarak period, which was initiated by Sadat in the mid-1970s and flourished under Mubarak in the 1990s, constructed a vicious capitalist system that took from the poor and gave to the rich under the claim of supporting political reform or promoting democracy. In his endeavor to get his son, Gamal, to inherit the presidency, Mubarak made a mockery of the basic tenets of the Egyptian political system and its constitution. And that made the youth of the 2011 Revolution relentless in their demand for a new constitution.

If the Naguib-Nasser era strongly supported the poor, many of whom were farmers, the Sadat-Mubarak one inhumanly took from the poor and gave to the rich. The wide gap between the haves and have-nots of the Sadat-Mubarak era was unprecedented. While Nasser sided with the Russians because he needed their support to build the High Damn, the foreign policy of both Sadat and Mubarak was entirely pro-American. This has led to the rise of political Islam to a level much higher than it was under Nasser because of his engagement with the Russians. Nasser also sought strong ties with African nations and those of the Non-Aligned Movement, with the latter being a move which he championed with four other leaders.[507] Hence one can argue that the 2011 Revolution constructs a third period, one that is different from the past two ones because it has simultaneously stressed the need for both democracy and social justice.

On March 19, Egyptians voted in favor of changes to the country's constitution. If elections are "carnivals of freedom," the Egyptian referendum has asserted the success of the "first test" of democracy for the Egyptian people, observed Mohamed El-Shafey of *El-Dostour*.[508] The referendum was a day that has brought back trust in ourselves, proclaimed Mohamed Amin in *Al-Masry Al-Youm*. It was indeed a "wonderful symphony."[509] In the opinion of Ibrahim Nafie of *Al-Ahram*, "There are no losers and winners from the referendum of freedom and democracy because everyone knows where the road is and wants to reach it." The referendum has proved that the revolution belongs to all the people and not just a certain group, added the former chairman of the giant Al-Ahram Press Group.[510] "I have no doubt that the January 25 Revolution is the greatest revolution in the modern history of the Egyptian people because it has perfectly expressed the conditions of its time while benefiting from the lessons of the past," observed Sadeq.[511]

In a decree announced on March 30, the military issued an interim constitution (based on the amended articles) under which the transitional government will run the country until a government is elected and power is transferred to it. It was, as one legal figure put it, a "condensed constitution."[512] Enacting changes approved in the March 19 referendum, the sixty-two articles interim constitution included amended sections of the old constitution that were endorsed in the referendum, opening the door for presidential elections that are fair and competitive. Read by the SCAF, the decree also keeps a quota that allocates 50 percent of parliament's seats to "workers and peasants." It conserves a constitutional article stating that Islam is the state's religion and the "principles of the Islamic Sharia are the primary source of legislation," and that no political parties could be established on "religious basis." Sharaf and the SCAF were to run the country until parliamentary elections were held in September and the presidential elections in October (or November) of the same year. Once the country's members of parliament and a president were elected, Egyptians were to then begin working on drafting a new constitution, one that is not necessarily founded on the 1971 Constitution.

If all goes well and according to plan, the commission's members (whom to be entrusted with the task of drafting a new constitution) were to be selected by the People's Assembly following the parliamentary elections. But Egyptians, even after the declaration of the interim constitution, continued to be divided in their views with some insisting that a constitution should be drafted prior to the parliamentary and presidential elections because there is always the fear that powerful politicians could try to make future amendments to the constitution to benefit them.[513] Listen to what these distinguished figures have to say. Rules ought to be instituted before elections for the People's Assembly and Shura Council are held, emphasized law professor Nour Farahat at a conference held in Cairo on the changing political system in Egypt. Writer Samir Morcos, likewise, feared that drafting the constitution after the parliamentary elections could cause problems. Kamal El-Menoufi, a political science professor at Cairo University, cautioned that while the symbols of the former regime has fallen its social base remains active.[514]

Despite all that division on the constitution issue, Egyptians humor (which I have been touching on throughout this book) has continued unabated. In the days that followed the declaration of the amendments, I got a message in Arabic on my Mobile that echoed Egyptians' deep and never-ending sense of wittiness. The message read: "An important announcement: We need a president for an excellent country with a sea on two sides—the Red Sea and the Mediterranean—and an eternal river: the Nile. It has three pyramids and a great people of a grand civilization. Rent is for eight years only."

Sabah El-Kheir magazine published a caricature in which a father is standing next to his son and tells the teacher: "My son is excellent in politics; he memorizes all the national songs and the Constitution."[515] And Egyptian humor continued. In early March 2011, I was standing by a bakery to buy bread and a number of customers were all speaking loudly. asking the salesman to hand them their orders. Dazzled by all the competing voices, the salesman laughingly said: "Wait, folks! Everyone will get his order in time. It seems that the revolution has unleashed people's appetite."

Chapter 8. Trial of Al Mubarak

The trial of the deposed Egyptian president Hosni Mubarak, on August 3, 2011, was an extraordinary scene. History in the making; the soul sinks at the picture of him and his two sons dressed in white prison robes behind bars (the norm in criminal trials in the North African state). The hearing, which was broadcast live on state television, was an event which many Egyptians never thought they would witness. It was not just they who were watching; the whole world was watching what the Egyptian press called "the end of the pharaoh." It was an unforgettable moment, as this was the first time an Arab leader had stood trial in person behind bars in his own country. The trial also proved the good intentions of the Supreme Council of the Armed Forces (SCAF) which was facing mounting criticism. After the trial was held it seemed that every Egyptian was talking about nothing but that scene: Mubarak in cage. Messages about the event were in abundance on Facebook and Twitter. There was also a sense of cynicism and sympathy on the faces of some people. But before studying such a historic event in detail, let us have a quick overview of the events that took place prior to it.

Following Mubarak's downfall on February 11, a transitional government was appointed to run the nation's affairs for not more than six months, when parliamentarian election was scheduled to be held. Early in March Essam Sharaf was appointed as prime minister in place of Ahmed Shafiq, a military man who was Mubarak's last prime minister, but was forced to quit later that year. His government was the second since SCAF assumed the responsibility of running the country.[516] The appointment of Sharaf (an engineer who served for a short period as minister of transport in the Mubarak government before resigning following a deadly train accident which he lamented was the result of lack of resources and corruption) was welcomed, particularly by youth with whom he went and demonstrated with at Tahrir Square on February 4. In his twenty-five-member government only four ministers were from the Mubarak regime. After assuming the premiership, he also went to Tahrir and spoke to demonstrators and promised them that he would do all he could to meet their demands. In the months that followed the ouster of Mubarak, the Egyptian media focused on unveiling political corruption in the land of the Nile under his rule. By early March, twenty-eight businessmen, including Gamal Mubarak's father-in-law, were detained on charges of exploiting their National Democratic Party (NDP) membership for personal profit. Bank accounts of many officials and businessmen were frozen. Mubarak did also submit his financial statements to the General Prosecutor. On March 8, the Cairo Criminal Court ordered the freezing of Egyptian bank accounts of the Mubarak family, including that of his wife Suzanne and sons Alaa and Gamal. This came following documents published in the independent newspaper *El-Osboa* revealing that Alaa and Gamal held LE100 million ($17 million) deposited at the National Bank of Egypt. It also showed that Suzanne held a secret account with some $145 million deposited in it at the same bank which allegedly contains donations from European countries for the Bibliotheca Alexandria (Library of Alexandria) which was established in 2001.[517] The director of the distinguished library Ismail Serageldin denied any knowledge of Suzanne's secret account. Similarly, a statement by the Mubarak family, released on March 2, denied the allegations. It was in fact the British daily *The Guardian* which first broke that story, by quoting a Middle East expert saying that the wealth of the Mubarak family could be as high as $70 billion. Other British papers, such as the *Financial Times*, put the number to between $2 to $5 billion.[518]

The outgoing Mubarak government feared that they might be called for trial, and rumors spread of many of them escaping the country. Rachid Mohamed Rachid, former minister of trade, and Youssef Boutros Ghali, former minister of finance, were outside the country and sentences were issued against them in absentia. But most members of the regime did not escape the country, and this, according to journalist Mohamed Ali Kkher, was because the regime never thought that they would stand trial.[519] On April 17, it was reported that the former Prime Minister Ahmed Nazif was to stand trial for misusing public funds. Many top members of the Mubarak regime, such as Zakaria Azmi, Mubarak's chief of staff; Fathi Sorour, speaker of Parliament; Ahmed Nazif, prime minister; and Safwat El-Sherif, secretary-general of the NDP and head of the Shura (consultative) Council, minister of interior Habib El-Adli, among others, stood trial. Mubarak and his son Alaa and Gamal were arrested on April 13, 2011, and placed under interrogation. Three days later, the Egyptian judiciary issued a decree that dissolved the NDP and returned all its belongings to the state. Businessman Hussein Salim, who until this book went to print was in hiding abroad, is said to have embezzled millions of dollars from U.S. arms aid to Egypt provided under the Camp David peace agreement and that Mubarak ever since he was a vice president had benefited from those arms scams. It was alleged that Salim monopolized, with Mubarak's help, the export of Egypt's gas to Israel (this was reported by the independent newspaper *El-Fagr*) and that Alaa and Gamal had received millions of dollars in commission.[520] A study by an economics expert, Ahmed Adam, highlighted that businessmen escaped their money out of Egypt right before the revolution with the help of their bank executives.[521] The well-acclaimed journalist Adel Hammouda, editor in chief of *El-Fagr*, wrote in mid-April that the Qatari ambassador Bader Al-Dafa[522] said that a member of the Mubarak regime once saw the yacht of the Emir of Qatar in the French Rivera city of Cannes and asked for one like it as a gift for Gamal Mubarak. After his request got met, he then asked for one for Alaa. Hammouda said that the price of both yachts was estimated to be 60 million Euros. It was because of this luxurious gift, argued Hammouda, that the Qatari station Al-Jazeera was offered a carte blanche to criticize, if not altogether "double" its criticism of the Mubarak regime.[523] Hammouda furthermore claimed that Gamal "sold" Egypt's debt and made profit out of it for himself.[524] And the stories on the corruption of the Al Mubaraks continued unabated in the Egyptian press.[525] In an article published a day before the arrest of Mubarak and his sons, the state-owned *Sabah El-Kheir* magazine cited the dozens of bank account numbers which Gamal, Alaa, and Suzanne held at various Egyptian banks—in dollars, euros, and Egyptian pounds—and which value millions of pounds each (a dollar is worth approximately six pounds and a euro exceeds seven and half pounds). The Mubarak family, except for Susanne, also owned twenty properties—palaces, villas, and super apartments spreading across the country. They held stocks in companies and used their power to influence the stock market, added *Sabah El-Kheir*, further claiming that Gamal and Alaa owned foreign corporations (or shares in them) abroad.[526]

Conflicts among political powers or between political powers and the SCAF were a daily feature from the time constitutional amendments were made late in March 2011. (Until this book was completed Egypt did not draw a constitution). In almost every month of the months that followed Mubarak's demise, violent spar did take place in parts of Egypt and not just in Cairo. Some of these clashes were said to be sectarian driven. In March 2011, over a dozen of people were killed in clashes between Muslims and Coptic Christians. In May of that same year, similar sectarian clashes did also take place with a dozen of people dying in attacks on Coptic churches. Many, particularly the Coalition of the Youth of the Revolution, charged remnants of the Mubarak regime and intelligence officers of being behind the clashes and the incitation of Muslim-Christian disunion and called for a one-million-man march in Tahrir Square. Demonstrators at Tahrir often shouted "Long Live the Cross with the Crescent." Mosques and churches adjacent to each other hanged Egyptian flags that joined them together. Others blamed the Salafists[527] for the escalating hostility towards the Coptic community and the lack of concrete action by the country's military. These clashes, together with street violence, weakened the image of those running the nation and caused a state of lawlessness.

The Trial Scene

Mubarak was flown to Cairo from the Red Sea resort of Sharm El-Sheikh where he had been under arrest since April at a hospital getting treatment for a heart condition. In the courtroom of the Police Academy where the trial was held, Mubarak showed up reclining on a hospital bed inside a large metal defendants' cage. This was his first public appearance since the remarks he made on February 10 in which he showed no intention to resign. In the cage with him and his two sons (who were dressed in white and holding copies of the Quran) there were also seven co-defendants, including El-Adli (already sentenced to twelve years for bribery) and six senior police officers. Only El-Adli was in blue because he was accused in the bribery, while four of his assistants were dressed in white because they were facing charges. The remaining two were dressed in normal clothes because they were not facing jail charges. The trial, which many characterized as the "trial of the century," began at noon and its procedure was aired life on state television from 8:30 a.m. to 3:00 p.m. Judge Ahmed Refaat presided over the Cairo Criminal Court. Names were announced and Mubarak said "Yes, I am here," raising his hand slightly high from his gurney to identify himself. The charges of corruption and involvement in the killing of hundreds of protesters were read and eighty-three-year old Mubarak replied: "I deny all these charges completely." Alaa and Gamal were charged with corruption and after Judge Refaat said you heard all these charges they denied them.

No one expected Mubarak to be tried in open court; just the fact of him and his sons seeing inside that metal cage was electrifying, a thirty-eight-year-old Egyptian man told me. My seventy-one-year mother described "Mubarak locked behind bars" as an "unforgettable scene." Without a doubt, the trial of a man who, according to many Egyptians, once ruled Egypt with an "iron fist" was an extraordinary and shocking event because many Egyptians doubted that he would stand trial. Ordinary Egyptians who were interviewed by television stations before the trial conjectured that Mubarak would not show up in court. Others said there would be duplex of him. (In fact, while in court one of the plaintiff's lawyers claimed that Mubarak had died in 2004 and that the man in cage was not him.) When watching the trial on television, many commentators quoted this verse from the Quran: "Say, 'O Allah, owner of sovereignty, you give sovereignty to whom you will and you take sovereignty away from whom you will. You honor whom you will and you humble whom you will. In your hand is [all] good. Indeed, you are over all things competent'" (Surah 3:26).

Following Mubarak's trial, many members of political movements gave their views on television and in the print media. Tariq Zedan, founder of the Free Egypt Alliance, commended Egypt's justice system and the military for making the trial open for the public to witness. Today, said the media spokesperson of the April 6 Movement, we are delighted to see such action taking place, and this is not out of a desire to degrade Mubarak; all we want is to see justice being served. He called on the SCAF to rush toward implementing the other demands of the revolutionaries. Abdelrahman Samir, a member of the Revolutionary Youth Alliance, spoke of how families of the victims were not happy with the performance of the lawyers who were filling on their behalf. But, he added, "this trial will stand for 100 years as a cautious reminder for any leader" who wishes not to abide by the law. Independent television stations echoed similar opinions about how the trial gives us hope that justice will prevail. "We are still a nation that respects justice," said the popular journalist Adel Hammouda of the independent TV station CBC.[528] In a column in the independent paper *Al-Shorouk Al-Jadeed*, political analyst Amro Hamzawy said he does not doubt that most Egyptians watching Mubarak being trialed felt a sense of honor for the victory of the will of the people and the supremacy of law.[529] An op-ed in the state paper *Al-Akhbar* compared two scenes. The first was when Mubarak stood at the People's Assembly in 1974 to receive the army's badge of honor for his military accomplishment in the 1973 War, and the second was when he landed at the Police Academy, arriving by airplane on a rolling hospital bed to be charged with corruption and complicity in the killing of protesters.[530]

Procedural measures dominated the scene at the courtroom with defense lawyer Farid El-Deeb wanting to summon more than sixteen hundred witnesses. There were angry crowds outside the courthouse of the Police Academy located in north Cairo and which once bore Mubarak's name. Over fifty individuals were injured in clashes between pro- and anti-Mubarak protesters outside the courthouse. In general, some were angered by the delay of the trial and how it should had been held immediately after the toppling of Mubarak; while others were content and said justice has been served. "We now can feel that there is justice in Egypt," said an Egyptian in an interview with the state TV station Al-Oula. "I can now say that I am proud to be an Egyptian." We now feel that the SCAF backed our cause, said another on the same TV channel.[531] We are now witnessing "justice" being served, said a third in an interview with the state television channel Al-Masriya. We are now seeing an event that the modern world has never seen before: Egypt is putting its president on trial. "We are proud of our judicial system," said another on the same TV station. According to another interviewee, this trial has comforted the public and the nation; it is a decisive moment in the history of Egypt, a nation which has never tried any of its leaders for thousands of years. There should be no suspicion of the role of the SCAF after today, said another. We are pleased with our judiciary.[532]

Abbas El-Tarabilli, a veteran columnist with the party paper *Alwafd*, pointed out how Mubarak used to enter the same Police Academy as the top man and how he is now entering it as an accused man. He, like other commentators, quoted early in his piece the same verse from the Quran which says: "You give sovereignty to whom you will and you take sovereignty away from whom you will" (Surah 3:26). El-Tarabelli ruminated over what Mubarak was saying to himself when he was laying in cage listening to the plaintiff lawyers, particularly the one who said that the man in cage was not Mubarak but a duplex. He wondered if Alaa and Gamal used to read the Quran in the past or ever abided by what the holy book says. The Egyptian people want justice; they want to know who killed the innocent protesters.[533] Khaled Kassab mockingly wrote: We have never gotten used to seeing Gamal holding the Quran in hand during the conferences of the NDP. As for Alaa, we rarely did see him and hence we cannot say that carrying the Quran was a habit of his.[534] There was no need from either of them to carry the Quran because it is mainly held when one is reading it. Kassab also ridiculed the minister of interior for holding a *Sibhah*[535] (a kind of rosary which Muslims use for the glorification of God after prayer) while behind bars. "Perhaps he was carrying it to count on it the number of Egyptians whom he ordered killed during the January 25 Revolution. Or perhaps he was using it to count the number of prisoners whom he ordered released from jail to trigger disturbance and spread horror on Egyptian streets."[536] Like El-Tarabelli, Mohamed El-Dsouky of the independent paper *El-Youm El-Sabaa* also inserted the same verse from the Quran in the first paragraph of his column. He asked those who sympathized with an effete Mubarak and others in cages not to do so and instead think deeply of the acts they had committed against Egyptians—not just the victims of January 25 but also against the sick and poor. Mubarak treated us like "his slaves," convinced that he had the power and right to pass his presidency to his son.[537] In "Mubarak in Cage is Best Gift for the Future," Emad Eddin Hussein also began his column with the same verse from the Quran.[538]

The trial was concerned mainly with the crimes committed in the period between January 25 and February 10—the day of Mubarak's departure. The deposed president is facing charges of conspiring in the killing of over eight hundred individuals. Furthermore, he, his sons, and businessman Salim (who at time of the trial was in hiding in Spain) are charged of misusing power and plundering state money to make profit. Mubarak's and his sons' trial was adjourned until August 15, and Judge Refaat said Mubarak would be staying at the International Medical Center which is located on the outskirts of Cairo until the next hearing. The trial of El-Adli and his six assistants resumed on the following day, August 4. After allowing cameras to film the first sessions, the court rescinded its decision and Judge Refaat ruled that the hearings should not be televised. In the months that followed, the trial was adjourned a number of times, raising some criticism of Judge Refaat in public opinion.

Findings

Like in all chapters of this book, the research method we have employed in Chapter 8 is news framing and discourse analysis. We mainly examined opinionated articles printed in the state owned (national), independent (privately owned), and party (opposition) daily newspapers on the day that followed Mubarak's trial, August 4, and we found 28 of them. (Because we could not find enough articles printed in *Alwafd* on that day, we decided to also include articles from that paper's August 5th edition.) Besides the discourse debate echoed on the Mubarak trial in the Egyptian press, we also wanted to see whether there was a difference in the way the three press genres referred to Mubarak. Did they describe him as the "ousted/deposed" president or the "former" president? We decided to carry out such a measure of coding after noticing difference in coverage when reading all articles. Even though the state press was critical of Mubarak we found that the majority of its articles (91.67%) referred to him as the "former" president rather than the "deposed/ousted" one; while 63.64% of articles in the independent press and 60% of articles in the partisan press used the word "deposed/ousted" in their reference to him. In all, 60.71% of total articles examined referred to Mubarak as the former president and 39.29% said he was the ousted/deposed president. Table 8.1 below shows results in more details.[539]

Table 8.1 Description of Mubarak

Press Genre	Former (%)	Deposed/Ousted (%)	Total (%)
State	11 (91.67)	1 (8.33)	12 (100)
Independent	4 (36.36)	7 (63.64)	11 (100)
Partisan	2 (40)	3 (60)	5 (100)
Total	17 (60.71)	11 (39.29)	28 (100)

From the finding above it seems the state media were insisting on recording Mubarak in history as a former president rather than one who was ousted by his people. When I asked a journalist at the state-owned, liberal magazine *Sabah El-Kheir* of why state publications are mostly reluctant to refer to Mubarak as an ousted president and used the word former instead, he said that such process in the change in lingo demands some time because it is "difficult to turn 180 degrees at once." He observed that some of the journalists at state publications are also "men of Mubarak's inner media circle" and denouncing the former regime means denouncing them too. He added that chairpersons of political parties whom during Mubarak's rule avoided standing in confrontation with the regime still follow the same path and this has an influence on how their newspapers cover the post-revolution period. He concluded: "There is, after all, no such a thing as absolute freedom. The business of journalism is also about making money and serving interests. If the editors of state publication (who are appointed by the government) serve the interests of those in the regime, the heads of political parties and businessmen also insure that their newspapers serve their interests—be it gaining political clout or making profit."

On the day following Mubarak's trial, pictures of him and his sons and El-Adli standing behind bars filled the cover pages of the newspapers of Egypt's three press systems giving them salience. State newspapers jockeyed to be balanced. The state paper *Al-Ahram* carried the main headline "Mubarak and His Regime Standing at the Hold of Justice" and the subhead "Former President and His Two Sons Behind Bars Accused of Killing Revolutionaries and Plundering Money." *Al-Akhbar*'s main headline read: "Mubarak at the Cage: Now the Revolution Has Won." Below it was the subhead: "The Trial of the Century Has Begun." *Alwafd* ran the main headline "Gang Leader in Cage" and the subhead "Mubarak Denies His Crimes." Independent papers printed more screaming headlines on its cover pages. The main headline on the cover paper of the independent paper *Al-Masry Al-Youm* read: "The Pharaoh in Cage: 'Yes I Am Here'." *Al-Shorouk Al-Jadeed* borrowed the following words from a verse from the Quran and placed it as its lead headline: "That you may be a sign to those who succeed you" (Surah 10:92).[540] The independent paper *Al-Tahrir* carried the main headline: "Viva the Revolution" and the subhead, "Egypt's Pharaoh in his Cage." *El-Youm El-Sabaa* cried: "3-8-2011: Brightness on All the Oppressed; Darkness on All the Oppressors."

To some extent the depiction of and debate on Mubarak in the state press was softer than those in the independent and partisan press, but it was by no means befriending to the ousted president. After describing the scene at the courthouse, *Al-Messa* newspaper wondered about what hopes run in the minds of Mubarak and his sons at that critical moment. "Does the former president whose age is exceeding 83 wishes to live longer and freely like ordinary citizens or is the devil of desire luring him more toward returning back to power and taking on the revolution and revolutionaries and everyone who stood against him?" The state paper further wondered if a psychiatrist can be able to invade Mubarak's mind and explain to us how he feels and what his hopes now are. What about the feelings and hopes of Alaa and Gamal, particularly the latter who was preparing himself to inherit the presidency? How will they be record in history?[541] At last, the trial of former president Hosni Mubarak and his sons has started, celebrated *Al-Ahram*, stressing that the scene ascertains the seriousness of the trial and increases the degree of its transparency. But it cautioned that the trials will take time and called on Egyptians to end their protests because they "have affected the nation's production" and caused "chaos" on the streets and an increase in the incidents of burglary and violence.[542] A commentator in *Al-Akhbar* stressed that he never believed that he would ever see the "former president" in court, let alone in cage. The stand of Mubarak in a cage is a fact which should now snub those who have been trying to insinuate division. It shows that "no one is above the law."[543] As we are witnessing the "former president," his two sons and the minister of interior and his six assistants on trial we can say that "a new history for governing in Egypt, a new history for justice," has indeed begun.[544] In their criticism or Mubarak or reference to him as a "deposed president," state papers also denounced the rule of the former Egyptian president. In covering the "trial of the century," *Al-Akhbar* concluded, the state owned media, along with those owned by affluent businessmen who accumulated wealth under "Mubarakian corruption," portrayed the deposed president as the "one and only devil—the big devil—and finishing him is capable of bringing down the regime, solving all of Egypt's problems, comforting martyrs' hearts, and calming down protests." But that is all wrong. The youth of the revolution, and we along with them, want to bring down a regime whose leaders — from Gamal Abdel Nasser to Anwar Sadat through to Mubarak — have eradicated political life in Egypt.[545]

Today, observed Adel El-Sanhory in *El-Youm El-Sabaa*, we are witnessing the first trial of an Egyptian president in the country's history. The political history of Egypt stands at a true decisive moment today because Egypt before August 3 is not the same as Egypt after August 3. The time now is not suitable for showing any sympathy with the "deposed" man because he is a leader and not a father or a god, added El-Sanhory. It is time for a just trial. "Mubarak committed lots of crimes, including starvation, poverty, and submission of his people. He should be held responsible for the deterioration and backwardness that took place in Egypt for 30 years." El-Sanhory's article was titled, "No Time for Pity."[546] Wael Quandil, chief editor of *Al-Shorouk Al-Jadeed*, accentuated: "Those who think that the deposed president and his two sons and their assistants could have been held behind bars had it not been for the struggle of protesters at the squares of the revolution would be mistaken."[547] Citing how Saddam Hussein was trialed by the Americans, by an outsider, columnist Abdel Moneim Yousseif expressed how he was pleased that the deposed president stood in front of an Egyptian judiciary with the freedom to select his lawyers, and that he was trialed in a civilian court and not a military one as some struggled to bring about. "One of the great things about this revolution is that it trials its enemies and those who did harm to Egypt in a just way, because this revolution is all about justice." In this sense, added Yousseif, Mubarak and his companions enjoyed what their victim did not enjoy: The right for a fair trial. This revolution erupted mainly to insure justice.[548]

And Egyptians' jubilations kept rising. Mubarak's trial has placed Egypt's name high up in the "sky of justice" and has showed that oppression must have an end, celebrated a commentator in *Alwafd*. That day "was not a normal day in my life and the lives of millions of human beings in Egypt and around the globe; it was a day of bringing the oppressor and the tyrant to trial." The "deposed president" and his sons stood next to each other trying to hide their father from cameras.[549] In "Devils of the Presidential Palace," Essam El-Ebadi wondered whom should we blame for Mubarak's faults. He argued that some say it was his wife and two sons, but the reality is that there was a "group of devils" surrounding the man. After all, added El-Ebadi, presidential palaces are often inhibited by devils. Members of the inner circle that engulfed the "deposed" president were all corrupt and driven by avarice. With them around, Mubarak became "head of a gang rather than a president of a state." El-Ebadi named in order the following five officials as being Mubarak's inner circle of corruption: Safwat El-Sherif, secretary-general of the NDP, Zakaria Azmi, Mubarak's chief of staff, Ahmed Ezz, NDP secretary for organizational affairs, Fathi Sorour, speaker of parliament, and Anas El-Fiqi, minister of information.[550]

The Themes

Many impressions were recorded in the Egyptian press—particularly in the independent and partisan press—about the trial of the deposed president, his sons, and the interior minister and his assistants. In all, the Egyptian press focused on the following four main themes, or issues, in its discourse on the Mubarak trial.

A Pharaoh and an Obstinate Man

Over the past decades, Egyptian thinkers have often spoken of how the Pharaohs of ancient Egypt had always tried to be the sole source of legislation.[551] Within this context, media discourse on Mubarak at times depicted his rule as pharaonic. Mubarak's obstinacy, noted *Al-Akhbar*, has made it hard for us to sympathize with his old age and effeteness. "He came to court with his hair dyed and wearing a posh watch similar to that of his younger son." Mubarak failed, as he had done during the revolution, in gaining public sympathy due to his stubbornness and reluctance to step down. There is no way out for him, and Egyptians will know about those "snipers who stood on high buildings at Tahrir Square and shot protesters," added the state paper. Former Vice President Omar Suleiman must give his testimony; yet, and in spite of its importance, it must not be in open court because the man holds lots of secrets that can endanger the nation's security if made public.[552]

Al-Ahram's distinguished columnist Salah Montassir observed that what was surprising about the trial was that Mubarak looked and acted fine for his age and showed no sign of sickness, and this comes in contradiction to what had been reported before, let alone that he also continues to have his hair dyed. He added that Mubarak wore his watch and spoke with a strong voice; the only exception was that he was lying on a medical bed.[553] *Alwafd* wondered why did not Mubarak escape and preferred to stay in Egypt after the downfall of his regime. Why did not he run with his "crimes" and the money he "stole" to another country? "Has his stubbornness reached such a degree?" Here he is in his old age lying on the medical bed to give testimony. No one can stand such a scene, but we must also know whether or not he ordered the use of live ammunition on protesters and whether his sons embezzled money or used their father's power to benefit themselves, added the party paper which supported making the trial closed to the media.[554]

In "The Egyptian Have Done It," Ibrahim Mansour of *Al-Tahrir* described the trial as a "historic scene," one which will be recorded in Egypt's name in the history of nations. The Egyptians have succeeded in trying their pharaoh, their president, and making him stand in a cage like in any other ordinary trials.[555] "This is a unique trial in the Egyptian history; it puts an end to the Egyptian people's submissiveness to the pharaoh. Israel will no longer brag that it is the only civilized country in the region that puts its rulers on trial," proclaimed the renowned *Al-Akhbar* columnist Ahmed Ragab.[556] The trial, according to an *Al-Masry Al-Youm* op-ed, proves the truthfulness of the Athenian philosopher Aristotle's theory of tragedy as exhibited in *Poetics*, because the Egyptian president also miscalculated it like the hero in Shakespeare's *The Tragedy of Macbeth* who commits regicide to rise to the throne and Sophocles' *Oedipus Rex* in which its hero kills his father and marries his mother in fulfillment of a prophecy. Mubarak, continued the independent paper, is a stubborn man who forged elections and made a mockery of his people. Worse still was the way he showed no relentless in leaving office following the eruption of the revolution, and that "was not just his end but the tragedy of those closest to him: wife and two sons." There is no alternative for Mubarak now but to either go insane or die because no human being can bear such a tragedy.[557] If this is how the trial in life looks like, Mubarak (and we along with him) must now think about the Day of Judgment.[558] But we must also remind ourselves that taking revenge on Mubarak is not the way to build a safe future, stressed *Al-Ahram*. We must let our judicial system determine whether Mubarak is guilty or innocent.[559]

Egypt is changing; the revolution has changed it, pointed out *Al-Tahrir*. It is building its own new state, a state of law—a state without pharaohs. Egyptians are putting on trial their own dictators but not assassinating them. "Trying a gang of oppressors is the result of our peaceful revolution," added the independent paper. "This is the miracle of oppressed nations."[560] After today, a ruler will no longer act as if a state is a property of his. This is the end of the "god ruler," of the "pharaohism of rulers," said *Al-Akhbar*. We are putting Mubarak on trial not for revenge but to achieve justice and build a better Egypt free from dictatorial rule.[561] Mubarak is an obstinate man, wrote Mohamed El-Brghoty in *Al-Masry Al-Youm*, alleging that it was his "corrupt" policemen who blew up the Two Saints Church (or Al-Qiddissin Church in Arabic)[562] in Alexandria on the 2010 New Year's Eve. The man, who "stole thirty years of our lives," cared about nothing but passing his throne to his son, Gamal, whom El-Brghoty alleged assigned the snipers to shoot protesters at Tahrir. We have every right today to feel "joyful" as we witness these "killers and thieves" stand trial. Egyptians have lived to see members of a regime characterized with "cruelty, obstinacy, mighty, and lying" stand trial at the same place they gathered six months ago. It was at that place— the Mubarak Police Academy—that they often celebrated victory, including the forged 2010 parliamentary elections.[563]

In "The Trial of the Century," *Al-Akhbar* commented: "No one had ever imagined or visualized to see the former president, his two sons Alaa and Gamal, and the former interior minister Habib El-Adli and his assistants in cage." Mubarak came dying his hair and with the same tyranny on his face even though his is stretched on a medical bed. This made no one sympathize with him. Had he done like Saddam Hussein and appeared in ruffled hair and kept a long beard the Egyptian people would have shown some sympathy toward him.[564] In short, all attempts to "add glory" to the pharaoh or win people's empathy while at court have failed because of Mubarak's egotism as shown in his looks, dying of his hair, and putting his finger in his nose at times, observed Belal Fadl in *Al-Tahrir*. From today this will be the destiny of every tyrant who "kills" his people and "steals" their country's wealth.[565]

"Strong" Defense Lawyers vs "Weak" Plaintiff Lawyers

The stance and performance by lawyers calling for victims' rights were poor and unprofessional, according to journalists and political analysts. The flocks of the more than thirty lawyers representing families of martyrs were chaotic and disorganized unlike Mubarak's veteran lawyer El-Deeb who took a professional and well-organized position. One of them shouted that Mubarak was a serial killer, while another denied that it was Mubarak who is standing in the cage. The chief editor of *El-Youm El-Sabaa* wondered why there was an "absence of big lawyers" in the courtroom defending the plaintiff against the "big lawyers who stood in defense of the camp of evil inside that cage." In his criticism of some plaintiff lawyers who in his opinion were competing to show their faces on television screens, *El-Youm El-Sabaa*'s chief editor Khaled Salah sardonically wrote: This trial is a "true test" of justice and law, and we either achieve it or just "clamp to appease the 'pasha lawyers' dazzling on the television screens."[566] Making reference to presidential candidates Hazem Abu Ismael, Mohamed Selim Al-Awa, Hisham El-Bastawisi, Quandil contemplated: "If it is a requirement upon us to thank those noble revolutionaries, it is also mandatory that we ask the distinguished lawyers who are running for the presidency this question: Where do you stand when it comes to defending the causes of the martyrs and the injured?"[567] It is a mockery not to see eminent lawyers defending the plaintiffs, stressed *Al-Akhbar*. None of these high-priced lawyers who often appear on talk-show programs bragging about how we should protect human rights came to defend the weak. Referring to a number of Egypt's top lawyers, the state paper further cried: "Why did you leave the families of the martyrs alone?"[568]

A number of commentators pointed out that Mubarak should have been put in normal jail, and tried and treated for health problems under the same conditions that ordinary prisoners undergo. In the "Trial of the Deposed," Nowara Nigm of *Al-Tahrir* argues that when she saw Mubarak behind bars she remembered pictures of the "martyrs" who died due to torture in Egyptian detention camps since the eighties and nineties. She mocked how Mubarak, the "pharaoh," is now sitting on a comfortable chair in an air conditioned jail with his two sons shielding him from cameras and having distinguished lawyers to defend him.[569] It is shameful to see this absence of good lawyers standing in defense of the families who lost their loved ones at Tahrir Square, lamented *Al-Akhbar*.[570] Likewise, *Al-Tahrir* disdainfully asked: "Who are these plaintiff lawyers, my friends?" We have never heard or seen them before. What is this all idle talk which they uttered? Where are Egypt's great lawyers whom we see day and night on satellite television stations? Would it not have been better for Al-Awa to defend the rights of the martyrs of the revolution than run for the presidency? Why did not Abu Ismael and other big lawyers and businessmen employ their legal background and wealth to defend the martyrs? "The people want serious lawyers and not a flock of comedians?"[571]

Containing Turmoil on the Street

The trial was seen as helping in containing some of the turmoil that gripped the public since Mubarak's downfall on February 11. Prior to the trial one could see anger on people's faces and in their lingo when Mubarak's name was mentioned; many often shouted: "Why has not Mubarak stood trial until now?" As we mentioned above, many doubted that there would be a trial of him, held, let alone one broadcast on television. On this, *Alwafd* contemplated: The appearance of the toppled Mubarak standing in court after months of disappearance from public view should calm things down on the Egyptian street; after all, what we are seeing is the fulfillment of the will of the Egyptian people.[572] Akram El-Kasas of *El-Youm El-Sabaa* called for a serious trial to be held against Mubarak, a man whom he accused of "impoverishing the poor" and "ailing the ill." We do not want entertainment episodes. El-Kasas conjectured, "If Mubarak was concerned with history he would have admitted that he is the one responsible for the crimes committed against protesters in January and February, because it was him—and only him—who told the authorities to issue instructions that turned into laws and decrees. It was him who headed the police council and gave information and orders to the minister of interior." If this trial is carried out correctly, it will calm down the uproar in public opinion and give a lesson to those who hold power.[573]

According to *Alwafd*, the trial has accomplished three goals. It has shown that government is capable of carrying out a top trial and exhibiting that its institutions are operating fine. This is the "initial lesson of the new Egyptian democracy, of post-revolution Egypt." Secondly, the trial has emphasized Egypt's leading role in the Arab world for the whole world to witness. Thirdly, it has helped in "regaining trust" between the state and the public. But there was also this sense of worry among some journalists about what comes next. For example, Ibrahim Issa, one of Egypt's most popular journalists and political commentators, pointed out: I am worried that Egyptians will "pay a heavy price for trying Mubarak." He added that those running the country can now pass the "wrong laws and issue the wrong decisions," and when the public complains they will say: What more do you want? Have not we put Mubarak in cage for you? Egyptians must always remind those who are in power that the Mubarak trial is a natural outcome of the revolution and not a gift or a reward from anyone, added Issa who serves as the editor in chief of *Al-Tahrir*.[574] *Al-Shorouk Al-Jadeed* called on Egyptians to celebrate this victory. We should all be proud to be Egyptians because we have succeeded in getting our dictator and his tyrannical regime to stand trial. We should start dispatching ourselves from the past and begin laying the foundation for "a state of law" that stands against dictatorship and supports the "weak and oppressed."[575] The trial will take a long time; there will be a long road ahead for us to achieve freedom, civility, progress, ending military rule, and building a big state in which justice prevails, declared Fadl.[576]

State papers in particular, such as *Al-Messa*, emphasized that the trial should put an end to the claim that there is a conspiracy between "Mubarak and the army, or that the SCAF will not allow for Mubarak to stand trial." We now have every right to "praise" our military and the SCAF. The trial is a "badge of honor on the chest of Egypt's judiciary and military, and on the chest of every Egyptian."[577] An *Al-Shorouk Al-Jadeed* columnist spoke of how none of his relatives or friends believed that Mubarak would show up in court, and that if it happened it would not be Mubarak himself but a duplex. He lamented how the Egyptian people have lost trust in their institutions because, as one of his friends told him, they are being bilked out of their wealth for a century by greed and thus they cannot immediately trust what is being said to them. He called on Egyptians to trust their judiciary and the military.[578]

In the opinion of *Alwafd*, Egypt expressed itself in two major steps: the first was in producing the revolution and the second was in getting its president to stand trial.[579] Kudos to every person or group of individuals which contributed to making Mubarak's trial open for the public to watch, proclaimed Hussein of *Al-Shorouk Al-Jadeed*. He added:

> The scene of Mubarak standing in cage is a message to every tyrant or despotic or corrupt ruler that no matter what his feeling of power or the security entourage that protects him or his corruption reach, his downfall and trial will take place sooner or later.

> The picture of Mubarak lying on a bed inside the cage exhibits that the Egyptian people have for the first time overcome their pharaoh. The people were in the courtroom or sitting in front of television screens while their former president, his sons and senior aid were in cage.

> Mubarak's picture in a cage is the best achievement of the revolution, continued Hussein. Today we can feel a sense of comfort, a sense of justice.[580]

Symbolism for Arab Uprisings

Mubarak is the first Arab leader to go on trial, which is coming at a time when a wave of revolts is sweeping the Arab world. The trial added panache to the unfolding Arab uprisings; autocratic Arab leaders must have thought of their own fate when they saw Mubarak in cage. The symbolism of an untouchable ruler brought before the law in a historic trial offered an ineradicable lesson for Arab autocratic rulers, with many Egyptian commentators describing it as a milestone that will give a push for democratic change in Arab states. Hence, many incumbent Arab regimes—from Syria to Saudi Arabia, Bahrain, Yemen, and through to Morocco—were fearful because something grand was taking place in the Arab world. They feared of ending in the same dock as Mubarak. The only live coverage that was broadcast of the trial outside of Egypt was in Tunisia and by the Lebanese-based, Hezbollah-owned Al-Manar television station.

The Egyptian press portrayed the trial as a victory for democracy. "The Mubarak trial is a model that should be taught to all societies, including democratic ones," proclaimed *Al-Messa*.[581] It is the first trial of an Arab leader seen held in cage; it is a scene not just for Arabs to record but for the whole world, observed *Alwafd*.[582] The question now is: "Will the remaining Arab leaders such as [Moammar] Gadhafi, [Bashar] al-Assad, and [Ali Abdullah] Saleh, learn a lesson from seeing the first Arab leader standing in a cage or will they continue shedding the blood of their people to keep their seats—which no matter what they do, will not last?"[583] If Mubarak, Ben Ali of Tunisia, Ceausescu of Romania, among others had thought for a moment of the wisdom that says "if others had stayed in place for so long, you would not have been here," they would not have found themselves in those critical and horrible situations, wrote *Al-Ahram*. Mubarak is now standing in cage after it was impossible in the past to whisper a word to him or his family, or come closer to a man who ruled for thirty years as if there was "no one but him suitable to govern" in a country of eighty million.[584] This trial, like the Egyptian revolution itself, will inspire the oppressed in other nations to rise against their dictators and bring them to justice, accentuated Mansour.[585] Focusing his debate on Syria, Hamzawy ruminated over the following issues: Will Mubarak's trial make Syria's Assad feel a bit of "fear or worry? Will he reconsider acts concerning his horrible and criminal treatment of his people for fear of an end similar to Mubarak's?" Other dictatorial regimes in the Arab world—presidential be they or parliamentarian—are following the scene in Egypt, "searching for a path to avoid a Mubarak-like end."[586]

Conclusion

On August 3, 2011, the world watched a long and complex trial in what used to be the Mubarak Police Academy, and we must remind ourselves that the trial is the product of stepped youth protests. Few Egyptians—a few Arabs—did in fact expect to see the day when Mubarak stand trial on charges of complicity in the killing and corruption. Some claimed that the SCAF did not want Mubarak to stand trial, and that had it not been for the persistence of protesters the trial would not have come into being. Indeed, the trial set a lesson for every upcoming ruler that they must abide by the law and accept the other. Many Egyptians anticipated that hearings will continue to be broadcast to the public in an open court but that did not happen and the court was closed to the media and the public after that first session. In all, the trial has comforted most Egyptians and fulfilled the demands of protesters. Egyptians viewed it as a victory for the revolution and a genuine move toward reducing the atmosphere of distrust that was mounting between the public and the SCAF. The eyes of many were, however, focused on what the final verdict would be. Yet one can also argue that on August 3 Egyptians have witnessed history in the making. Gone are the days of the pharaoh from Egyptian governing. Gone are the days that autocratic Arab rulers think they can rule for ever and commit atrocities without being trialed. The Mubarak trial is indeed a milestone in uprisings in the Arab world. Or as Abdel Hakim, son of Egyptian President Gamal Abdel Nasser, said in an interview with the private Al-Hayat television station that if the funeral of his father has been characterized as the "funeral of the century," Mubarak's trial is the "trial of the century."[587] Certainly that scene must have terrified Arab autocrats facing popular uprisings in their countries.

The demise of a modern pharaoh, and his trial later, has surely inspired revolutionaries in the Arab world. It has given Arabs' hope that they too can not only change their regimes but put them on trial. It has invigorated the youth-led wave of uprisings that were sweeping the Arab world, giving a push to the Libyans, Syrians, and Yemenis in particular to complete their task of toppling their corrupt regimes. Autocratic Arab rulers were left with a few choices: cling to power at any cost like Assad is doing, negotiate immunity like Saleh of Yemen has done, or seek a foreign sanctuary like Ben Ali of Tunisia has done. The question now is: Will the trial heal or open Egypt's wounds? Seeing the deposed president standing in court made many people around me calm down; there was a lot of drama in it. The spectacle of a frail, eighty-three-year old man on a medical bed was sad. It was a sight that people never thought they would witness but all Egyptians wanted to see justice served to the mothers who lost their loved ones in the revolution. There was also this fear in people's eyes about what comes next. In the trial sessions that followed, and which showed no accusation against Mubarak, many wondered at the time of whether the SCAF is searching for a way to absolve and forgive Mubarak whose lawyer has been claiming his innocence. Bud I did also hear others on the streets speak of how Mubarak's trial is nothing but an attempt by the SCAF to distance itself from Mubarak and convince Egyptians that they stand with their revolution. Nonetheless, some remained skeptical that the military would allow Mubarak, a former head of the air force, to be persecuted. After all, indicting Mubarak means implicating the army's top authority.

Certainly lawyers of the plaintiff were weak and ill prepared while those of the defense were strong and well prepared. In the months that followed, Egyptians have denounced the slow pace of the trial. Members of the judiciary said this was not their fault but because of the long procedures. The trial was put on hold for three months after the plaintiffs' lawyers filed a complaint against Judge Refaat accusing him of being biased against their civil rights cases but the complaint was rejected. The fifth session of the trial was resumed in late December after the three months break, with the author of this book listening to Egyptians—both opponents and supporters of Mubarak—stressing that its procedures were going in his favor. It was stated then that a verdict will be announced before the SCAF leaves the duty of running the county on June 30.

Then came the ugly day of June 2, 2012, in which the final verdict was announced, sentencing Mubarak and El-Adli to life imprisonment but acquitting six of the former interior minister's police chiefs. None of the members of the former Mubarak regime were held directly responsible for the deaths of protesters. Mubarak and his two sons were acquitted of corruption charges on technical grounds, and Alaa and Gamal were to be released. When Judge Rafaat completed his controversial rulings, plaintiff lawyers and families of the victims shouted in the courtroom: "People want to cleanse the justice system." Almost all Egyptians whom I had spoken with or were interviewed on television called the trial a "scandal" and the verdict as too lenient and denounced the presiding judge. They called for a revolutionary court to be established because they said the defendant lawyer will appeal and acquit Mubarak in the not-too-distant future.

Indeed, the flimsiness of the rulings outraged the public and sparked a new uprising, a new revolution, in Egypt with anger seen on people's faces wherever one went. Once they were declared, people, particularly youths, started pouring into Tahrir Square and in other major squares and gathering areas not just in Cairo but in all parts of Egypt, from Alexandria to Suez down to Luxor and Aswan. Like at the courtroom, Egyptians called for "cleansing" the country's justice system and demanded the removal of not just the general persecutor but members of the SCAF. They denounced the verdict as a "politicized" and "hypocritical" one, a "political farce," with hundreds of them marching from Tahrir to demonstrate in front of the Supreme Judicial Council located not far from the Square. These demonstrations continued in the days that followed, with protesters demanding the following:

1. Ceasing the then-ongoing presidential elections and removing Shafiq from the race on legal grounds: that he was Mubarak's last prime minister.

2. Instituting a presidential council to be entrusted with running the country's affairs until a new election is held.

3. SCAF to leave duties of running the nation to the presidential council and return to its task of securing the country's borders.

4. Firing the general persecutor and appointing a new one.

5. Establishing a new constitution as soon as possible and before a presidential election is held (some even called for running a new parliamentary election because the one held before was unconstitutional).

The rulings did also have an impact on the June 16-17 presidential run-off between Shafiq and Mohamed Morsi as we shall discuss in more details in Chapter 9.

Chapter 9. The Presidential Debate

If no one in Egypt or the Arab world ever expected to see Hosni Mubarak in cage, not many did also anticipate seeing a presidential debate being held in the Land of the Nile on the pattern of those conducted in Europe and the United States. Just as America's first televised presidential debate between John F. Kennedy and Richard Nixon on September 26, 1960, caught the hearts and minds of Americans, Egypt's first-ever presidential debate of May 10, 2012, between presidential hopefuls Abdel Moneim Aboul Fotouh and Amr Moussa did also capture the hearts and minds of Egyptians to the extent that the hustling and bustling streets of Cairo, a city of eighteen million, were said to be unusually vacant of people because everyone was watching. Egyptians were waiting for that moment as if it was a world soccer cup final. The debate was something new, something Egyptians had never seen before neither in their homeland nor in the Arab world, (this is if we of course overlook that a presidential debate was conducted in Mauritania on March 22, 2007). This debate, as one of its moderators said in its introduction, would not have taken place had it not been for the January 25, 2011, Revolution.

The American-style Aboul Fotouh-Moussa debate was fierce on television screen, and it sure made everyone tune in to the box at their homes and in outdoor cafes. It was something foreign to Egyptians, and the ordinary citizens I spoke with after its conclusion said they liked it and portrayed it as a step in the right direction. The reason for selecting those two candidates in particular of the thirteen registered presidential ones was because polls steadily placed them at the front of the presidential race. Chapter 9 offers an analysis of the issues raised in the debate, and how each candidate's views on them were. The debate is analyzed from the perspective of news framing. News categories included a candidate's views on the ousted Mubarak regime, health care, education, security, role of religion in public life, and foreign policy issues such as Egypt's position in the Arab world and Africa and whether Israel is viewed as a strategic enemy. The chapter will study the frames that were constructed by the country's state-owned and independent newspapers in an attempt to answer the following questions:

Did newspapers in general favorably link either Aboul Fatouh or Moussa to certain issues, such as domestic or international ones?

Was there a considerable difference in coverage between the country's independent and state newspaper systems?

Who was covered more favorably and by which newspaper system?

In this chapter we studied articles published in independent and state newspapers in the two days that followed the debate (May 12 and 13). Because not enough articles were found in the country's two daily party newspapers,[588] we excluded the partisan press from our study. We were mainly interested in the favorability of an article toward either of the two candidates. We read the whole article and then coded it accordingly. An article which took a critical or favorable stance toward both candidates or did not express a position at all was coded as "neutral." But before examining the debate's themes let us have a quick look at the major events that took place in the country since the first Mubarak hearing was held on August 3, 2011, and which we detailed in Chapter 8. Protests continued in Tahrir Square and other major squares in the country and in front of major government buildings, including the state television building (known as Maspero), ministry of defense, among others. Conflicts among political powers or between political powers and the Supreme Council of the Armed Forces (SCAF) were a common daily feature. In October 2011, twenty five people were killed and more than three hundred injured in clashes between predominantly Coptic Christians and the military and security forces. There was also the ugly deadly soccer match riot that erupted on February 1, 2012, and in which seventy four Egyptians were killed and over two thousands injured in the Mediterranean city of Port Said. Parliamentary elections were held and the People's Assembly conducted its first session since on January 23, 2012, with SCAF transferring legislative authority to its newly-elected members. The parliamentary elections were described as the "fairest" elections in post-Mubarak Egypt, though skepticism was raised about whether they were "entirely free" because of questions about its methodology and the repetition involved. There were also questions about its constitutionality. Most Egyptians were apathetic to the second and third repetition of the elections, and that was evidenced by the very low turnout, including in my home constituency, Qalubiya, which saw a second and third run-off of the single-winner seats.[589] Yet, my seventy-one-year-old mother was far from phlegmatic in going to vote on all three rounds of the parliamentary elections. On January 14, 2012, she went out and voted and said that she would continue to vote until she sees a "better Egypt." Members of the country's once banned Muslim Brotherhood group,[590] which was recognized in June 2011 as the Freedom and Justice Party, won the majority of seats (47%), followed by the ultra-conservative Safafist[591] Al-Nour Party (24%) of the total 498 members of the People's Assembly (another 10 more members are appointed by the president, or in this case by the ruling SCAF). There was disagreement over the establishment of the constitutional committee and the categories used for selecting its members, resulting in a crisis between the Islamist-dominated People Assembly's and the government and the SCAF which heated in May 2012. During the first week of that month Egyptians witnessed the ugly clashes of the Abbasiya Square between protesters and the military near the headquarters of the Ministry of Defense building in Cairo on May 2, and which left over a dozen of people dead and three hundred injured. The protest was over the disqualification of the Salafi leader Hazen Abu Ismail from the presidential race, and the military used water cannon and tear gas to stop the crowd from reaching the Ministry building.

The Debate

The May 10 live television debate between the presidential elections' two-front runners Aboul Fotouh and Moussa was conducted prior to the first round of presidential elections which was to be held on May 23 and 24. As we stated above, there were thirteen presidential candidates from liberals, Islamists, and the Mubarak era and a second round was inescapable. Among the prominent presidential candidates besides Aboul Fatouh and Moussa were Mohamed Morsi, the voice of the Muslim Brotherhood, Hamdeen Sabahi, a leftist with a Nasserite bend, and Ahmed Shafiq, Mubarak's last prime minister—though many Egyptians resented having the latter on the ballot box and anticipated that a legislation, the Political Disenfranchisement Law, which was passed in Parliament a month earlier, would be enacted to prohibit all members of the former Mubarak regime from running for the presidency or engaging in politics.[592]

The Aboul Fatouh-Moussa lengthy exchange was formed of two main sessions with each lasting roughly two hours including a half hour break in between. Generally, the first session centered on domestic issues—the constitution and presidential powers, minimum wage, campaign finance, period of future reign of military, role of religion in a state—while the second session focused on foreign policy, electoral platform, the judiciary, health condition and financial status of each candidate, expatriates, among others. Some of these issues were debated continuously and interchangeably during both sessions, however. The outline is that each candidate is given two minutes to answer a question (twenty four questions were divided between the two sessions) by a moderator and is allowed after two questions to remark on, or rather refute, the answers of his contender. Each contestant can also ask a question to his rival after three questions. At the end of each session, a candidate can ask his opponent one question. The tone of the debate was sharp and questions were asked by distinguished journalists Yosri Fouda and Mona El-Shazly of the popular private-owned television stations ONTV and Dream2 respectively, in cooperation with two of the country's leading privately-owned newspapers: *Al-Masry Al-Youm* and *Al-Shorouk Al-Jadeed*.

Aboul Fatouh

The sixty-year-old Aboul Fatouh is a progressive Islamist, a retired physician, and a former member of the Muslim Brotherhood. He struggled to gain the support of both moderate and hard-line Muslims and later in the campaign won the backing of the Salafists of Al-Nour Party. He is described as a symbol of the revolution and a man who is suitable for the presidency. He was the one that spoke first in the debate and quoted the main slogan of the revolution: "Bread, freedom, social justice, and human dignity." He then moved to speak about Islamic jurisdiction and his religious and revolutionary background. In answering a question about the relationship between religion and the state and the issue of citizenship, his reply connoted that in Islamic jurisdiction there is the answer to everything and that it meets the demands of citizens in all fields of life. When Moussa asked him about his view on apostasy, he appeared slightly confused but he quickly said that God has given human beings the right to believe or disbelieve. He added that although a disbeliever should be blamed, no one ought to intervene to coerce him to belief. He asked Egyptians to vote for him because he embodies "all political and social currents—liberals and Islamists—that represent the spirit of January 25." He said that he is against the "minority" terminology in Egypt because the Copts have the same rights as any citizen.

At the onset of the debate, particularly during the first session, Aboul Fatouh attacked less but scored, while Moussa embraced a somewhat critical stance of his rival's viewpoints. Aboul Fatouh tended to give long answers rather than the concise ones that Moussa made. In doing so he often exceeded the time framework allocated. He prefers a presidential parliamentary system for Egypt in which a president's powers are limited and are split with government—what he referred to as the balance of power. He stressed that he belongs to the camp of revolutionaries and consistently ridiculed Moussa for being a member of the former Mubarak regime. He charged Moussa of receiving campaign finance from businessmen loyal to the Mubarak regime. During the first session, Aboul Fatouh appeared more grouped together, cautious not to get tense or lose points, and more in control of himself; he rarely showed any sign of nervousness. To some extent he spoke more than his rival about the poor, low-income citizens, and often blamed that on Mubarak's "thirty years of corruption" governing. He repeatedly stressed the rights of the martyrs who died in the protests. He observed that he does not need the presidential palaces left from the Mubarak era and suggested that they be placed as Egyptian monuments for tourist attraction. He proclaimed that he can live in his private house while serving as president.

In the second session, Aboul Fatouh abandoned his somewhat calm position and pushed it more in an attempt to gain more points by attacking his opponent, and with this we began to see more hand movements and body gestures from him in his bid to assert his viewpoints. In doing so, he appeared less confident and less clear than in the first session; he at times even showed signs of nervousness (for example, he rubbed his nose at least once while talking). It is possible that that Achilles heel in his confidence was due to his counterpart's attacks on him, particularly when Moussa attributed a statement—which some later said was taken out of context—to Aboul Fatouh charging him of accepting and encouraging violence as a moral code when he was a member of the Muslim Brotherhood. Moussa also charged Aboul Fatouh of making comments in the past about applying Islamic Sharia law and pushed him to explain what he meant by that. That did make Aboul Fatouh more aggressive in his criticism of his rival. Yet Aboul Fatouh maintained his speech and harmony in his choice of words and often used fingers to count. He showed a document stating his health condition and that he slightly suffers from diabetes and high blood pressure. He said he opposes political parties established on religious "grounds" but does not oppose having political parties with religious "background."

In trying to list his achievements, Aboul Fatouh spoke in the plural, often using the personal pronoun "we" in his vocabulary: "Our revolution," "our vision," "our program," "our project." He may have also cleverly used it to show that he has his audience, his supporters, or that when in office decisions will not solely be made by one man, as Mubarak did, but by a presidential administration. On foreign policy, Aboul Fatouh was vicious in his criticism of the Mubarak regime's weak engagement with Africa and the Arab world, claiming that after the assassination attempt in Ethiopia in 1995 (he mistaking said "1994"), Mubarak paid farewell to the continent. Israel, said Aboul Fatouh, is an "enemy" which owns a huge military arsenal, opposes international law, and occupies the land of Palestinians and rejects their right for a homeland. Our peace treaty with Israel should be reconsidered every five years as stated in it, he added.[593] He contended that

Cairo has no conflict with Tehran. "We are not fearful of Iran but will not allow it to disseminate the Shiite sect in Egypt."

Moussa

Seventy-five-year-old Moussa is a former diplomat and a liberal nationalist who has more experience in politics, particularly foreign affairs, than other candidates. After all he served as a foreign minister under Mubarak for ten years (from 1991 to 2001) and as chief of the Arab League for another decade (from 2001 to 2011). He asked people to vote for him because of all the posts he had held and which he performed "efficiently" and "honestly." He stressed that his goal would be to bring stability to Egypt and promised to offer a secular balance against the Islamists-dominated parliament. Egypt, he added, is in a "crisis" and it must be led by a man who "understands the world and how things are run." He cunning evaded offering a concrete answer about his health condition and wealth, alluding that his health is well by saying the phrase: "knock on wood." He said he handed a financial statement to the country's High Election Commission. But Aboul Fatouh immediately lampooned him for refusing to present on air statements about his financial status and health condition as he had did. An aristocrat, Moussa said he prefers that a president be granted wide powers. He characterized Aboul Fatouh as one of his rivals but not the sole one, stressing that his opponent has experience in humanitarian affairs but not in politics. He cautioned that Aboul Fatouh will remain loyal to the *morshed* (religious guide) of the Muslim Brotherhood. "What does it mean that Mr. Aboul Fotouh swore allegiance to the guide of the Brotherhood," said Moussa. "Does it mean that if elected president, you will have a person in command or a particular path through which you have to go before taking a decision?" He emphasized that he is against parties founded on religious bases, at times referring to Aboul Fatouh's campaign organizers as "your brothers." Aboul Fatouh replied: Moussa appears to be a man who "does not follow the news closely" because I left the Brotherhood last year. When Aboul Fatouh asked him about the issue of exporting gas to Israel, he denounced that question by arguing that that incident took place years after he had left office. Moussa spoke of the necessity of keeping the presidential palaces of Mubarak in operation to house visitors and hold meetings because they are "treasures" of the state.

Moussa felt that attack is the best means of defense, and he embraced that from early on in the debate. He often used the pronoun "I"—even though it was a rule that a contender speaks in the third person—perhaps because of his long experience in politics and an expression of him being a diplomat and a statesman. He in fact spoke as if he was a president seeking another term in office. He also spoke in the passive voice unlike Aboul Fatouh who used the future tense. He, nonetheless, maneuvered well and abided more than his counterpart by the element of time. But he appeared exhausted at times and this is possibly due to the length of the debates and his age. In his opening remarks, he tried to focus on his points of strength, of him being a former statesman. He used the word "state" a number of times, declaring that he wants Egypt to be a respectable state that meets the demands of its citizens and plays a stronger role regionally and internationally. He asserted his respect for the law and the Constitution, particularly Article 2 which recognizes Sharia, or Islamic law, to be the foundation of the law of the state, while respecting the rights of people of other religions. In doing so, Moussa was courting the country's Muslim majority while comforting the minority Copts who constitute 10 percent of the Egyptian population. He, nevertheless, said he refuses "religious parties because they are established on dividing and discriminating against people." He was less critical of the ousted regime and spoke of a traditional presidential system as his role model. He did not mentioned the rights of martyrs (he, in fact, hardly mentioned the word "martyr") and was shaken a bit when Aboul Fatouh charged him of being a member of the former regime and of achieving little while serving as a foreign minister and head of the Arab League, asking him to tell the audience about one word of opposition he had made whilst serving Mubarak and whether he can deny that in 2010 while serving as head of the Arab League he made a comment in which he supported electing Mubarak for another term. Moussa's response was that he meant he was against a hereditary system of government, and that if he had to choose between Mubarak and his son for a president he would choose the earlier. He stressed that he was an opponent of the former regime and that pushed him to leave his post. "I was in contention with the policy of the state and that is the reason why I left or was forced to leave," he observed. He noted that he declared at the Arab League summit held six days before the January 25 evolution that the Tunisian Revolution epidemic "is not far" from us. "We all overthrew the regime," continued Moussa who further charged that Aboul Fatouh was in opposition of the regime not as a representative of the people but of a group—the Muslim Brotherhood. At that summit, I spoke of oppression in Egypt "not to defend a group but the whole nation." He further criticized Aboul Fatouh for voting "yes" for the constitutional referendum of April 2011 when in fact most "true revolutionaries" said "no."

He contended that Egypt needs a highly experienced statesman such as him who knows how a state is run and has strong relations with politicians and officials both on the regional and international levels. Throughout the debate, Moussa also artfully and skillful used his body postures more than Aboul Fatouh and tried at times to confuse his opponent and win audience support. He used his feet to turn around, and this is possibly to convey to his audience that despite his old age he remains fit and capable of running a country. When Aboul Fatouh tried to place blame on him for the deterioration of Egypt's stance in the Arab world while serving as a prime minister, Moussa replied that Egypt's relations with the Arab world and Africa was good when he was a foreign minister, adding that the first country he visited while holding that post was Ethiopia. He even went further to claim that his departure might have caused that deterioration in Egyptian foreign policy. He said he will reconsider Egypt's relations with Israel because they should be founded on solving the Palestinian cause and establishing East Jerusalem as its capital, and as long as Israel opposes this there will always be "tension and disagreement." Taking the right position, he concluded, will not affect our relations with the United States. "We have our problems with Iran but this does not mean we will agree on an attack on it." He observed, "I was the first one to connect with Iran, overlooking established rules at the time [at Egypt's ministry of foreign affairs]."

Common Viewpoints

In the debate disagreement over issues were constructed primarily in the framework of a *Falul* (remnants of regime) versus Muslim Brotherhood battle. Aboul Fatouh repeated over and over again (more than two dozens of times in fact) that Moussa is part of the former regime and Moussa focused on that Aboul Fatouh is a Muslim Brotherhood member and a hard-line Islamist who is deceiving people by telling them that he is a moderate who welcomes all viewpoints and beliefs. To put it more succinctly, Aboul Fatouh said to Moussa: You are a continuation of the former regime, a residue of the regime. The return salvo from Moussa was: You are liberal when speaking with the liberals and Islamist when speaking with the Islamists. Moussa cleverly raised fears about his rival's unclear ties with the Salafists. Both candidates spoke of the need for a democratic system of government and a constitution, but Aboul Fatouh stressed more than Moussa that it should be a constitution that goes hand in hand with Shariah, or Islamic law. There was resemblance in the way each of them dealt with issues concerning the military, taxes program, and heath care. Both also expressed their respect for the armed forces in protecting the nation but added that it should be confined to that. They argued that there should be a minimum wage agreed upon, and that a vice president be appointed once a president is in office. They, nonetheless, spoke little on the issue of high unemployment in Egypt, particularly among youths. Both candidates gave little or no attention to the role of women who constitute 50 percent of Egyptian society.

During the first session, Aboul Fatouh consistently looked at the camera and addressed his audience directly while Moussa often bent and looked on the side at his rival. In the second session, both candidates abandoned any form of defensive stance and traded barbs, at times even without watching for plausible words; the moderate language disappeared. They also focused on the past and spoke little of their vision for the future. This made Aboul Fatouh look more at his opponent. During the whole debate, Moussa mentioned the words "Muslim Brotherhood" six times and "foreign ministry" nine times. Aboul Fatouh mentioned the words "former regime' eleven times. Aboul Fatouh completed his answers prior to the allocated time on three questions only while Moussa was more observant of the element of time. Aboul Fatouh said elect me because I am the spirit of the January 25 Revolution and because I am the one who can unite liberals and Islamists together. Moussa said elect me because Egypt needs a ready-made statesman, an expert who knows the world and how things are run. In other words, Aboul Fatouh addressed the revolutionaries and Islamists and Moussa reached to the popular class and courted those who are vying for security. Each contender accused the other of getting outside funding to finance his campaign in violation of electoral rules. Each of them also said he would insure the right for peaceful protests if elected and engage in dialogue with future protesters. They both stressed they will not deal with or appoint members of the former Mubarak regime. They also agreed that the constitutional council that will be entrusted with writing a new constitution should be representative of "all" political currents. They criticized Israel and denounced it as an occupier but Aboul Fatouh was more outspoken in his criticism. Although they promised to abide by and respect articles of the 1979 peace treaty between their country and Israel, they both said they would renegotiate parts of the treaty.

Findings

Public perception of the debate was divided. Some said Moussa won; others said Aboul Fotouh was the winner. Supporters of Moussa claimed that Aboul Fotouh was confused; while backers of the latter observed that the former ascertained his affiliation with the Mubarak regime. In reality, though, Moussa appeared more confused than his arch rival at times but both cared about attacking the other rather than answering questions. Neither of them came out as a true winner, in my opinion, and despite some who said that Aboul Fatouh's answers were clear and of higher quality than Moussa's.[594] In the second session, and as he tried to be aggressive like his opponent, Aboul Fatouh showed some confusion. With that being said, one must point out that Egypt's diverse media—both print and broadcast ones—welcomed the debate as a step toward their Arab and North African state joining the camp of democratic nations, with some describing the debate as "Egypt's lesson one democracy." It is a "historic debate," accentuated the state-owned paper *Al-Akhbar*, and "an honor for the emerging democracy." It was characterized by its "seriousness, profundity and excitement."[595] It is "a unique and important experience," said the state-owned paper *Al-Gomhuria*, though it is sad that many important issues were not addressed in it. Yet we must not diminish the level of its success.[596] After all, we are still experimenting with democracy, proclaimed columnist Ibrahim Mansour of the independent paper *Al-Tahrir*, and the debate is a "positive and important step that nobody ever imaged to take place in Egypt after 30 years of despotism, corruption and bullying to implement a hereditary system."[597]

In an interview with Dream2 satellite television station, a political expert proclaimed in joy that the debate is "our first test" with presidential debates. We are experimenting with it, and as time goes by we will become professional at holding them.[598] The process of running the debate was "generally fine," said a member of the committee that observes the election process, and we look forward to future ones.[599] Cairo University's Journalism Professor Hisham Attiah sarcastically said that both candidates came out as losers from the debate with the true winner being the satellite televisions stations which amassed huge amounts of money from advertising and have strengthened their popularity among viewers.[600] Moussa tried to escape from the past because it forms his main point of weakness, said Mohamed El-Mahdi, a professor of psychology at Al-Azhar University. Aboul Fatouh, he added, brought in the past in his speech because he views it as his point of strength. "One escapes the past while the other invites it in," concluded El-Mahdi.[601] Moussa is a "man of authority" and a failed foreign minister who "does not know the culture of apology," noted Seif Abdel Fatah, a Cairo University political science professor. He was not subtle in his answers; while Aboul Fatouh stood like a statesman. Moussa laboriously tried to exploit Aboul Fatouh, and in doing so the former statesman revealed his weakness.[602] According to Bassiouni Hamada, a professor of public opinion, Moussa's team produced to him more subtle details on Aboul Fatouh's background—such as his relations with the Muslim Brotherhood and its spiritual leader—while Aboul Fatouh depended on his memory and personal talent.[603]

History will undoubtedly record this Aboul Fatouh-Moussa face-to-face encounter as a groundbreaking debate on the characteristics of the individual capable to lead the Arab world's most populous country. Each candidate scored goals in the debate; Aboul Fatouh when uncovering Moussa's support of Mubarak for the presidency in a 2010 statement and associating him with Mubarak's "failed foreign policy," and Moussa when he unveiled the contradictions in Aboul Fatouh's previous speeches. Aboul Fatouh reached to people's passion rather than their minds. "Is it possible that one of the men of the regime which created the problem could come to solve it?" he asked. Moussa's answers were more prag-matic and often used foreign policy terminology. He advocated the importance of embracing the politics of mutual interest coming from experienced policymak-ers. He freed himself from any blame Aboul Fatouh endeavored to place on him with reference to the issue of the invasion of Iraq.

In their coverage, and based on our coding of the collected articles from both the newspaper systems, we found that roughly 17% of state newspaper articles took favorable position toward Moussa and 83% were neutral in their views. As for Aboul Fatouh, roughly 11% of state newspaper articles were favorable and 89% were neutral. Table 9.1 below shows results in more details.

Table 9.1. State newspapers stance toward each candidate

	Favorable (%)	Neutral (%)	Total (%)
Aboul Fatouh	11.11	88.89	100
Moussa	16.67	83.33	100

Table 9.2 below shows the stance of independent newspaper articles toward each candidate, with Moussa and Aboul Fatouh each receiving equal distribu-tion: 5% favorable and 95% neutral.

Table 9.2. Independent newspapers stance toward each candidate

	Favorable (%)	Neutral (%)	Total (%)
Aboul Fatouh	5	95	100
Moussa	5	95	100

In all, the two press systems—state and independent newspapers—exhib-ited some degree of differences in their favorableness toward each contender. State newspapers showed higher praise of Moussa (60%) than of Aboul Fatouh (40%); while in the independent press favorability toward both Moussa and Aboul Fatouh was evenly distributed, with each receiving 50%. This once again shows that the state press was more supportive of Moussa—a man who served as foreign minister for ten years in the Mubarak administration—while the inde-pendent press evaluated both candidates evenly or rather did not favor one over the other. Table 9.3 below shows the overall degree of favorableness toward each candidate in the two press systems.

Table 9.3. Overall degree of favorableness toward each candidate

	State Press (%)	Independent Press (%)
Aboul Fatouh	40	50
Moussa	60	50
Total:	100	100

Press Coverage

State Press

State newspapers' criticism of Aboul Fatouh mainly built on Moussa's denunciation of his rival's relationship with the Brotherhood and his unclear ties with the Salafists. In a piece addressed directly to Aboul Fatouh, *Al-Gomhuria* columnist Mahfouz El-Ansari said that he was disappointed because he thought Aboul Fatouh's departure from the Muslim Brotherhood would make him structure a new vision rather than just changing his colors to appease everyone. Aboul Fatouh has shown that he specializes in nothing and has no political vision for his country. It was idiotic from him to unleash criticism at a skilled diplomat such as Moussa and at members of his ministry of foreign affairs, added El-Ansari. Egypt is in need of a "true leadership," a true statesman, rather than empty "slogans" and "false" bravery.[604] I have known Moussa as a "genuine" and "charismatic" diplomat who has always had a passion for the Arab world, Africa, and the Muslim world, accentuated the longtime *Al-Akhbar* journalist Ibrahim Saada.[605]

Articles in state newspapers charged Moussa of escaping answering questions. Moussa tried in vain to save himself from a corrupt regime of which he was a key member, proclaimed columnist Mohamed El-Zarqani of the state paper *Akhbar El-Yom*. Moussa threw accusations on his rival who succeeded in answering them in an objective way, yet the former foreign minister did not answer the questions which his opponent posed to him. Within this framework, Moussa resembled "a failed theatre actor whom audiences wish to make him leave."[606] According to a different commentary in the same paper, the debate "has unveiled the negative sides of Moussa in many aspects, making public opinion reevaluate the situation and reconsider its view of him." There were those who characterized Aboul Fatouh as a noble figure of the revolution and rejected drawing a comparison between him and those who were associated with the former regime. Aboul Fatouh has shown that he is more capable of running Egypt toward a better future.[607]

Articles that neither supported Aboul Fatouh nor Moussa expressed certain viewpoints. The debate has revealed the deep gap between the two candidates and within each candidate, observed *Al-Akhbar*. "It has succeeded in convincing Egyptians not to support either of them—and perhaps even in rejecting them both," mainly because each of them lacked an "independent vision." Moussa appeared confident but less clear on issues; he did not introduce anything new. Aboul Fatouh was more confused and tense and uncovered his pro-Muslim Brotherhood stance even though he had claimed he abandoned the group.[608] The same state paper made the following comment in another article

Moussa resembled an old lion opting to determine the battle but did not hold the tools. When he tried to stand on his feet he discovered that they were made of cotton, and when he tried to get his history to support his position he discovered that it is all delusion. Aboul Fatouh looked like an eagle that went color-blind, unable to distinguish the colors of different political currents and losing the ability to decide his direction. I do not think that someone like him holds the compass to lead and direct the nation.[609]

Doubt about each candidate's skills to hold the office of the presidency continued in the state press. Both contenders offered their audiences "wide promises" but without directly stating the kind of state they want to establish.[610] In some way, said El-Zarqani, it was not Aboul Fatouh who defeated Moussa; it was "Moussa who defeated himself by uncovering his political faults and clear participation in the corrupt rule of the former regime, although he repeatedly tried to claim heroism and propagate himself as one of the most important opponents and denouncers of the politics of the deposed president." El-Zarqani added, "Moussa continued to serve as a foreign minister for [ten] years and Mubarak granted him an end-of-service reward by appointing him as head of the Arab League, and he did gain many benefits and made profits from such post with money and gifts pouring on him from every corner. Was this then a punishment to an opponent or a reward to a lower head who labored to appease his benevolent governor? El-Zarqani maintained: I want to ask Moussa this: If you were against the politics of Mubarak why did not you resign while serving in his administration?[611]

Independent Press

Despite Moussa's age, said the independent paper *Al-Masry Al-Youm*, he fared well in the debate; in fact, Aboul Fatouh at times forgot questions and asked to be reminded of them.[612] However, wrote media analyst Yassir Abdel Aziz, Moussa must realize that it is "very difficult to be in two places at the same time." Aboul Fatouh also needs to grasp that it is very difficult to "satisfy the devil simultaneously."[613] Moussa looked like "an experienced old fox who never ceased attacking Aboul Fatouh by every means, and when Aboul Fatouh shot a bullet at him he stood behind the curtain, overlooking the matter and pointing his artillery at Aboul Fatouh," wrote Tarek El-Shinnawi of *Al-Tahrir*. Yet, Moussa's image is damaged simply because three months from Mubarak's departure the former foreign minister offered his ex-boss all service of obedience, including supporting him for a six term in office. On the other side, added El-Shinnawi, Aboul Fatouh's team "did not know how to surprise the opponent."[614]

There were those political commentators who did not see difference between what Aboul Fatouh and Moussa said in the debate. The political agendas of both contenders were similar in many ways, commented Ahmed El-Sawy in the independent paper *Al-Shorouk Al-Jadeed*, with each of them failing to weaken the support of his rival. Each candidate focused on what he views as his positive sides and the negative sides of his contender. Others perceived drawing any comparison between Aboul Fatouh and Moussa as a shame. America, contemplated *Al-Tahrir* journalist Osama Ghareib, elected an "idiot with no skills such as George W. Bush as president for eight years, yet the country did not crumble. It also managed to have an ignorant and narrow-visioned leader such as Ronald Reagan with no catastrophes taking place during his rule, simply because the country's firm institutions were skillfully running the nation's affairs on all fronts." But in our "wounded Egypt" the situation is different, added Ghareib. The nation is still bleeding from the corrupt politics of the former regime. Hence, the Egyptian people are searching for hope, for a leader who can heal these wounds. It is a "shame to compare one of the noblest symbols of the revolutions such as Aboul Fatouh to one of Mubarak's secretaries [Moussa or Shafiq]."[615] (Of course, one may dispute the accuracy of Ghareib's analysis. I have heard some Americans who claim that much of the turmoil in their country today stems precisely from policies initiated by President Ronald Reagan and the Bush family, and by the "firm institutions" that carry on with their agendas, whatever they may be, no matter who holds the White House.)

In the opinion of El-Sawy, the strong voice of Aboul Fatouh helped him in making his words more trustworthy and Moussa's body movements were his greatest asset. Moussa spoke as if he is a president seeking another term in office and Aboul Fatouh as a new candidate seeking the presidency.[616] Aboul Fatouh appeared "more frank and enthusiastic and Moussa was more experienced and knowledgeable."[617] According to *Al-Masry Al-Youm*, Moussa has gained Egypt's first presidential debate with considerable points and Aboul Fatouh lost because of his failure to prove his "capability to be a leader of a big state such as Egypt." Moussa's mind was more present than Aboul Fatouh who succeeded only in asserting his anger toward the Mubarak age. In all, some of the questions they were asked were "too naïve," while others needed writing "a book" for an answer, added the popular independent paper. It argued that the question with reference to Egypt's relations with Israel should not have been "do you consider Israel a strategic enemy?" but rather "how do you qualify Israel?" The paper stressed that "objectivity" must be embraced in everything we do.[618]

I do not know how Aboul Fatouh fell in the trap of extensively focusing in his questions on Moussa's relations with the former regime to the extent that the latter mastered the technique of answering them, argued one *El-Youm El-Sabaa* columnist. Moussa also never stopped concentrating on that he is the "beloved foreign" minister who faithfully and diligently served his country.[619] He seemed unable to liberate himself from the burden of being a former member of the deposed regime, argued the popular Egyptian political commentator Gamal Fahmi in *Al-Tahrir*. Aboul Fatouh's fault was in his attempt to create an "all-size-fit-all election picture of the right and left," of liberals and religious groups.[620] One commentary mocked how both candidates often did not observe the time element. If the candidates did not abide by the element of time how can we "trust" them "containing the nation's budget deficit and maintaining the timeliness of the decision-making process."[621] An *El-Youm El-Sabaa* column was titled: "The Result is Nil—Nil."[622] The true winner of the debate, declared *Al-Tahrir*, is the team that orchestrated it and helped in disseminating it around the globe.[623]

In celebration of the event, *Al-Shorouk Al-Jadeed* posed this question: Had anyone ever imagined that Hosni Mubarak stand in a face-to-face debate with one of his contenders—both exposed to those kinds of detailed questions? The reality we must admit is that the "notion of the pharaoh ruler has met a fatal blow."[624] Our nation will be ruled by a leader "selected by the people—a leader who will not be a pharaoh," proclaimed Abdel Aziz. We will hold respect for him, but he must attentively listen to the demands of his people.[625] Truly, wrote *Al-Masry Al-Youm*, both Aboul Fatouh and Moussa were respectable in the views they have exhibited; they are an example of the "educated and knowledgeable presidential candidates. The deposed president is illiterate in comparison." With that being said, the debate was history in the making; after all, party leaders in the past used to battle to get half an hour of television time during elections, added the independent paper. But will Aboul Fatouh and Moussa agree to work together in the future in the same manner that Barack Obama and Hilary Clinton have done.[626]

In "Mistakes of the Moussa-Aboul Fatouh Debate," columnist Mohamed Shoman of *El-Youm El-Sabaa* noted that Egyptians are stepping on the first step of building a democracy, but "sadly in the process of how a debate is run we have begun from where others started and not from where they finished." He denounced the amount of ads that were interwoven during the four-hour debate, stipulating that no debate in the word had ever lasted more than two hours. He called on Egyptians to establish a committee to be entrusted with running the debates (similar to the United States' Commission on Presidential Debates,[627] which was established by the Republican and Democratic parties in 1987, to guide how presidential debates are run) and insuring that it is a fair and a non-profit process. Selecting the two candidates from among the other eleven ones was not based on fair, scientific measures and was a "mistake," added Shoman.[628]

Rising Support for Sabahi

After the Aboul Fatouh-Moussa debate, I witnessed supporters of Sabahi talking in the streets and on social networks that he was the true winner of the televised debate. "We have enjoyed watching this historic debate as well as following the comments of pro-Hamdeen Sabahi on social networks," observed the independent paper *El-Dostour*, "and many of his supporters have agreed on the failure of both candidates and that Sabahi is the winner."[629] The debate has weakened support for both Moussa and Aboul Fatouh, argued *Al-Akhbar*. Neither of them has introduced anything new.[630] The single winner from the debate is Sabahi, posited *Al-Gomhuria*, because Egyptians have admired him once they knew about his background, about a man who does not belong to the far left or the far right. His "struggle" and "civil project" for building a "modern state" has made every Egyptian feel that he is "one of them."[631] He is a "shinning face among the symbols of the revolution," expressed *Al-Tahrir*, and his "history of struggle is an evidence of this."[632]

The socialist candidate Sabahi emerged more victorious from the debate than Aboul Fatouh and Moussa and cut the gap on front-runners. The Great Debate has showed how democracy can work in the digital age. But did it have influence on voters? Yes, indeed, it did as we saw Aboul Fatouh and Moussa ranking fourth and fifth respectively in the results of the election.[633] The debate came in Sabahi's favor and buttressed his position which was clear in election results in which he ranked third, an outcome which previous polls never predicted. On television, according to many commentators, both candidates lacked smooth delivery and charisma which they said saw more in Sabahi. Abdel Aziz wrote, "Hamdeen Sabahi: You have achieved a rare result in the history of political debates; you have won in a debate which you did not take part in because you were more consistent with yourself in your words and deeds than others."[634]

Some Egyptians told me that those who abandoned their support of the two presidential candidates and inched more toward electing Sabahi were youths—revolutionary youths. But I also witnessed strong support for Sabahi among Egyptian farmers because of his proposed policies that aim at buttressing the farming industry which has deteriorated under Mubarak's rule. Yet, commented

Al-Masry Al-Youm, while examining the viewpoints of Aboul Fatouh and Moussa we cannot overlook the agendas of other powerful presidential candidates besides Sabahi such as Morsi and Shafiq.[635] The outcome of debate came in favor of candidates such as Shafiq, Sabahi, and Morsi, emphasized *Al-Shorouk Al-Jadeed*.[636] In short, stipulated *Al-Akhbar*, none of the two contestants has gained from the debate; it was Sabahi—who was hindered from participating in the debate without justification—who came out as the "big winner."[637]

Conclusion

Television debates in Europe and America have been an essential part of campaigning, and Egyptian audiences were riveted by their country's first U.S.-style presidential debate. If the Mubarak trial was characterized as the "trial of the century" in which an Arab leader for the first time stood in cage, the Aboul Fatouh-Moussa television debate was the debate of the century because it was the first time to take place on Arab soil. Debates normally attract the biggest audience, and in a nation of over eighty million that was a big and high-stake event. Egyptians clustered around their TV sets avidly watching the debate as they often do with big soccer matches. On Facebook and Twitter discussions also flared on the debate—some of them were even humorous. Moussa, for example, wrongly said in the debate that Iran is an "Arab" state, and a number of individuals on Facebook ridiculed him for such mistake. One individual contended: "If politics does so to persons who practice it, then it should be outlawed internationally because it makes people lose their minds."

The Egyptian media failed at cajoling the two finalist presidential candidates to debate a range of vital issues to the public, such as what they should do to help in uplifting the failing economy and easing public anger toward trying those responsible for the killing of over eight hundred Egyptians on the Friday of Anger of February 28, 2011. These issues, together with working diligently toward finding a solution to the Palestinian cause, will pose the biggest challenge to the future Egyptian president. With their homeland located at the center of the world, Egyptians must not separate the line between domestic and international issues. It is also worth noting that the Egyptian press's coverage changed as the 2012 presidential campaign progressed and the public was left with only two candidates (Morsi and Shafiq) to choose from rather than thirteen, with many describing the results of the first round of presidential elections as "strange" and "unanticipated" as we shall discuss in Chapter 10.

But did Egyptians favor one candidate over the other on certain issues? Most of the individuals I spoke with said both Aboul Fatouh and Moussa came out losers because candidates focused on trading slights than on debating issues. It seems that Moussa was told by his strategists to be aggressive and attack. But sadly neither him nor his counterpart were presidential in the debate; they both lacked a vision. The debate was more of a discussion with attack and defense than it was a debate. Had each of the two moderators adopted a more prominent role with turn-taking being more decisive and less of interruption between candidates, things might have gotten better. The nature of the questions posed to contenders also lacked depth and did not help in unveiling differences on main issues. There was not one question on how to fight growing poverty, rising unemployment, and forming better relations with the European Union. The two leading candidates traded barbs and that might have contributed in weakening public trust in them. In that war of words, some claimed Moussa had a much more coherent and disciplined method. When it comes to foreign policy Moussa did certainly emerge victorious. But on domestic issues he embodied the same Mubarak politics of not caring much about the poor and unemployed and about Egypt's youth and those who gave their lives during the revolution. Furthermore, Moussa's preference that a president be granted wide powers made some fearful of him turning into a pharaoh.

Once again, the Aboul Fatouh-Moussa debate was Egypt's first-ever presidential debate, and it is hoped that it will become an important feature of political discussion not just for Egyptians but for the whole Arab world. No matter what have been said, or will be said, about the debate one thing is certain: Had it not been for the January 25 Revolution Egyptians would not have seen that presidential debate—surely not under Mubarak's rule. The debate has set an example for future campaign in the Land of the Nile and scholars should give it the attention it deserves because it is indeed a form of electoral populism. The true winner from the debate is the Egyptian people themselves who are experiencing for the first time how free elections in democratic states are often carried out.[638] From now one I anticipate that Egypt will build its own history of presidential debates. Based on our analysis one can conclude the following:

- In general, state newspapers framed Moussa as a candidate more electable than Aboul Fatouh.

- State newspapers covered Moussa more positively than Aboul Fatouh on foreign policy issues.

- Independent newspapers equally framed both Aboul Fatouh and Moussa as candidates suitable for the presidency and on the attributes of domestic and foreign affairs issues.

Surely, and as results have shown, the Aboul Fatouh-Moussa presidential debate, which the United States described as a "good and healthy thing," had an impact on voters. One can also hypothesis that the way the media framed candidates following the debate did have greater influence on candidate evaluation following the debate as our study of post-debate media coverage has shown. Moussa's image has been shaken in the eyes of his supporters because of his inability to be eloquent and straightforward in his answers, and this may have lifted the aunts of Shafiq, and Sabahi of course, as one party paper said.[639] His weakness was in that he was a member of the Mubarak regime and Aboul Fatouh's flaw lied in the fear of him getting his instructions from the religious guide. Moussa laboriously tried to distance himself from the Mubarak regime while attacking Aboul Fatouh for being associated with the Muslim Brotherhood. In doing so, he tried to break what some called the "iconic and revolutionary figure" of Aboul Fatouh—the man who battled with words with Sadat in a conference while he was a medical student. In many ways, Aboul Fatouh succeeded in countering the attacks by the intelligent former diplomat, according to Hamada. But the former diplomat did not succeed at the end because the public realizes that corruption, human rights violations, and the rigging of elections did not only emerge after his departure from the Mubarak regime but had been accumulating over years.[640]

By all means, Moussa could be characterized as a realist and a down-to-earth pragmatist while Aboul Fatouh inched toward being an idealist with a new vision that politics and religion can jointly be embraced. In some way, their waffling on certain issues served to embroil matters rather than explain to their audience what their agenda would be; it turned into political waffling rather than a serious debate—a *Falul* vs. Muslim Brotherhood battle. Both candidates spoke little of their foreign policy agendas, an important topic for a nation that plays a vital strategic role for peace and stability in the Middle East. For example, Ahmed Abdel Hameed, a professor at the Cairo-based Ain Shams University, said both candidates were not successful in attracting new supporters. He noted that Moussa's image as a statesman failed because of the way he answered questions by posing questions and not introducing clear answers. Both candidates did not stick to the rules of the debate. He added that while Moussa failed in presenting himself as a suitable candidate, Aboul Fatouh's words got stock at times and he forgot parts of it, let alone the way he prolonged his answers which caused him more harm than good.[641] One can also add that Aboul Fatouh felt that attacking Moussa's roots and links with the Mubarak regime was enough to make him a winner.

In general, the Aboul Fatouh-Moussa debate marked Egypt's entrance into presidential politics, and both candidates deserve applause for engaging in the country's first presidential debate. It, together with the trial of Mubarak, helped somewhat in absorbing anger on the street and weakening the voices of some who were shouting that the revolution was a ruse. One also believes that the debate had more influence on the opinion of the middle class than the lower and higher class of the Egyptian society. That view was also asserted by Egyptian academics. The outcome of elections will affect only the opinion of the middle class strata of our society, observed Hamada.[642] Yet, we can argue that Egyptians lived an enjoyable time while watching the debate. Watching may not be the right word here; Egyptians saw for the first time democracy in the making.

In conclusion, elections in Egyptian remain primitive in nature and in the way each candidate run his campaign. If a presidential candidate in America or Europe presents a false piece of information in his campaign he or she is likely to be pushed out of the race. But in Egypt candidates inject false information and they get away with it. Although the Aboul Fatouh-Moussa debate was driven by sound bites and shout fests, it is a genuine step toward implementing a democratic system of governing in the North African state. It was one memorable moment for Egypt and Egyptians. After all, it was Egypt's first presidential debate and Egyptians need to reshuffle the structure of presidential debates by allowing a wider range of highly-experienced journalists and foreign policy analysts to participate in and ask questions. To generate the "big debate," rather than the somewhat polarized one which we witnessed, the moderators need to press candidates to expand on their positions on main issues. They need to revive the spirit of a debate, and they can learn from the world outside—from the Europeans and the Americans, just as the Europeans and Japanese learned from the Americans after the Kennedy-Nixon debate. After all, election, and as Alas de Tocqueville wrote in 1840, "intrigues" and brings "agitation."[643] And so should presidential debates.

And as usual, there is the Egyptian humor echoed in political cartoons. An *Al-Tahrir* caricature—composed of three drawings joined together—shows two men sitting on a sofa with one of them saying: "This is the first time we have 13 presidential candidates." He then points his hand to a television screen in front of them showing Aboul Fatouh and Moussa debating, and he says: "And television debates like in America." The other man, sipping from a cup of coffee or tea, responds: "Seeing this, one might think we've had a revolution."[644]

Chapter 10. Mohamed Morsi: Egypt's First Civilian President

On June 24, 2012, and after a fierce battle, Mohamed Morsi of the Muslim Brotherhood won the presidency against Ahmed Shafiq—a military man who served as Hosni Mubarak's last prime minister—in what has been described as the first time in which Egyptians elect a civilian president after the 2011 Revolution ousted Mubarak from office. The result of the first round of the presidential elections was released on May 27, showing the victory of Morsi and Shafiq for the run-off. Sixty-year-old Morsi, who won 52% percent of votes, was to be officially inaugurated in office from the beginning of July and for a four-year term. Political turmoil was high before and after the final run-off between Morsi and Shafiq, which was held on June 16 and 17; in fact it took nine days before election results were declared. This run-off between the top two vote-getters was held because no candidate rose with a majority of voting in the first round of May 23-24. The Political Disenfranchisement Law, which was passed in Parliament in April 2012, was not enacted and Shafiq was not disqualified from running in the presidential elections.

Morsi is the Arab world's first freely elected Islamist leader and the country's fifth president since the overthrow of British rule in 1952. He did not win with the vote of Islamists alone; seculars and leftists who believe in the separation of politics from religion voted for him. They did so because they did not want one of Mubarak's top men, Shafiq, to win. Like at the time of the referendum on constitutional amendments of March last year, there were those propagandistic voices that claimed following the results of the first session of the presidential elections that Coptic Christians voted for Shafiq and that the majority of Muslims voted for Morsi, or that those in support of a return of the Mubarak regime voted for the earlier while those who backed the revolution voted for the latter. I do not hold this to be a true, though, because I know of a number of relatives who said they did not vote for Morsi.

The emergency law was lifted on May 31, and the Supreme Council of the Armed Forces' (SCAF's) duty of running the country was expected to be completed on June 30—the day Morsi was sworn in as president. The June 2 rulings which acquitted Mubarak's two sons and six police chiefs had an impact on the Morsi-Shafiq presidential race. (Mubarak and his interior minister were sentenced to life in prison for their role in the killing of protesters during the revolution.) The verdict enraged Egyptians and protesters took to the streets in major cities shouting the slogans: "We either get their rights [rights of martyrs] or die like them," "military ruling is outlawed," and the "people want capital punishment for the president." Many of the Egyptians I spoke with said the ruling, particularly the acquittals of Mubarak's sons, is full of flaws—that it is a "politicized" verdict. I heard many around me insisting that Mubarak should be executed. Then came the "dirt" of the constitutional decree issued on June 17 by SCAF, limiting the powers or the president and giving the military greater prerogatives. The decree granted SCAF legislative and financial powers and the right to form the constitutional assembly. Most Egyptians were infuriated by those SCAF acts, which blunted the power of the presidents; some described them, together with the dissolution of the Islamist-dominated Parliament on June 14, as a military coup. This resulted in protests in major squares of Egyptian cities in what had been called the "June 19 Revolution" against the generals of the army and a "corrupt" judicial system.

When election results were declared, many were wondering before whom Morsi will take his oath as president (which is normally taken before parliament): Supreme Constitutional Court, members of the dissolved People's Assembly, or people in Tahrir Square. And Morsi cunningly tried to appease them all. He took his symbolic oath as president before his supporters in Tahrir Square on June 29. On the next day he gave swearing-in speech before the Supreme Constitutional Court. Later on that day, Morsi also gave a speech at Cairo University to members of the dissolved parliament, SCAF generals, and foreign diplomats. In the latter, he praised SCAF's role in the revolution and the election of Parliament as a victory for democracy but without acknowledging its dissolution. Yet he also called on the army to go back to its main task of protecting the nation's borders. At Tahrir, Morsi delivered a vigorous speech to tens of thousands, most of whom Islamists, promising to regain the presidential powers the SCAF generals stripped him off. His supporters at Tahrir yelled: "We love you Morsi." He later joined them in their celebration shouting: "Revolutionaries and free, we will carry on the journey." (On July 8, President Morsi ordered the dissolved People's Assembly to reconvene in a surprise move that failed.)

It is also worth mentioning that hours after the announcement of his victory, Morsi delivered a speech on state television in which he offered some words of comfort to the Egyptian people, focusing on finding solutions to national crises: 1) maintaining security on the street; 2) improving traffic; 3) removing garbage; 4) offering quality subsidized bread; 5) insuring availability of petrol and gas. But there was this fear among Egyptians because a new system of government utterly unknown to them is now in office. They feared its leadership could cause them harm despite their deep desire to see change in their homeland. In his first speech as president, Morsi promised to be a president for all Egyptians, achieve goals of the revolution, and offered his thanks to its martyrs and injured and to the military, police, and judiciary. He said: "I am a servant of the people and an employee of citizens. I was appointed to head you but I am not your best, and I'll do my best to keep my promises. Help me if I implement righteousness and justice among you, and if I fail I do not then deserve your obedience." He added, "I call on the great Egyptian people to strengthen our national unity," accentuating "the revolution will continue until all its goals are achieved." He also stressed he will abide by international agreements, protect human rights, and treat all Egyptians equally. Immediately after his TV speech some young Egyptian political activists launched Morsi Meter, a website that records and assesses Morsi's performance and progress on certain issues during the first one hundred days.

Chapter 10 will examine the victory of Morsi as president in what has been characterized as the "fairest" presidential elections the Arab world has witnessed. It focuses on coverage of the event in the state and independent press and how each press system framed it differently. We found it sufficient to draw a comparison only between those two press systems because we collected a large number of articles from the state and independent newspapers just for one day, June 26.

Findings

The Egyptian (and Arab) press and the revolutionaries of the Land of Nile spoke in pride of what they described as Egypt's first free presidential election. Some even said it is the country's free elections in five thousand years; other observed that Egyptians will not be just electing a president for themselves but for the entire Arab world. Such sentiments were echoed in the Lebanese paper *As-Safir*. The pan-Arab paper wrote on the day the Egyptian presidential elections were held, May 23, that Egyptians today are not just voting for a president for their country but "a president for all the Arabs."[645] On the same day, Tunisian

President Moncef Al-Marzouki also noted: Egyptians today will determine the destiny of the Arab world. An Egyptian farmer laughingly told me: This is the first time that we do not know who the next president for our country will be. The connotation is that it is the freest elections Egyptians have seen so far. But there were those Egyptians, though a few in number, who feared the vote may be rigged.

As we have noted above, public opinion was divided on whom Egyptians should elect for the presidency. When the issue was thrown for discussion in the a few days before the elections there were tense arguments even between family members, at times mixed with humor. This was often reiterated in television interviews. For example, a journalist with the independent TV Al-Nahar station asked a couple who were walking in central Cairo about whom they were going to elect. The man, an ultraconservative Islamist with a long beard, said he was going to elect Morsi. When his wife said she wishes to elect Moussa the husband jokingly shouted at her. She then told the journalist he would divorce her if she did so.[646] There was a case reported in the press following the Morsi-Shafiq run-off about a man who divorced his wife because she did not vote for Morsi.

The State Press

In its coverage of the election of Morsi as President, the state press tackled the following five themes.

1. Free Elections

The state press focused on that the presidential election is free and a badge of honor on the chest of all Egyptians. Its journalists described Morsi as the first freely elected president of Egypt in modern history. It is natural, said the state paper *Al-Akhbar*, that Egyptians celebrate the victory of the country's first post-revolution president in the first free presidential elections. Before the January 25 Revolution a president often won with sweeping victory (over ninety percent of votes); Mubarak's men mastered the craft of "forging" elections.[647] Today the will of the Egyptian people has won after a clean democratic experience recognized by world governmental and non-governmental organizations and the mass media, commented the state paper *Al-Gomhuria* in a piece titled: "Egypt Has Passed the Democracy Test." At last, and for the first time in their history, Egyptians have managed to elect their leader away from the forged elections which they got accustomed to before the 2011 Revolution.[648] We should all back the man Egyptians selected in the "first, free elections in Egypt's history. Let us write a new history for our nation in which all political powers bond together to reestablish stability and build a democratic state that meets the demands of the January 25 Revolution," *Al-Akhbar* proclaimed.[649]

One should emphasize here that this sense of admiration for and extol of the "free elections" was widespread in the state press except in one or two articles. Egyptians should be proud of what they have achieved toward "building a democracy," because their election of Morsi was "free" and "transparent," noted *Al-Gomhuria*. This is an unprecedented development, not just in Egypt but in the entire Arab world.[650] It is the first time since President Gamal Abdel Nasser in which we have a president who wins not with a "fake majority" of over ninety percent, but with "real voices of real people," proclaimed Salah Montassir, a veteran journalist with the state newspaper *Al-Ahram*.[651] The day of June 24, 2012, is undoubtedly a critical day in the history of our country, commented *Al-Akhbar*, because we at last have a president elected by the will of the people in an election which the whole world has witnessed its transparency."[652]

2. A Civilian State: "The Second Republic"

There was this debate that Morsi's victory is the first in which a civilian leader—and a not military one—will be ruling Egypt since the 1952 coup d'état declared the North African country a republic. Within this framework commentators characterized the post-2011 revolution Egypt as a second republic, the republic of democracy, borrowing from a statement president Morsi made when he was inaugurated in office on June 30.[653] In an editorial titled "Egypt Begins Age of Second Republic," *Al-Ahram* declared: "Egypt is beginning a new stage; it is the age of the second republic. It is unprecedented in Egyptian history with all political and democratic measures. It is the first time that the Egyptian people elect a civilian president at the ballot box after a revolution," one that brought down the Mubarak regime and its symbols.[654] Egyptians have every right to celebrate the election of the first civilian president in sixty years, even if he is slipped from his powers and is restricted by the constitutional declaration.[655]

It is time that we have a civilian president after sixty years of military rule, observed *Al-Gomhuria*. America, the most powerful nation in the world, is ruled by a civilian president. So too is Britain and France. Is Egypt (a country of seven-thousand-year civilization) less than those states whose history does not exceed five hundred years?" Morsi's winning of the presidency is "an honor to all Egyptians, the revolution, a protection of the blood of the martyrs, and a continuation of the path of giving and change which we have awaited for decades. . . . It places the dignity of Egyptians—which the Mubarak regime ruined—up high."[656] There were those voters who, however, elected Morsi not because they admired him but because they rejected having Shafiq to be president because of the latter's military background and attachment to an "unwanted" regime, argued Montassir.[657] On the issue of before whom will Morsi take his oath, an *Al-Akhbar* article was titled: "The President's Crisis."[658] A caricature in *Al-Ahram* showed Morsi taking oath in front of a giant woman who represents Egypt and was sitting on a chair. With her hands on his head and him placing his hands on her knees, the giant lady says: "Oh! A civilian president at last after 60 years, but your rule must be in a civilian state."[659]

3. Cautious Optimism

There was hope and optimism in the way the state press reported on the election of Egypt's post-revolution president, but there was also a sense of cautious optimism. Once Morsi's victory was announced, voices shouted in fear from every corner about the possible scenarios in which Egypt could plunge in. In the opinion of *Al-Akhbar*, the new president faces "great challenges and numerous problems" that need to be tackled immediately. On top of them is the issue of lack of security on the street, eradicating corruption, containing rising food prices, and fighting poverty that is spreading among more than half of the population. "God be with the elected president," added the paper.[660] *Al-Ahram* columnist Ashraf El-Ashri prognosticated that:

> despite the end of the marathon of the presidency, many Egyptians are very convinced that what has happened is nothing but a first step for the preparation of a new elections anticipated by the public. The ills and crises this nation is mired in today need a hundred presidents like Morsi, and thus the time of the next presidential elections will not be far—possibly by the beginning of next year or the middle of it at the most. Morsi's modest victory will neither convince Egyptians nor enable the President to implement his program. His movements will remain crippled.

The struggle between the Muslim Brotherhood and SCAF will persist for a long time, added El-Ashri, and neither of them will surrender easily. The *Al-Ahram* journalist's column was titled: "In Search of a President."[661] Likewise, a piece in *Al-Akhbar* cautioned, "The struggle for power will persist, and the danger of clashes does unfortunately exist."[662]

Big figures in the state media called on Morsi to observe and abide by domestic agreements. Some expressed worry about Morsi from those surrounding him. In "A Message to the President," Nabil Amr of *Al-Ahram* asked—like many others in the state press—Morsi to remember that he came to the presidency with a very slim victory, and that those who did not vote for him are fearful now that many of the individuals surrounding him are "men of religion who claimed that voting for you is a jihad for Allah."[663] Mr. President, cried the state paper *Al-Massa*, we pray that those around you do not make of you "another Mubarak" and turn the Freedom and Justice Party into a National Democratic Party.[664] In his first speech, which he addressed to all the classes of the Egyptian society, the president-elect Morsi laid the foundation for a "new ground for national reconciliation," noted Makram Mohamed Ahmed who headed Egypt's Syndicate of Journalists and was said to be the one who wrote President Mubarak's speeches. We are all Egyptians, no matter how different our views and political affiliations are. Morsi should respect all court rulings—including the one that dissolved Parliament—and international agreements.[665]

4. Unity and National Reconciliation

Journalists at the state press often spoke of the need to unite the nation and on members of the Muslim Brotherhood to accommodate different opinions, with some of them even going as far as stating that Egypt and its institutions are on the brink of collapse. They stressed that it is incumbent upon the Muslim Brotherhood to work jointly with different political parties over issues of concern to the nation's stability and unity. *Al-Gomhuria* argued that whether we agree or disagree on the election of Morsi as president we must all put our political affiliations and views aside and stand by him so that he gets the "full chance to play his role as it should be."[666] It is time that we now "correct what we have corrupted;" it is time that we stand by him, observed *Al-Ahram*. But he must also realize that the forty eight percent of Egyptians who did not vote for him feel a sense of fear now. Morsi's first task must be to "comfort all Egyptians" without regard to their political association and views. The country's oldest state paper proclaimed, "The one-man-one-party age has ended."[667]

Morsi has won, stressed *Al-Gomhuria*, and what remains is for him to be a "president for all Egyptians" and march toward Egypt's "renaissance." His victory must be seen as the "beginning of a wide national reconciliation movement."[668] According to columnist Fathi Mahmoud of *Al-Ahram*, the main task ahead of the president-elect is to exist us from the "atmosphere of division and fanaticism prevalent these days in Egypt." Words alone are not enough, added Mahmoud. Morsi and his supporters, particularly the Muslim Brotherhood, should carry the heavy burden of eradicating this fear by initiating a wide dialogue among all Egyptians. "I wish that the first visit Morsi makes as president be to the Coptic Orthodox Church, and that one of the first meetings he holds as president be an open discussion with the largest number possible of Egyptian intellectuals, particularly his opponents. I also wish that his first tour in the nation be to the governorates which he did not win in the elections."[669]

Al-Massa made the following comment: The choice of a president in a fair election should make us forget the "past" and its atmosphere of division and opt towards a future of unity and reconciliation. After sixteen months of turbulence, national reconciliation and implementing a state of law should be Morsi's priorities, emphasized an *Al-Ahram* article which proposed composing a presidential council from the failed presidential candidates (such as Shafiq, Amr Moussa, Hamdeen Sabahi and Abdel Moneim Aboul Fotouh) to work side by side with the president.[670] President Morsi should work diligently towards granting people "their rights and offering utmost care to the poor and working class, which has lived in misery and despair for thirty years to the extent that the poverty level in some governorates has reached 70%."[671]

Al-Gomhuria cautioned: When the new president begins his work he must have all Egyptians by his side "without discrimination against women or men or based on religion. Egypt is for all Egyptians." Egypt is laying its feet on the ground of a new future and we must all stand by its side.[672] We no longer want to see Egyptians divided into two groups—supporters and opposers, said *Al-Massa*. "Morsi has proved that he will be president for all Egyptians." Now it is time for us to work and produce and not just utter words.[673] In this "critical moment in Egypt's history," it is incumbent upon us all to support him as long as he respects the constitution, law, and protects people's interest. We must all unite to accomplish people's hopes and aspirations.[674] To achieve unity and democratic rule, *Al-Ahram* emphasized, political opposition must be given a voice. By electing a civilian president for the first time, Egypt is beginning the "age of democracy and social justice. With all national powers uniting together, our country will be able to stand any challenge."[675] We should name Morsi "Egypt's Mandela" because he, like the South African leader Nelson Mandela, spent time behind bar in service of his country. Morsi is a humble man, and we must back him throughout his journey because the burden placed on his shoulder is heavy.[676]

In "Files of the President," *Al-Ahram* columnist Emad Ghoneim argued that no wise person expects from the new president to achieve miracles in a few months, but people are waiting anxiously to see his method in selecting members of his administration which govern us during these next four years. We all are waiting to see how he will launch what he has described as a "renaissance project," added Ghoneim. We must remind him that what our country is in dire need of now is the institution of a "crisis government to heal the wounds of the transitional period and to regain trust by restarting normal life in an atmosphere of justice and the supremacy of law."[677] We ask president Morsi to prove to Egyptians that they are "people worthy of getting bread, freedom, social justice, and human dignity." These are the demands for which the martyrs gave their lives in Egyptian squares.[678] We will be watching closely how Morsi will carry out his renaissance project.[679] God be with him because Egyptians are craving for stability.[680]

Under this theme, fear of the Muslim Brotherhood mingling in the political process and affecting Morsi's decision-making process was echoed in the state press. After the declaration of his victory, it is expected now that Morsi is no longer a member of the Muslim Brotherhood, pointed out *Al-Massa*. And Egyptians, whose population is close to ninety million, will not allow for a political group whose number does not exceed three million to control the nation's political decision-making.[681] The group publicly declared that the elected-president has departed them but it seems that they have not departed him.[682] Morsi must show that he governs in support of all Egyptians and not just of his "backers" or those that voted for him.[683] We want Morsi to distance himself from the Muslim Brotherhood and rebel against the *morsheed* (religious leader) of the group for the sake of establishing a "modern, democratic civilian state and not an extremist Islamic caliphate," concluded *Al-Akhbar*.[684]

5. Tribute to Judiciary and SCAF

A large number of journalists and commentators who wrote for the state press commanded the Egyptian judiciary for what they described as the diligent role it had played during the elections. In the opinion of *Al-Gomhuria*, Egyptians should be proud of their country's "honest judiciary" which has shouldered the heavy burden of insuring a just and fair elections during tough times in the country history.[685] We have in Egypt judges who raise the flags of nothing but justice, emphasized *Al-Akhbar*, and we pay them our utmost respect and appreciation for their role and virtuous mission.[686] We have a reputable judiciary system that deserves all respect, and the way it managed the election process is a clear evidence of that, proclaimed *Al-Massa* in a piece which offered strong praise to judicial consultant Farouk Sultan who headed the Presidential Elections Committee.[687]

Many called on political parties to reconcile their differences over the issue of the dissolution of the People's Assembly. When the state press praised the "free elections" it also stressed that the Supreme Constitutional Court's decision to dissolve the People's Assembly must be respected, and that it is legitimate. However, a few did accuse SCAF of deliberately fueling disorder in a bid to fashion the electorate to its authoritarian agenda. Hence, they argue, the elections are illegitimate. Tackling the issue of the dissolution of the People's Assembly, Awwad Salem, poses a number of thought-provoking questions: Who put into place the unconstitutional law upon which parliamentary elections were held? Were they not legal figures? And so, who permitted them to piece together such an important law allowing for parliamentary elections to be held? "Why did not we consultant the Supreme Constitutional Council—which I question its constitutionality—before implementing it? In fact, those who implemented that law are constitutional experts among whom are two members of the Supreme Constitutional Court." How did they miss on this?[688]

Many also applauded the role played by SCAF during the presidential election process, though it was clear that the state press was reluctant not to separate the SCAF members—whom the public wanted to see criticized because they were the ones making decisions—from the army as a whole. In other words, commentaries insinuated that a criticism of the SCAF generals would mean a criticism of the entire army. Within this framework, glorification of SCAF's role continued unabated in the state press. In a column in *Al-Akhbar*, Mahdeha Azzab extolled SCAF and argued that "we have done it injustice" because we now know that it has dealt with the election process in a fair and objective way. I wish satellite television station stop denouncing and distorting the image of others, she added.[689] Egyptians should be proud of its army as represented in SCAF, which has proved its "neutral stance and support of justice, democracy, and the nation's public interest by protecting elections and not intervening to bolster one political current against the other."[690] An *Al-Ahram* Op-Ed called on the president-elect to "fully cooperate" with the SCAF because it has carried out a "great nationalist role," despite some critical viewpoints of it.[691] Our praise goes to the SCAF, stressed *Al-Gomhuria*, for the role it has played in supervising elections and insuring that they were conducted in a "transparent" and "fair" manner. The police also deserve applause because its staff worked diligently to assure the safety of the elections. In fact, all Egyptians—including the other twelve presidential candidates—have won in the elections and not just Morsi.[692]

The Independent Press

There was little talk in the independent press about the theme of the "second republic" that advocated that Egypt is entering the second republic—the republic of democracy. Only two articles in the independent press tackled the theme as opposed to the state press which gave it much coverage. The Mubarak regime has ended with Morsi's victory, noted the independent paper Al-Masry Al-Youm, and we have begun a new system in the second republic.[693] Those who have been claiming following the election results that Egypt is witnessing the birth of the second republic are wrong because the new constitution which endorses it is not yet in place, noted another Al-Masry Al-Youm article. Even if it is stated in a constitution, this republic will not begin until the exchange of power is complete. Or else we will be "moving from one dictatorial regime to another."[694] After all, under the new constitutional declaration a president serves as a "secretary" for the SCAF, commented the state paper El-Youm El-Sabaa.[695] There was also much more criticism of Shafiq in the independent press than in the state press, with many denouncing him as a remnant of the regime and a close ally of Mubarak. Here are the main five themes we found in the independent press.

Fulfilling Promises

There is a strong focus in the independent press on the president's duties and the fulfillment of the promises he has made, including development of democracy and protecting human rights and the rights of religious minorities. The state paper *Al-Tahrir* urged Morsi to stick to the promises he launched during his campaign. The president-elect needs to launch a national reconciliation project that encompasses all sects of the Egyptian society—women, Copts, and youth.[696] In an open letter to the president, an *El-Youm El-Sabaa* columnist asked Morsi to remember that the "blood of the martyrs" is what has gotten him to the "presidential palace, or else you would have been back lying in the darkness of prison." We ask you for justice to all our people—Muslims and Christians, men and women.[697] Morsi must cut all his ties with the Muslim Brotherhood and form a reconciliatory government that includes all "ministers of the revolution" with all their different political currents, observed the renowned novelist and political commentator Alaa El-Aswani. All those accused of fraud—Shafiq on top of them—must be tried, police must be cleansed of corruption, tryingcitizens in military courts must come to an end, and the twelve thousands civilians detained in military jails must be released and trialed in civilian courts. We must set minimum and maximum wages, end unemployment and poverty, added El-Aswani. Offering the best treatment to those injured in the revolution and tryingthe killers must also be a priority. After all, this is what this revolution is all about: Freedom, dignity, and justice.[698]

Other writers, such as Anisaa Essam Hussouna of *Al-Tahrir*, argued that many Egyptians demand too much from Morsi. Sadly, she wrote, Egyptians expect Morsi to achieve miracles: uplift the economy, pay the country's debt, raise wages, solve the traffic and garbage problems, tackle the security issue, insure social justice, protect human rights, institute freedom, and defend protesters. "We are with Morsi if he proves he is a president for all Egyptians," she wrote, including women, Copts, youths, and members of national political movements. She added

> We are with him if he associates himself with youths—youths who faced injustice until he assumed power— and women whose skills have been overlooked and were distanced from leadership posts and the decision-making process. We are with him if he revives the spirit of the revolution of countering corruption and protecting human rights. We are with him if his allegiance is to Egypt and not the Muslim Brotherhood group, if his aides are working under the framework of the agenda of national reconciliation and in consultation with the People's Assembly and not the *Morsheed* [religious guide]. We are with him if he respects Egypt's diversity. . .[699]

Emad Ghad, an expert on Israeli affairs, praised Morsi for stating in the speech he gave hours after his victory on June 24 that he would abide by all international agreements. This, added Gad, will record the first, official public endorsement by the Muslim Brotherhood of Egypt's treaty with Israel.[700]

Defeating Remnants of Mubarak Regime

Some commentators claimed that Morsi's victory means that activities of remnants of the Mubarak regime in political life are about finished. The election of Morsi "carries many meanings, most important of which is the end of a regime," accentuated *El-Youm El-Sabaa*. The regime which had kept on "changing its colors" and launching attempts to regain powers—the latest of which was Shafiq being a presidential candidate—is "inching toward an end."[701] Thanks God, wrote Zaki Salem in *Al-Tahrir*, "at last we have gotten rid of the horrors of the deposed [ruler] and his students—killers of our noble martyrs in the Battle of the Camel. We have gotten rid of them completely, and in the next days we will get rid of all the residues of the corrupt regime." The joy of our revolutionaries is not because of the victory of Morsi but rather happiness for our dignified people who went to the polls in millions to defeat a candidate (he described Shafiq as "the military's candidate") who is supported by men of the counter revolution. Salem's column was titled: "Defeat of an Entire Regime."[702] Other writers denied that Morsi victory puts an end to residues of the Mubarak regime, proclaiming that Mubarak's men will remain active and ambitious to reclaim power. Morsi's mission will not be easy because he will face remnants of the Mubarak regime who are "still in control of the state."[703]

Commentators spoke of why they voted for, or had to vote for, Morsi and not Shafiq. Morsi, said the state newspaper *Al-Shorouk Al-Jadeed*, must admit that more than half of those who voted for him did not approve of the Muslim Brotherhood's program, and that they voted for him as a form of rejection of his opponent Shafiq because of fear the latter may "get the revolution lost."[704] Ziyad Bahaeddine, an economics expert, spoke of how voters at times experience "negative voting," that is the desire to vote against an opponent candidate, in our case voting for Shafiq because of fear of Muslim Brotherhood rule and voting for Morsi to insure that the candidate of the former regime does not win.[705] Within this context, we congratulate all those who voted for Morsi even if they did so because they "could not stand Shafiq."[706] An *El-Youm El-Sabaa* column titled "Don't Make a New 'Mubarak' of Morsi," cautioned Egyptians not to glorify Morsi too much but to be realistic in their opinion of him so that he does not turn into another Mubarak.[707] "Yes, we will remain on the opposition side until the revolution has achieved all its goals of dignity, freedom and social justice." We will not accept that the elected president "turn into a new pharaoh."[708]

A Big Victory: Congratulations to Egypt

Commentators at the independent press spoke less of the issue of "free elections" and focused more on how the election results should be viewed as a "big victory" because Egypt passed a big hurdle by electing a president who is not from the military. There was a consensus among those in the independent press that the election was closest to being free. Everyone who believes in democracy, contended *Al-Masry Al-Youm*, must accept the election result because it was conducted in a "free" way in as much as possible. After all, there is no such a thing as an absolutely free, ideal election; hence, everyone who believes in democracy should accept the Morsi-Shafiq election results.[709] Morsi has won and with it we have folded the page of the presidential election which almost gotten the country to the brink of division, proclaimed *El-Youm El-Sabaa*.[710]

Not all those who celebrated the election results were from the Muslim Brotherhood, and their celebration was more of the loss of Shafiq than the victory of Morsi.[711] In the view of El-Aswani,

> The Egyptian revolution has achieved great victory by electing Morsi and dropping Shafiq no matter what our political differences with the elected president are. He is the first elected civilian president in Egypt's modern history. This is a victory of the determination of Egyptians that will have an effect not just in their country; it will also push the wheel of change in Arab states that aspire to get rid of despotic rulers that have been holding on the breath of their people for decades.[712]

A new president for Egypt has arrived, celebrated *Al-Masry Al-Youm*. The "historic fact" is that we are before a new age. Egypt is changing but it has not changed yet, and the president's leadership will decide the nature of its change.[713] The defeat of candidates of the Mubarak regime means a victory for all revolutionary streams, accentuated *El-Youm El-Sabaa* columnist Abdel Rahman Youssef. The revolution has moved a step forward even though it is a "symbolic" or "restricted" step; we have won "a half victory" and not a full one. Whether or not it will prove its full success will dependent on Morsi's performance. We want "a civilian state and not a religious one," one in which there is "no monopoly of power or capital," added Youssef.[714] Similar to French President Francois Hollande, Morsi should now arduously work to convince those who did not vote for him that he is worthy of their vote, and that the state he is going to implement is a civilian one.[715]

Portrayal of SCAF and Judiciary

There was little extolment of SCAF in the independent press; the state press adulated SCAF more than the independent press. There was also less glorification of the country's judiciary in the independent press. On certain circumstances, there was joint praise of both institutions in the independent papers. Listen to this, for example: Morsi's victory, proclaimed Al-Masry Al-Youm, has proved that "our Egyptian judiciary is fine as usual and that our great army has fulfilled its promises."[716] A piece in *El-Youm El-Sabaa* demanded that Morsi and his men should publically declare the honesty and transparency of our judiciary. It was unjust from them to unleash criticism at it and SCAF.[717]

The SCAF

El-Aswani was critical of the role played by SCAF before and after the elections. He lamented, For sixteen months now, "SCAF has abstained from achieving the goals of the revolution and has rejected any change in the structure of the Mubarak system." El-Aswani claimed that there were plans to forge the elections and get Shafiq to win by placing pressure on the ordinary Egyptian citizen via the issue of lack of security, and that it was that man—Mubarak's last prime minister—who can regain security to the country. Faced with the anticipated victory of the Muslim Brotherhood's Morsi, SCAF members felt they are in a crisis and issued a constitutional decree (an addition to the constitution) just hours before the final election results were announced, restraining a president's powers and placing SCAF above all authority.[718]

From the beginning the plan by the SCAF generals was to "keep everything as it is, including maintaining the traditional confrontation between the regime and the Brotherhood. It was clear that the role for them was one of frightening the public, and which they had often been able to cleverly use," said Al-Masry Al-Youm. And it seems that the "military was confident that it would reach the same results, that of re-installing the staff of the regime and asking Egyptians to celebrate because their fire is better than the heaven of the Brotherhood."[719] The influence of SCAF on the political process has not come to an end yet. Morsi "will not be ruling alone," stressed Hussouna, but has in fact another partner: SCAF.[720] The constitutional declaration means the president does not hold enough powers to be able to decide the nation's future in the next period; it means that SCAF will be a "partner in running Egypt's affairs and a guardian on the process of producing a constitution, if not the main actor in its writing," contended *Al-Shorouk Al-Jadeed*. But this should be of no surprise to us because in fact there has not been a time in Egypt where the military has not been the powerbroker—the "real ruler" in Egypt.[721]

Criticizing SCAF's rule and describing it as despotic was noted on some cases. Morsi, declared *El-Youm El-Sabaa*, should eliminate public's suspicion of him and his Muslim Brotherhood group; he must distance himself from America's support of him and his group because foreign intervention in Egypt's internal affairs will dismantle "public's unanimity against SCAF's despotism."[722] *Al-Masry Al-Youm* criticized the way SCAF took crucial decisions and implemented laws concerning the nation just days before it is scheduled to hand power without running a referendum to seek public opinion. Under them, President Morsi will be "a mere official overseeing the services of education, health, transportation, agriculture and commerce" without any right to exercise any authority on the army. "In short, the army which is feared and is terrifying people of a fake enemy named the religious state has turned Egypt into a religious state."[723]

Fahmi Howeidi, an expert on political Islam, ruminated over how the SCAF generals made mistakes when they said Egypt should benefit from the Turkish democracy experience, lamenting that instead of them promoting the democracy of Tayyib Erdogan they followed that of Mustafa Kemal Ataturk which was far from being democratic. When Turkey's Development and Justice Party assumed power in 2003, wrote Howeidi, Erdogan skillfully existed the military from politics and broke the "alliance between the judiciary and bureaucracy," making Turkey emerge as a modern democracy. But sadly in Egypt, the recent constitutional decree has granted SCAF the legislative power and the final decision of its execution. The power of SCAF is now above the law and the constitution, he added. "SCAF is now a state within a state." If disturbances break out in Egypt and necessitate military intervention, SCAF's approval is mandatory for the execution of the president's decision. SCAF can object to any article in the constitution which it does not like. "It has the right to issue any laws it desires without anyone being capable of rejecting them in front of a judicial body." Howeidi concluded that he first described what SCAF did as a "soft coup," but he later moved away from that and considered it a "beautification of an ugly act."[724]

It is worth noting that we found only two articles in the independent press that extolled the role of SCAF, and they were in *Al-Masry Al-Youm*. The first visit Morsi should make as president ought to be to the headquarters of SCAF "because it was the institution that governed the nation before him and was one of the important reasons for the success of the revolution, if not its most important one."[725] One article mourned how SCAF, and its chief in particular, Defense Minister Mohamed Tantawi, carried an unbearable burden and faced "accusation, rumors, lies and attack." Yet it has stood firm in protecting the country.[726] By guiding the elections in such a "responsible" and "marvelous" manner SCAF has "risen to a historic responsibility level and recorded its name in history, despite all attempts to hurt its image," observed Montassir El-Zayeat, a popular lawyer who often defends Islamists and members of the Muslim Brotherhood.[727]

The Judiciary

To some extent criticism of the judiciary in the independent press was much less than that of SCAF, but there was criticism contrary to what we found in the state press where one could hardly find articles that disapprove of judges or courts or the way they supervised the elections. *Al-Shorouk Al-Jadeed* alleged, "There has not been a day where civilian bureaucracy—with the judiciary at the top—has not been a tool for passing the will of the ruling authority and imposing it in a legitimate framework."[728] According to popular political commentary Amr El-Shobaki, the election of Morsi came via the ballot box and under the supervision of a judiciary that deserves "applause and respect." Yet, the Muslim Brotherhood has launched vicious criticism on the judiciary, accusing it directly or indirectly of rigging the election. What if it was Shafiq who won in a free and candid election?[729]

In "What After the Presidency," Bahaeddine proclaimed that Egyptians must give the judiciary the respect it deserves because it has offered them a "free and clean election." It is foolish to celebrate the victory of Morsi and the outcome of presidential elections and yet still call for ignoring the decision of the Supreme Constitutional Court which dissolved parliament. "It is possible that the judicial system may be in need of development, of more independence or resources. Criticizing legal decisions is not a crime, but refusing the notion of law and justice is a completely different thing. Society is essentially in need of agreement on the piety of the principle of the supremacy of law. We can search in details after that," added Bahaeddine.[730] Likewise, El-Aswani pointed out, "Even though the judicial system in Egypt is not independent and comes under the power of the executive branch we have judges who take independent decisions and have conscience and courage that push them to say the truth no matter what the cost will be."[731]

Cautious Optimism

Unlike in the state press, the independent press did not wide openly raise a sense of fear about Egypt's unity. Commentaries stressed the issue of religious diversity and called for a president for all Egyptians. According to *Al-Shorouk Al-Jadeed*, Morsi can truly prove that he is a president for all Egyptians by embracing a national reconciliation initiative and forming a wide reconciliatory government with a rescue program aimed at solving the security and economic problems.[732] We want from Morsi to be a president for all Egyptians—Muslims, Christians, and those who offered him their trust and those who did not, qualified El-Zayeat.

"We want from the elected president to immediately declare national reconciliation, to melt all Egyptians in the fabric of the Egyptian society without rejecting the other based on ideology, belief or political stance"[733]

In many ways, the caution raised was much about how Morsi will rule in a state that has no constitution or parliament. There is no constitution that defines the powers of the president, of Morsi, proclaimed Hussouna. El-Aswani charged the Muslim Brotherhood of engaging in an unwritten agreement with SCAF after the revolution, and this has led to us failing to "write a new constitution."[734] The absence of parliament will make Morsi operate in "a legislative vacuum."[735] Journalist Lamees El-Hadidi wishes that before judging Morsi's performance he is granted a period of at least one hundred days to unveil his political performance. She asks: Whom will he choose as prime minister and what will be the shape of his government? What about his ties with SCAF? What will he do about the dissolved Parliament? Will he distance himself from the issue or try to use his power to bring back Parliament into operation? How will his foreign policy be like and his ties with Hamas, Qatar, and Iran? What will he do to improve the stand of women and Copts? Morsi has a chance and he should not waste it or else people will be waiting for him at the ballot box.[736]

Moreover, there was this fear of Morsi trying to appease in order to win support. In making his upcoming decisions, Morsi will be driven by his weakness and necessity to win the majority, qualified *Al-Tahrir*, and we should start closely monitoring this before it is too late.[737] One writer also demanded that Morsi must ask his two sons (who were born in America) to give up their U.S. citizenships.[738] The road to democracy is long, and we have achieved in months what took other nations years to achieve, noted columnist Mohamed Amin of *Al-Masry Al-Youm*. "There is a chance for the president to prove that he is a president for all Egyptians," to prove that the interest of Egyptians comes first. There is no need for confrontation with the military or the public. "Let Morsi's first decision be the appointment of Commander Shafiq as his vice president," suggested Amin. Decisions should also be taken to appoint in his cabinet members of other sects of society without discrimination.[739]

Summary

Egyptians had to choose between the old regime of Mubarak and a new one in the form of the Muslim Brotherhood, and many chose none as fifty percent of registered voters abstained. I'll never vote for an Islamist or a former member of the Mubarak regime to be my president, a recent college graduate told me. This stance was exhibited in how many Egyptians, particularly youths, declined to vote in the final run-off between Morsi and Shafiq. I too abstained from voting because that would have meant me accepting Shafiq as a presidential candidate—a man who I continue to see his hands stained with the blood of those who died on February 2, 2011, known as Black Wednesday (Battle of the Camel) which we discussed in details in Chapter 5. A victory of the ex-air force commander, who served as prime minister for a little over a month (from January 29 to March 3, 2011) would have meant the end of the revolution and the loss of hope of tryingthose who killed the innocent—revolutionaries who died over the past sixteen months. In that sense, I viewed the whole electoral process as flawed and that it, together with many of the country's ills, could have been corrected had a new constitution been written early on. For sixteen months we waited in vain for a constitution to be drafted and this raised suspicion in the minds of many that the SCAF members were corrupting the political process to achieve personal gains. When Egyptians went to vote on the constitutional amendments in March 2011, they were promised that a new constitution will be drafted in six months but that promise was never fulfilled. Egyptians have waited for months, and it looks as if they will be waiting for more months before they see a new constitution in place—a constitutional that represents all Egyptians and wins public support.

Shafiq's victory in the first session of the presidential elections made some claim that the revolution was a ruse, and that the deposed president's repression machines are still alive and well; it has just changed its attire and looks. Morsi did not win with an overwhelming mandate, and right after his victory he tried to be reconciliatory in his political endeavors reaching to all political parties. When he was delivering his Tahrir speech, I intentionally walked in poor areas of my home city Benha, a suburb of Cairo, and mingled with people on the streets to get their response. In that hot summer day, people in that working class area were sitting outside their houses or stores watching Morsi's speech on television. When he said he would work diligently to free detainees from jail, people applauded. And they applauded even more when he said he would work to free Sheik Omar Abdel Rahman and bring him home from America. One man looked at me and said: "Morsi will straighten things up—Allah be with him." Another said with his hand pointing to a mosque nearby, Morsi should clean those mosques up. The implication of that phrase, as I understood from the words that the man later made, is that the imams, or religious leaders, of Egyptian mosques under Mubarak rule have been mere voices of government and never reflected the voice of the public. On June 13, and just days before the final run-off, I witnessed from the balcony of our apartment a scene that echoes the true revolution. I saw over fifty cars filled with people carrying posters of Shafiq and microphones on them shouting: "We want Shafiq." As the line of car proceeded, kids who were playing in the streets stood on the sideways and started shouting: "No we don't want Shafiq; we want Sabahi."

Egyptians' eyes have remained wide open for the moves Morsi takes. By the time I finished writing this book Morsi completed five months in office and critical voices were rising against him for selecting cabinet members with Islamist blend. There was a considerable delay in the way he appointed his cabinet and the prime minister, whom many claim has weak political experience. Then all of sudden, Egypt's first freely elected president was on the move, removing on August 12 a number of military generals followed by Field Marshal Tantawi and his deputy, Armed Forces Chief of Staff Sami Anan, and ending his power struggle with SCAF. He has annulled the June constitutional decree and reclaimed power from the military.[740] Morsi's powers are no longer circumscribed; he has cemented his power. We have also witnessed Morsi appointing Islamists in his government and state governors in what some describe as an attempt to remove loyalists and remnants of the Mubarak regime from politics. Others, mainly non-Islamists, were alarmed by such move, complaining that the weight of Islamists on political life in Egypt has been growing.

Even though we command the efforts embraced by the SCAF to insure that the presidential elections were conducted fairy, the contradictions in decisions made by SCAF are crystal clear and one can but hail Morsi's decision to rush to push them off the political process. It has surprised Egyptians beginning with its proposed constitutional amendment (amending eight articles of the 1971 Constitution) in March 2011 through to constitutional declaration of sixty three articles which was announced in mid-2012. The SCAF organized "free" parliamentary elections but then turned angrily on parliament and dissolved it. It issued the constitutional decree and based on its content it produced the elections law, but we then discovered that the "latter does not reconcile/conform with the former. Furthermore, SCAF called on us to elect a president but then shocked us by seizing legislative authority, announcing the constitutional decree and granting itself the right to veto decisions made by the established constitutional committee; it even granted itself the right to form a new constitutional committee. It cancelled the emergency law in mid-2012 but then surprised Egyptians—if not at all frightened them—once again by offering the country's intelligence apparatus (both of the police and the military) mass powers, a carte blanche to throw in jail whomever it wishes without the right for fair trial, violating all international norms established after World War II for protecting the decency of fellow human beings. All Egyptian youths were asking for is a decent life—for "bread, freedom, social justice, and human dignity."

A revolution means change and the Egyptian revolution is continuing. The revolution of Poland lasted for thirteen years until it achieved its goals. The true challenge for Morsi in the days ahead lies in his ability to solve a bundle of problems which a number of post-revolution nations faced. Most important of which is the duality of being the "man of the state" and the "man of the revolution," because the Egyptian revolution is continuing via public protest on one side and building the state of law on the other. Each of these two scenarios need not only different skills and capabilities but also world backing—particularly from the rich Arab Gulf states—to be achieved. The Egyptian President must distance himself from the Muslim Brotherhood. Morsi's Egypt will not pursue a political Islam track—implementing a strict Sharia (Islamic law) as the rule of law—as some are advocating in the Egyptian and Western media, simply because Egyptians will not allow that. The military will remain strong in influencing the political process, even though SCAF is no longer in power. This is because the military as an institution is deeply founded in the Egyptian society, including the making and unmaking of the decision-making process. If the economy does not improve to help Morsi implement some of his promises on enhancing the lives of Egyptians, he will face difficulty from the public. People will go out on the street again in masses, this time demanding that he steps down. Seculars will also keep the pressure on him for fear of turning Egypt into a religious state. On the international level, one cannot prognosticate that Egypt's relations with the United States and Israel will be weakened under Morsi, but it is possible that we will see more ups and downs in ties; we will see his foreign policy bandwagon frequenting states such as China and Russia more than the United States.

The revolution has up-ended the longstanding authoritarian regime of Mubarak but the democratic transition will be a long-term process because the secular-Islamist and civil-military tension will continue. The firing of the top generals is not the final move. Egypt will continue to undergo a period of political limbo until a new constitution is drafted, the People's Assembly is in place, and courts are cleansed of corruption. The separation of politics from religion is also a vital issue if Egyptians are to establish a true democracy that is compatible with those in the West. In the upcoming years, or decade, it is possible that both seculars and Islamists will jostle to form the new Egypt; they will navigate until they shape a union that paves the road toward democracy. In many ways, my viewpoint here goes in harmony with one made by an American academic three years before the revolution. In his 2008 masterpiece *Egypt after Mubarak*, Bruce K. Rutherford defines the constitutional, judicial, and legal constituencies of Egypt's major political forces, contending that liberal and Islamist opponents of the regime are navigating a middle path, a "convergence," that can counter the state's intrusion on political and civil rights and result in a distinctively Islamic style of liberalism—and possibly democracy later.[741] Morsi's military shake-up should be a positive step for a future civilian-military dialogue because it means an end to military constraints on the political process such as the drafting of a new constitution which often faced SCAF's veto. But one cannot rule that a power struggle will not remain in the backyard between the army's generals on one side and Morsi and the Brotherhood on the other. Egyptians also realize that a coterie of rich, dishonest businessmen—mainly men of Gamal Mubarak—remain active; these Mubarak-age veterans are anti-revolutionaries and they still hold powerful positions in and outside of government. There remains also the fear of Morsi and the Brotherhood accumulating too much power hurting the democratization process.

In the eight months that followed Morsi's inauguration until this book was sent to the publisher late in February 2013, protests continued against him and what they denounced as the Brotherhood's intervention in the President's decision-making process. Liberals, leftists, and members of opposition parties rejected many of Morsi's political decisions as damaging to Egypt's diverse cultural and religious background. Morsi encountered a number of crises, most difficult of which was over the draft constitution which heated late in November. The controversial draft constitution, which was written by an Islamist-dominated assembly, resulted in strong rival protesters by supporters and opponents of Morsi. Tens of thousands of protesters gathered in Tahrir Square on November 30, denouncing the draft and calling for the downfall of Morsi and his government which they charged of promoting only the opinions and values of the Brotherhood which Morsi once chaired. A day later, thousands of supporters (whom the Egyptian press described as Islamists allied to Morsi) gathered by Cairo University showing support for Morsi. On that day, Morsi delivered a speech calling on Egyptians to go to poll on December 15 to vote on the referendum of the draft constitution. On December 2, the Supreme Constitutional Court stated that it would not convene until its judges can operate without "psychological and material pressure." The Court was forced to take that decision after Morsi's supporters surrounded the Court building and hindered the judges from entering it to rule on the legality of a shady constitutional assembly that put together the draft constitution. I saw this confrontation between Morsi's supporters and opponents—between Morsi and his supporters in the Muslim Brotherhood on one side and the secular opposition and the judiciary on the other—as constituting the biggest obstacle for the President, to such an extent that I came to believe that Morsi's time in the presidency would be limited. Only time would tell, though, what was to happen in Egypt in the days that followed, as we saw thousands of protesters marching on December 4 to the presidential palace and calling for the downfall of Morsi. Some shouted: "Down with Morsi and *Morsheed* [religious guide] rule" and "From Tahrir we'll bring Morsi down as we did with Mubarak."

Chapter 11. Conclusion

> In 40 years of writing about the Middle East, I have never seen anything like what is happening in Tahrir Square. In a region where the truth and truth-tellers have so long been smothered under the crushing weight of oil, autocracy and religious obscurantism, suddenly the Arab world was a truly free space. — THOMAS L. FRIEDMAN, *The New York Times*, February 7, 2011

Widespread corruption under President Hosni Mubarak's rule, which resulted in widening the gap between the rich and poor and high unemployment among youth, together with the iron fist of the country's security apparatus enforced on people's lives, were the propeller of the January 25, 2011, Egyptian Revolution. I personally knew that there was corruption in Egypt but I never anticipated it to be that vast—it was bedded in all institutions: government, health, education, and more. In the weeks that followed Mubarak's downfall, I heard daily of public figures who allegedly embezzled government money or used their position to accumulate wealth. One must admit, however, that there were attempts by distinguished Egyptian thinkers to draw our attention to that growingly pervasive culture of corruption under the Mubarak reign, particularly over his last two decade rule. But some rejected them, arguing that the country's economy was booming under his leadership, particularly in the last four years of his term in office and according to figures released by the World Bank and the International Monetary Fund. In his 2009 Arabic book on Mubarak's rule, Galal Amin, an economics professor at the American University in Cairo (AUC), prognosticated the beginning of the end of the Mubarak regime. "Presidents come and go except for President Mubarak. What a man he is!" wrote Amin. He added that globalization and unrestrained open market economies manipulated by those in the ruling regime—ministers who have been in power for many years—have turned Egypt into a state that "invites regret at times and derision at other times." He lamented that over the past two decades of Mubarak's rule corruption spread in politics, economics, and the media, resulting in an increase in the level of poverty and unemployment. In short, concluded the AUC professor, "corruption was legalized in the last twenty years" of the Mubarak regime.[742]

Half a century ago the distinguished Egyptian author and thinker Abbas Mahmoud El-Aqqad said that revolutions take place in Egypt either for bread or religion. The 2011 Revolution is the second revolution carried out and led by Egyptian civilians; the first was the 1919 Revolution which attempted to end British occupation. They were preceded by two military-led revolutions—military coups—namely the 1882 Urabi Revolution (led by Ahmed Urabi) and the 1952 Revolution. Similar to the 1919 and 1952 revolutions, the 2011 Revolution had no single leadership. The 2011 Revolution is the product of youth—of their struggles and sacrifices. More than half a century ago Tawfiq El-Hakim, another renowned Egyptian thinker and a playwright, released his famous Arabic book *The Revolution of Youth* in which he lays down the role of youth in introducing the peaceful values that lead a nation to safe shore. El-Hakim says, "Every revolution is evidence of vitality, and youth are the vital part of the body. It is no surprise then that a revolution is launched by youth."[743] And El-Hakim was right. The people who went on demonstration in Egypt on January 25 asking for their political and economic rights surprised Egyptians and the many who falsely denied that what took place in Tunisia could happen in Egypt. They were mostly youth aged between eighteen and thirty, unemployed and did not belong to political parties. These youthful revolutionaries practiced politics on social network groups. During the revolution some of them protected children, women, the elderly, and places of cultural heritage; while others stood steadfast in their protests in Tahrir Square. We even watched them clean the Square in the mornings. At that moment, we all knew that Egypt would endure no matter what difficulty it faced.

But let us have a brief look first at Egypt and its culture before debating this further. Throughout history, Egypt has passed through different ages and cultures: Pharaonic, Greek, Roman, Islamic, and the modern age. Today's Egypt occupies an important place because of its Arab, Islamic, and pharaonic history. Over the thousands of years, Egyptians have settled on the banks of the Nile River and despite the various occupations that the country experienced—from the Greeks to the Romans through to the Arab conquest and Ottoman Empire—Egypt has managed to absorb all those cultures, together with its pharaonic roots, to produce a unique cultural mosaic for the Land of the Nile. The Greek philosopher Sophocles once said that "Egypt is the gift of the Nile." The eminent Egyptian historian Mohamed Shafiq Gharbal wrote in the mid-twentieth century that "Egypt is also the gift of its people."[744] Today, the country is the most populous state in the Arab world and has one of the most vibrant intellectual communities in the region. Its culture, which dates back 5,000 years ago, continues to fascinate the world, including Arabs. Cairo's thriving media, movie, and television industry has a major influence on Arab culture. Educated Egyptians—teachers, doctors, and engineers—can be found working in almost every Arab state. Hence, it was natural that a political meltdown, a revolution, in it would affect and resonate powerfully in the entire Arab world. In addition to that is the role Cairo plays in maintaining peace and stability in the region. As the 1988 Nobel laureate for literature Naguib Mahfouz once put it: Egypt is an asset to all Arabs because of the mediating role it can play in any conflict, and its ability to defuse regional tension.

Many things come to mind when one reminiscences about the days of the 2011 revolution. Some believe that the revolution succeeded because it had a prime goal: regime change and restoring dignity to the Egyptian people. Compared to other revolutions, it was a clean, pure, and somewhat nonviolent revolution. A number of Egyptians even characterized it as a "white revolution," though many disagree with this as we later discovered that thirteen hundred Egyptians died and another thousand is still missing. Those missing were, according to distinguished political commentator and novelist Alaa El-Aswani, most likely "killed and their bodies buried in unknown places." Adding to this the thousands injured, many of them lost their eyes.[745] Those martyrs have written a new chapter not just for Egypt but for many countries in the Arab world. In a country of over eighty million, run for 30 years by one man, Egyptians were desperate for a change—for a fresh start. On this, the Arab world's most acclaimed journalist Mohamed Hasseinein Heikel complained that Mubarak badly tackled ethnic issues in Egypt, submitted to Israeli demands, violated human rights, and indulged in intelligence affairs to achieve his personal financial and political goals.[746] Following Mubarak's downfall, Egyptians called for a new president and a new government that would not be run for decades by one party.

If revolutions are good to watch on television screens, three events shocked Egyptians the most when watching their revolution. The first is watching Wael Ghonim (who, with other activists, formed the Facebook group "We Are All Khaled Said") breaking out in tears after being jailed for twelve days for seeing the pictures of dead protesters. He said the "deaths of these martyrs is not my fault but of everyone who clings to power" against his people's will. The second scene is of an army officer standing in support of demonstrators at Tahrir with one protester bending down to kiss his head, a sign of respect in Arab culture particularly for the elderly. The third incident is of an Egyptian cardiologist at Cairo University's hospital who had nothing to do with politics but was asked by his daughter, a protester, to join them at Tahrir and assist medically. He went there on January 28 and stayed thereafter doing all he could within his means to treat the injured—from those suffering dehydration to gunshot wounds and teargas inhalation difficulty. He vividly described to viewers the horrible scenes he had witnessed at Tahrir.

Egyptian Revolution and Arab Spring

The prospects of uprisings taking place in the Arab world have increased after Mubarak's ouster. Egyptomania, or love for anything Egyptian, has swept the Arab world, with Tahrir becoming a symbol of a revolution not just for Egyptians but for all Arabs. It has been called: "The January Revolution," "The Youth Revolution," "The Lotus Revolution," and the "The Uprising of the Young." But we must also not overlook the vital role the Tunisia revolution has played in the contagion of revolutions in the Arab world. Once Arabs witnessed the fruits of the Tunisian and Egyptian revolutions they began digging in their heels for ways to imitate them. Indeed, the Tunisians and Egyptians have shown the way toward democracy and the whole Arab world was watching. Both revolutions have ignited the flames of change in the Arab world, and suddenly we have begun to see winds of uprisings sweeping the Arab world. We have begun to see the Arab world go through a democracy epidemic—a demographic time bomb of tumultuous times. Whenever one heard ordinary Arabs criticizing their regimes, they often spoke of a need to launch a Tahrir-style sit-in. All of a sudden, Arab rulers have shown their age and their citizens are counting how long they have been in office. We have witnessed unrest in Libya and then Yemen, and concluding with Syria, and passing through Bahrain, Oman, and Jordan. We also saw protests in Morocco, Kuwait, and Sudan. In this democracy tsunami, Arabs who took to the streets all shared the same grievances: lack of human rights, government corruption, high unemployment, low wages, and skyrocketing food prices. Protesters in Yemen and Bahrain enchanted the popular phrase which the Tunisians and Egyptians coined: "*E'shaab Yo'reed es'qat al-nezam*" (Arabic for "The people want to topple the regime"). They also called—as Egyptian and Tunisians and later Libyans did—for a march to the palaces of their ruling leaders. Yes, today it is all topsy-turvy (though on and off) in the Arab world. No one should expect political change in the region to be an easy process; after all, Arabs have lived for half a century under a protracted stage of fear, unable to explain their views in face of their dictatorial regimes. But Arabs, and despite of the obfuscation that surrounds the events, no longer talk of fear—fear of being punished for speaking their mind.

In many ways what took place in Egypt and the Arab world is similar to what happened in Eastern Europe in the 1990s. I heard some speaking of the pro-democracy revolutions in Eastern Europe that began in 1989, stressing that the Mubarak regime was more authoritarian and corrupt than most of the centrally-planned regimes of Eastern Europe. Once again, one must emphasize that inequality, economic want, and political repression incited the Tunisian and Egyptian revolutions, and this has helped in the usurping of the uprisings that took place in parts of the Arab world thereafter. We have begun to see a symbolic gathering of Tahrir Square taking place in major Arab cities. The results of these uprisings came out differently in each country. What took place in Egypt has caught the world attention; it has had a strong effect on nations surrounding it, simply because of Egypt's strategic and cultural heritage which I touched on above. To some extent one can argue that the Egyptian revolution has succeeded, with some human losses—though not as many as in Tunisia, Libya, and Syria of course where bloodshed has been massive. Egyptians put their ousted leader on trial and did not kill him as the Libyans did with Moammar al-Gadhafi or injured him as the Yemenis did with Ali Abdullah Saleh. Nor did their leader escape as happened in Tunisia.

Yes, Egypt has astonished the world with its revolution and certainly Arabs took inspiration from it and the Tunisian revolution. They were galvanized by both revolutions and closely watched them and wanted a piece of the action in their own countries. Discontent with Arab regimes was high and autocratic Arab rulers strongly believed that only death could uproot them. Sadly, the aged Arab leaders never wanted to learn or give political reform a try—perhaps out of fear, or perhaps not. Had they read history they would have known that the Roman statesman Cato the Elder studied Greek at the age of eighty, and that Johann Wolfgang Goethe finished his masterpiece *Faust* when he was over eighty. The reluctance of aging heads of Arab states to leave office reminded me of Sophocles' famous aphorism: "Nobody loves life like an old man." These autocratic and stubborn Arab rulers have been determined to stay in power until the last minute. In fact, Mubarak once said that he holds a "doctorate in stubbornness." Yes, there are changing political realities in the Arab world today. Yet while the Arab Spring has brought down totalitarian governments in Tunisia, Egypt, and Libya, the monarchies of the Arab world (particularly of the Gulf region) have managed to weather the mayhem. This is a topic that deserves research from Middle East scholars.

Egypt today can also help in the process of accelerating the momentum of political reform in African countries south of the Sahara due to its large population and the affinity Africans hold to its culture and history. In 2011, the year of Arab uprisings and revolutions, we also saw political protests in the sub-Saharan African states of Uganda and the Ivory Coast. If Gamal Abdel Nasser was strong in his support of African states against foreign occupation in the 1950s and 1960s, Egyptians today must also stand side by side with their follow Africans in their struggle to liberate their nations from political corruption and autocratic regimes—and from growing Western influence also, which mainly aims at manipulating their resources. In this Facebook-Twitter cyberspace age, Egyptians must now look south and start engaging with and assist their troubled fellow Sub-Saharan Africans toward economic and political independence in the same manner that Nasser did. President Mohamed Morsi, Egypt's first civilian president chosen by the people, should engage from early on in his presidency in intensive dialogue with African nations, not just with ones north of the Sahara but also with those south of the Sahara. Social diplomacy should play a vital role in his administration's attempt to settle the dispute over Nile water between Egypt and its Nile basin African neighbors. Sadly, the Mubarak regime damaged relationship with the Nile Basin countries

End of "Clash of Civilizations"

The Arab revolutions have proved the West's misunderstanding of the Arabs—this Orientalist notion that they are "background" and resent living in a democratic sphere. The downfall of Mubarak and other Arab autocratic regime has proved the end of Samuel Huntington's "clash of civilizations" thesis that claims that the post-Cold War era will be marked by civilizational conflicts in which humans are divided into different cultural blocks: Islamic, Hindu, Western Christian and Jewish, and more. In his opinion, Islamic civilization will be the most problematic one. Their culture, he argued, lacks the core political value needed for the establishment of pluralism, democracy, and other liberal ideas. Arabs and Muslims' regard is to their religion and not their nation-state, added Huntington.[747] However, the Arab Spring revolutions have proven Huntington wrong because Arabs long for democracy and pluralism. They are nationalists and just like people in other nations. It is high time that we dismissed the myth of the clash of civilizations.

In the digital age, it no longer matters who you are, or where you are from, as one can communicate with people across the world. When the Tunisians took out to the streets, a twenty-year-old Egyptian said that he felt he is Tunisian educating us that home is not just a matter of birth certificate but of deep feeling. When the massive human tragedy happened in Japan due to the earthquake one felt he was Japanese. Our heart was with all of them and we wished we could be with them and help as much as we could. As technology speeds and distance shortens we will physically be able to move from one continent to another in short periods of time. With this we will see more demand for the downfall of autocratic regimes across the world. There will be more dialogue among nations and not less, one based on understanding and respect of each other's culture and social values. The massive political changes that swept the Arab world in such a short time are a perfect evidence of the death of the "clash of civilizations" proposition. And from this part of the world, the Middle East, which is rich in culture and history, I commend every Westerner institution and individual who has worked to wipe out this nonsense from the world's minds. And on top of them is *The New York Times*, which ran a column by David Brooks three weeks after Mubarak's ouster arguing that revolutions in the Arab world have closed the chapter of the clash of civilizations.[748] Nabil Abdel Fattaah, head of the Cairo-based Al-Ahram Center for Sociological and Historical Studies, agrees with America's newspaper of record, stressing that the change of regimes in Egypt and Tunisia has abolished the "so-called clash of civilizations" from the "lingo" of world affairs.[749]

Westerner intellectuals who claimed that democracy cannot be implemented in the Arab world were wrong. What worries me though is that a twenty-first-century form of democracy cannot be implemented unless it is founded on open market economies and the rise of the powerful—of people who have the wealth. This will further widen the gaps between rich and poor and among the Arab masses. Over the past decade, corporate greed in the Arab world has resulted in corporate dictatorship. Since I came back to live in Egypt in 2004, I saw a ruling corporatocracy championed by Gamal Mubarak and the capital greed of his friends in government, many of whom were businessmen. Gamal's corporatism with its unbridled greed and corruption was the propeller of the 2011 Revolution. They cared only about making profit while leaving hospitals and schools degraded. Following the resignation of his father, there were daily reports in the Arab press that lands were sold below market price to Gamal's buddies and Egyptian and Arab businessmen. Many Westerner leaders, who now speak with loud applause of Arab revolutions, were friends of Arab dictators; they were bonded together by a desire to make money. When visiting Tahrir Square ten says after Mubarak's demise, British Prime Minister David Cameron said that the view that Arabs cannot handle democracy is no longer applicable. But I also wish to remind Mr. Cameron of these words by Chinese writer Lu Xun: "Before the revolution we were slaves, then we became slaves to former slaves."

To sum up, the Arab world is no longer cut off from the outside world, but Arab ordeal will continue with tyrant rulers refusing to step down or to accept political reform that allow for a wider participation of their people in the political process. It is true that the West ought to change its perception of the Arab world because the brave work of Arab youth has proved that reform and political change can take place in the region. But it is also true that it takes years for a "true" democracy that is compatible with that in the West to be implemented. When pushing hard for democracy this often results in chaos, as we have seen in Somalia and in Iraq. Revolutions do not necessarily produce stable democratic regimes where human rights are respected, and one needs only to look at today's Iran to get a feeling of that. The West needs to exercise caution when helping Arabs to embrace democracy, for a Western-style form of democracy may not be applicable in the region where cultural norms still play a major role in daily life.

Rise of the Egyptian Dream

The two years that followed the Egyptian Revolution have been a trying time. Today's Egypt is staggered by economic mess, poor health care system, deteriorating social programs, and lack of security. Yet many of the Egyptians whom I spoke with in November 2012 remained hopeful and claimed that they were seeing signs of progress. But the confrontation between Morsi's supporters—who are mainly Islamists and members of the Muslim Brotherhood—and opponents that began late in November and heated up in early December (with thousands of Egyptians demonstrating at Tahrir and marching toward the presidential palace on December 4 calling for the "downfall of the regime" and denouncing Morsi's consolidation of power) indicated at the time that Morsi's period in office was limited. The greatest blunder of Morsi's government was its consolidation of power, a move that frightened many Egyptians.

No matter who is in office, Egypt's transition from dictatorship toward democracy will take time, simply because corruption remains widespread in the country. Undoubtedly, political unrest has hurt the country's economy and push toward political reform but signs of improvement in the Egyptian economy have emerged in mid-September 2012 due to talks held with the International Monetary Fund over a loan, attraction of foreign investors, and an increase in tourism. In that same month, a group of American businesspeople and government officials paid a high profile visit to the North African state and met with their Egyptian counterparts in an attempt to give a push to business between the two countries and tackle the issue of U.S. economic aid to Cairo. But one cannot deny that the visit also carried political implication, that of insuring American influence on the emerging regime of Morsi after the downfall of its three-decade-old ally Mubarak.

Following the detainment of members of the Mubarak regime, and the Arab uprisings that followed, some Arabs spoke of a Pax-Aegyptiaca—the rise of

Egyptian influence in the Arab world. Others were more precise in their definition, calling it the emergence of the "Egyptian Dream." The 2011 Revolution has revived a dream in the minds and hearts of Egyptians that their country's future will be a shining one. I was asked right after Mubarak stepped down of the characteristics of the president whom I view best to serve Egypt and the issues he or she should tackle right away. I said Egypt needs a president who is honest and vigorously works to promote the economy, insure a fairer distribution of wealth, and bring an end to corruption and political repression. But I cautioned that this is a process that takes time and Egyptians must be patient. Sociology professor Hoda Zakaria said she is waiting to see a president for Egypt such as Menes—the pharaoh who united Upper and Lower Egypt—and Mohamed Ali Pasha who modernized Egypt in the first half of the nineteenth century.[750] Professor Amin stressed that Egyptians must liberate themselves from foreign influence, from powerful Western nations imposing their control on poor nations. He added that he is optimistic, though, about the future of Egypt because things cannot get worse than it was.[751] The question once again is: Can the Egyptian dream of ending corruption and social division and enhancing people's standards of living be accomplished? Yes, it can, particularly if Egyptians focus their attention on the following issues which I see as crucial for their country's advancement:

- End corruption in politics and all aspects of life.
- Free their media from government restrictions and monopoly.
- Overhaul the country's education system.
- Do not primarily depend on income from tourism, Suez Canal, and gas sales.
- Produce and export more than they import.

Mahfouz described his masterpiece *Children of Gabalawi*—the first novel to write following the 1952 Revolution—as a search for justice and a big dream toward achieving it. And one can prognosticate that if the distinguished Egyptian novelist was living today he would have also described the 2011 Revolution as a dream for justice because of all the challenges Egypt is facing today. The January Revolution was a true test of not only Egyptians' patriotism but of their courage. Never before did I see an increase in national songs and in people's respect for others at public places—at supermarkets, gas stations, and crowded areas, which venturing into them before the revolution was a nightmare because of lack of organization. Never before did I see such a passion among Egyptians living abroad for their homeland, to see it rise again on the world center stage. But can Egyptians achieve their dream of economic development and democratization—of bread, freedom, social justice, and human dignity? The renowned Egyptian-British cardiologist Magdi Yacoub stressed that it is only through science and research can Egyptians achieve their dream. Professor Yacoub said he is "seventy percent" hopeful that Egyptians would reach their goal.

Like it or not, an Egyptian dream has risen in the minds and hearts of Egyptians and they will eventually achieve their dream; but the process may take longer time than they have anticipated. The revolution did not end on February 11 but has continued thereafter with more lives lost, and it is very likely that other lives will be lost in the months to come. Children at primary schools, such as my nine-year-old niece, are now sticking on their chests plastic cards with photos of the "Youth of the January 25 Revolution." The "Mubarak'" metro station was changed to the "Martyrs" station. An *"Encyclopedia of the Martyrs"* was founded by an Egyptian university. Egyptian flags now hang from the balconies of some private residences as a sign of happiness and pride—a tradition that I rarely saw in the country prior to the revolution. But I also continue to see men of the Mubarak regime instilling fear among Egyptians either by promoting cowardly acts or spreading rumors. And yes, the media have propagandized their lies in a manner that makes one wonder who is confusing the public. In the mist of this atmosphere of distrust that has been engulfing Egypt in the revolution's aftermath, there remains hope among Egyptians. As Lewis Greiss, former chief editor of *Sabah El-Kheir* magazine, said in an interview with the state TV station Nile Family in June, 2012, no nation could have lived for sixteen months in this atmosphere without suffering a shortage of bread, but Egyptians got by, simply because they are "kind" people who work diligently and help each other "in silence."[752]

Like other world revolutions, the main goal of the Egyptian revolution was ending corruption and the establishment of a better distribution of wealth, and Egyptians can learn from the past experiences of Turkey, Malaysia, Brazil, Singapore, and Spain. After Mubarak's demise, Egyptian intellectuals spoke of what political system would best suit their country. When speaking of imperialism in Egypt, some made reference to the Marxist-Leninist view.[753] Taha Abdel Aleem called on Egyptians to dispel the "capitalism of corruption" that governed Egypt prior to the revolution. With the help of advancements in science and technology Western democracy has become a model to follow in terms of improving the lives of its citizens. He added that we cannot deny that Soviet socialism has made "historic achievements in the fields of manufacture, science and technology, arms, and space. It has caught up with Western capitalism and even advanced ahead of it at times in these fields." But, continued Aleem, "we cannot overlook the great human cost of its unguided use of resources to achieve progress in the periods that followed." Progress is inclusive and failure of one of its foundation can result in stagnation followed by disintegration. Egypt's progress will be reached when we the country is economically self-sufficient; democratic-political progress will be reached when we have instituted a political system founded on the supremacy of law, political participation and a multiparty system, religious and racial tolerance, and peaceful exchange of leadership.[754] But there were also those who raised doubts that democracy as a system always works. From the day of Mubarak's departure, writers and cartoonist at the Egyptian press cautioned that democracy has its drawbacks and may not be easy to obtain as some think. A caricature in the party paper *Al-Ahrar* showed the word "democracy" in a huge sea wave that is reaching to an individual who represents the world and about to drown him.[755] If Egyptians succeed in building a unique form of democracy, theirs will be a model for Arab countries to emulate; it will be a giant elephant on the banks of the Nile River that the Arabs can examine every time they pay a trip to their neighbor state.

In Chapter 9, I stressed that one of the great victories of the revolution I witnessed at the time was the rise of presidential debate—a political practice which I have glorified. The second victory of the revolution is how it has revived Egyptians' interest in politics. Before the revolution, most Egyptians were apathetic to the elections, and that was evidenced by low turnout at the ballot box. But this is not to say that Egyptians never had an interest in politics. Egyptians have always had a passion for politics, but prior to the revolution they spoke of politics in private. After February 11, 2011, all this has changed, with politics becoming an adrenaline for public life in the Land of the Nile. Even senior Egyptian citizens speak politics today. My seventy-two mother asked her mom about whom she was going to elect for president? The grandmother, aged ninety, condemned Mubarak because she said his rule made people hate him. "Daughter," she said in a low voice, "this election is important because during King Farouk's time they used to inherit the throne from their fathers, and then came Mohamed Naguib, Nasser and Sadat, followed by Mubarak who held to power and never wanted to leave. He wanted his son to inherit the presidency. Damn him! It is good that he has gone. Life will be better after him." Now that my grandmother is gone, her words often inspire me hope about Egypt's future. Every time I see Egypt inching toward trouble, I remember her words.

Caution and Fear

It's hard to start a revolution. Even harder to continue it. And hardest of all to win it. But, it's only afterwards, when we have won, that the true difficulties begin. In short, Ali, there's still much to do. *The Battle of Algiers* (1966)

Egypt has been embroiled in protests demanding rapid political reform, trial of the regime of the ousted president and his family, and the drafting of a new constitution that wins people's approval. And with the exception of the latter, it has succeeded, and we witnessed Mubarak and his two sons and a number of members of his regime standing trial. But Egyptians should also remember that revolutions rarely follow the designs set for them; they are often diverged. The complexities of post-revolution politics in Egypt and months of periodic clashes since Mubarak's downfall have cast a show over the North African state's transition toward political reform. Till I handed this book to the publisher, Egyptians have continued to claim that the acts of violence taking place in the country was deliberately made in order to frighten people to get them to accept a Mubarak-like regime as seen in prime minister Shafiq running for the presidency. Incidents of violence and lawlessness—or what some have described as a "counter revolution"—have continued. From the time the first transitional government was formed in February, Egyptians, including journalists, have been speaking of a "counter revolution". "What I most fear about the Revolution is the counter revolution," wrote columnist Yasser El-Zayat in the independent *El-Fagr* newspaper. He cautioned that the counter revolution has the "mechanisms and tools" via which it can operate, the most important of which is an "alliance between corrupt businessmen and corrupt security intelligence men."[756] Such thought was further stressed when a Coptic church in the village of Sol in Atfeeh, south of Cairo, was set on fire in March 2011, resulting in violent clashes erupting and the death of thirteen people and injury of one hundred and forty. Other clashes and horrible acts did take place against Copts and in public places, such as the Port Said football stadium tragedy of February 1, 2012, often without definite answers to the question of who was the actual perpetrator.

Egyptians are in a state of political exhaustion due to repetitious shifts in the laws, struggles among political parties, contradictory decisions, and a monopoly of media coverage. This stagnated transition, this mounting revolt, is worrying. Egypt is not Tunisia and it is not Libya; it has a bigger population and more political stature on the world stage. And it is certainly not used to violence; the latest violent incidents have alarmed some Egyptians. Egyptians need a leader, not a preacher. Islamist cronyism must end. Morsi, a stalwart of the MB, has lost much of his appeal already and disappointed those who voted for him. Today in Egypt I've heard some people shy away from saying the word "revolution," their optimistic projections in 2011 already shattered. I have heard people question what has changed in Egypt since the revolution—with continued clashes and protests, no constitution, no parliament, and an economy on the brink causing instability. Immediately following the toppling of Mubarak, Heikel (who served as editor in chief of *Al-Ahram* newspaper and advisor to President Gamal Abdel Nasser) cautioned of the possibility of the emergence of a counter revolution, and he was right. Others—both journalists and non-journalists—also spoke from early on of a conspiracy theory taking place. To say that the prisoners who escaped during the revolution and have been absconding cannot be captured is, in my opinion, naïve and results in a false sense of security in Egypt. This sense of worry among Egyptians has resulted in the whirlpool of protests to continue. Many of the current protesters are public sector employees demanding better employment terms and tenure in their jobs.

It is a mistake to think that the nature of trouble in post-revolution Egypt is primarily economic or social; it is both political and systemic. What is sad about Tahrir Square today is how it has turned from being a symbol of the revolution, the Tiananmen Square of the Arabs, to being a place full of trash, burned tents, traffic chaos, and burglars. The question that many have been asking for months is what makes it difficult for the state and its security officials to clean it and bring it back to what it used to be—a symbol of the revolution. It seems that remnants of the Mubarak regime want to convince people that the revolution and revolutionaries should be the ones to blame. But Egyptians, particularly youth, are smart enough not to accept this propaganda.[757] Public distrust of the Supreme Council of the Armed Forces (SCAF) and also of leaders of the Muslim Brotherhood was mounting (clash between the Brotherhood and SCAF was also rising particularly after the dissolution of the Islamist-dominated Parliament). The unelected, aged military generals were really the ones running the country until Morsi pushed them into retirement. But aficionados of the military remain.

One pessimist, a teacher, told me in mid-2012 that after Mubarak's downfall Egyptians were anticipating a utopia but it turned out to be a dystopia. If Egyptians would have just followed the Tunisia model and demanded the downfall of the entire political system and those who were part of, or worked alongside with, the Mubarak regime things would have been fine by now. A new constitution should have been written immediately following Mubarak's departure. Egypt is in dire need of a constitution that respects the rule of law, individual rights, and basic freedoms, and this will be its next major challenge. Good times are not around for the country; Egyptians are tired and fear that their revolution may be dying. Remnants of the Mubarak regime still hold power at various governmental and nongovernmental institutions. But Egyptian youth have become revolutionaries and they will no longer accept any form of oppression. I often heard them say: "revolution until victory." They were the ones who did all the work; they fought tough battles and slept on the streets for days to secure a better future for their country. Some of them gave their lives for what they believed in; others are willing to do same. And as long as we live we'll demand justice for them, justice for the mothers who lost their loved ones—some of them were aged less than twenty.

In many ways, I see the incitement of division between Egyptian Muslims and Copts as nothing new; it resembles what the British did in Egypt right before and after the 1919 Revolution to counter the national movement which demanded Egypt's independence from British occupation. As they did in 2011, the Egyptians of the 1919 Revolution—Copts, Jews, and Muslims—were smart enough to realize that and quickly regrouped and stood united in face of the outside occupier. It is worth mentioning that the British also influenced the content of the Egyptian press to their favor in the same manner that the Mubarak regime did with the state-owned media. Throughout history Egypt's Muslim and Coptic communities stood side-by-side. We must all denounce and condemn extremism, but to say that the revolution was losing its vigor and dividing Egyptians is a condemnation of the Egyptian people themselves. At the end of the 1950s Egyptian movie "Between the Two Palaces," the director of this masterpiece (which is based on a novel known as *Palace Walk* by Mahfouz) showed real images of protesters of the 1919 Revolution. Published in 1956, Mahfouz's novel shows Cairo during and right after World War I. In it, we see a priest named Sergeous standing on the podium at a mosque preaching national unity among Egyptians in their fight against British occupation. It is a scene that has always captured the attention of Egyptians for decades and empowered the spirit of unity between Copts and Muslims. Sergeous believed that joining the Al-Azhar[758] imams in their work would form a symbol of national unity. In the years that followed the 1919 Revolution, many religious figures followed the footsteps of Sergeous.

The triumphant, popular Egyptian uprising has brought fruit but the road is still bumpy ahead. I have heard those who argue that the fate of the revolution has become cloudy because of some trouble-making Egyptians. I have heard those who said they got rid of a secular democracy to be ruled by an Islamist autocracy. Alas, there remains discomfort over the Brotherhood's political agenda and whether Morsi has actually detached himself from the group. Secular revolutionaries are concerned over Morsi running the nation. They fear that Morsi and "fundamentalists" in his government could turn Egypt into a religious state, but this is most unlikely because they know that the majority of Egyptians will not accept this. We are in fact beginning to hear voices calling for the downfall of Morsi. Egyptians must continue to keep an eye on Morsi's government, particularly at a time where there is no parliament in operation and the president holds massive powers—both the legislative and presidential powers. Even after this is achieved, the notion that the public is the "eye on government" must be installed in the minds of the Egyptian people. It is only through this notion that the West has been able to establish democracies that are the envy of the world.

Egyptian protesters used more perseverance, resolve, and heroism than violence to achieve their goals. But there remains until this day questions that need clear answers: Who opened the prison cells and burned police stations at the same time. Who is the beneficiary of the burning of secret police files? Who burned courts which held no secret information? Who benefits from spreading this state of chaos in the country—in sports stadium and government buildings? We may never find clear answers for all these questions, what I know is that I saw a community spirit rise among Egyptians from all walks of life and ages that later inspired many other Arab communities to revolt against their bureaucratic ruling regimes. I will never forget those little kids, which I referred to in Chapter 4, who walked out on the streets of our neighborhood holding sticks in their hands imitating what their parents and older brothers were doing in the evening of January 30, 2011, in order to protect their communities against looting and vandalism.

Post-Revolution Media

While journalists have gained a little more freedom in Egypt's independent and partisan press following the revolution, no improvement in the state media has been achieved. In the period that SCAF was running the country, the state media were consistently praising the generals until they were pushed out of power. You often saw criticism of officials who are from the Muslim Brotherhood but not of those who are "not Islamists"—a strange endorsement by editors which I believe was installed in the state media during Mubarak's days to justify his atrocity toward the group. Even though I entirely endorse the notion of the separation of religion from the state, individuals and groups should have the right to express their viewpoints as long as they not insult or dehumanize others. The state media cunningly cautioned of Islamists holding a majority in Parliament and the implication of that for Egypt's future political landscape and stability. Although I saw the domination of Parliament by Islamists as one of the drawbacks of democracy, dissolving the Parliament was clearly undemocratic—as undemocratic as the moves taken by Morsi in November to grant himself absolute powers. What is strange is that in the months that followed Morsi's inauguration in office, and until this book was completed, we have witnessed the state present more on the side of government—in defence of a government whose many of its members have direct or indirect ties with the Brotherhood.

On the other side, the independent press has enjoyed slight improvement but lack of investigative journalism founded on facts remains a major setback. Much of their coverage resembles the yellow press, focusing on political scandal but without any effort from journalists to go after the story and dig for facts. The rise of yellow journalism in Egypt (reminiscent of the era of Joseph Pulitzer and William Randolph Hearst in America in the early 1900s) is raising eyebrows among many Egyptians, with distinguished journalists denouncing today's Cairo press as being "sleazy and degrading." Egypt is a pivotal country in the Arab world, and so too should be its media. Egyptians are exasperated and alienated, and this in many ways is because their media do not exert enough efforts to try to offer them the truth—and nothing but the truth. The media, particularly the state ones, have contributed to their alienation by not laboring to report fully and objectively on the chaotic post-Mubarak political scene. There have also been talks among journalists that Morsi is attempting to silence criticism of him in the media, with journalists of the independent media cautioning that Egypt may soon be ruled by "another pharaoh," that they have replaced one autocratic leader with another. One journalist blamed the Egyptian people for that—for putting too much trust in Morsi and fully endorsing his moves. To show resentment of Morsi's consolidation of power and a draft constitution hastily embraced by his allies, many of the country's independent newspapers ceased production on December 4.

Sadly, editors of all different Egyptian press systems have cared more about the opinions of politicians and other political insiders than their audiences—particularly ordinary citizens—when deciding which stories to cover in the 2012 presidential elections. It was bizarre also to see how the state television stations in particular and a number of privately owned ones that directly or indirectly have links with the former regime were cautious not to downgrade those in power and often showed protesters at Tahrir generally as men in beards while in reality most of them represented a mixture of the whole Egyptian society, a blend of liberals and Islamists. In this sense, I must admit that the Western media have given a truer and more accurate picture of events in post-revolution Egypt than the Egyptian media themselves have done. I can attest to this; I have watched, read, and analyzed both their coverage. Yes, the Egyptian media have a long way to go to liberate themselves from this culture of manufacturing biased news and viewing their audiences as of little value.

Post-Revolution U.S.–Egyptian Ties

In the post-revolution era, Egyptian intellectuals hold various views of the United States and its relations with the Arabs—some are even suspicion of such ties. After all, American presidents have always supported autocratic Arab leaders. The hypocrisy is legendary. Gamal Asaad, a writer and thinker, claims America knows nothing but protecting its interests and that is why it has unwritten agreements with the Muslim Brotherhood. It was because of this, he added, that Hilary Clinton called for handing authority to Morsi. He stipulated that what pushed America to ally itself with the Brotherhood was Huntington's thesis of the clash of civilizations, with the aim of replacing ideological conflicts with religious conflicts in which "an alliance between Christian Europe and the Jews" is formed on one side to confront Muslims, Confucians, and the Orthodox of the East on the other side.[759] Hard-line Islamist Hazim Abu Ismail who ran as a presidential candidate but was dispelled from the elections because his mother carries a U.S. citizenship claimed that the United States still runs Egypt. The "political decision-makers of Morsi are America, and I am extremely amazed by the American cleverness in running Egypt's internal affairs." He added that Morsi's firing of the SCAF generals was a U.S.-approved act.[760]

The January 25 Revolution has dramatically changed the Arab world but not necessarily in the manner America has wished. Instability in the Arab world today can hurt America's economic and political interests in the region, from safeguarding oil to protecting Israel's security. American politics, particularly under the Barack Obama administration, has shown that it has no problem dealing with the Muslim Brotherhood or Islamist governments that rose after the Arab Spring had ousted long-standing Arab regimes. Islamist government has surfaced in both Tunisia and Egypt. But anyone who knows the politics and history of the Middle East also realizes that there will be hurdles in America's dealing with Islamist groups emerging in post-revolution Arab states, even though they said they would abide by international peace treaties. The role religion will play in politics in these states will pose challenges for Washington's future relations with Islamist governments.

Tension between Cairo and Washington over an American film which Muslims view as insulting to the Prophet Muhammad mounted in September of 2012, resulting in five days of protests in front of the U.S. embassy in Cairo and an attack on it. Protesters' attack on the embassy on September 11 resulted in its vandalism and U.S. flag torn down. Morsi did not quickly condemn the attack, which was aired on television worldwide, and this did further enflamed American public opinion. (The situation was worse in Libya where the American consulate in Benghazi was attacked resulting in the death of the American ambassador and three other embassy staff.) Morsi finally replied, stating that he "could never condone" the attacks on U.S. buildings in the region, but Washington was annoyed by Morsi's slow initial response. Following the attack, the U.S. President pointed out in an interview with the Spanish-language network Telemundo that he does see Egypt as either an ally or an enemy. "I don't think that we would consider them an ally, but we don't consider them an enemy." His comment has shown that ties between the two countries are passing through a delicate time.

The Obama administration's reaction was to condemn the film but reject censoring it because that would mean an infringement on free speech. The Morsi administration strongly criticized the film and called for placing a ban on it. In their speeches at the UN General Assembly conference which began on September 26 both Obama and Morsi held to their views. Obama defended freedom of speech in America and denounced "violence and intolerance;" while Morsi strongly condemned the U.S.-produced film that ridiculed Islam. In an interview with *The New York Times* on September 22, Morsi proclaimed that America needs to "fundamentally change" its approach in dealing with the Arab world by exhibiting more respect toward Arab values and assist in establishing a Palestine state. Morsi stressed that if Washington wants Egypt to honor its peace treaty with Israel, it should honor its own Camp David commitment to Palestinian self-rule. He observed that Egypt and America can be "real friends" but admitted that tension exists currently, adding that the ball is now in their court. He pointed out that it was up to the United States to mend ties with the Arab world and to rejuvenate its partnership with Egypt.[761]

In conclusion one must also cite here the sense of anger he has witnessed among Egyptians for what they called Washington's silence over Morsi's grab of sweeping powers. Most Egyptians say the Obama administration should have cautioned the Morsi government that unless it responses to people's demands Washington will not support it and could cut economic aid to Cairo. I have no doubt, however, that Cairo and Washington will eventually be able to repair their ties which have been strained over the past two years, simply because both nations have a long history of warm relations. And certainly meetings between leaders and intellectuals from both countries and debates over insuring the rights of the Copts and minorities in Egypt and countering Islamophobia in America can help in the process.

Final Note

Over the first six months of Morsi's rule, disillusioned Egyptians have been trying to decipher the meaning of events engulfing them, particularly following the clashes that broke out over the president's power grab and a draft constitution which was edited at the last minute to remove language explicitly guaranteeing the rights of minorities. Egypt sank into new chaos after Morsi issued a decree on November 22 that granted him overwhelming executive powers and an Islamist-dominated constitutional assembly hurriedly approved a new constitution to go to a referendum on December 15. (The assembly approved the draft constitution which advances the role of Islam and restricts freedom of speech and assembly.) Protests and clashes broke out between Islamists and liberals/

seculars in front of the presidential palace on December 4 in which seven people died and over six hundred got injured. This political crisis left the country in a state of uncertainty and raised doubts about Morsi's future in the presidency. It resulted in the deployment of the Republican Guard to separate the opponents and protect the palace. Six of Morsi's advisors resigned.

Morsi's dispassionate televised speech on December 6 offered little solution; it served as nothing but a call for more confrontation between Islamists and seculars. He refused to annul the decree and instead charged remnants of the Mubarak regime of being behind the clashes, insisting that the referendum on the disputed draft constitution will go as planned. The opposition denounced Morsi's speech and the protests continued; I heard people calling for the "downfall of the regime," the same chant which brought down Mubarak and captivated the West. There were others who shouted bluntly: "We want the downfall of Morsi." Morsi's irrational speech took place at a time when his aides were in the U.S. capital promoting their country as a new democracy. Washington urged both sides to engage in dialogue, and there were rumors that the Obama Administration was delaying Morsi's U.S. visit to February instead of December.[762]

It is anticipated that protests and sporadic clashes will be the norm in Egypt for a year or two more before we begin to see the fruit of true democratic reform showing forth in the Land of the Nile. Morsi's biggest error was not calling for a freeze on the drafting of the constitution and granting the staff judiciary the same power which he had stripped from them just days before the clashes erupted. In addition, both his supporters and opponents have been acting abominably, bracing more for confrontational rather than dialogue on various issues.

Many Egyptian intellectuals and public figures such as Mohamed ElBaradei, former head of the UN's nuclear watchdog, Amr Moussa, former Arab League head, and Mohamed Hasseinein Heikel who served as editor of the giant *Al-Ahram* newspaper and as an advisor to President Gamal Abdel Nasser, offered Egyptians a sense of cautious optimism. Morsi, said ElBaradei, must cancel the constitutional amendments and try to rescue what is left of his authority. In an interview with CBC television station on December 5, Heikel observed that these protests revived in our minds memories of the protests of January 25, 2011. He added that Morsi must carefully consider his decisions and their consequences at a crucial time in the history of Egypt. I wish the President does not place the country in "a dreadful end." He called on him to initiate dialogue with all political forces, including youth. Hamdeen Sabbahi, a former presidential candidate, cautioned that Morsi is "driving Egypt towards more division and confrontation."

Egyptians anticipated seeing a constitution which fully protects human rights, reduces military's role in public life and prohibits its persecution of civilians, and enhances the rights of women. They were not opposed to the appointment of a new general persecutor but wanted that to be conducted not by the president himself but via election supervised by the independent judiciary. Successive waves of street unrest continue as of this writing. Among the events that took place during those two months and which led to polarization in Egyptian politics was a court order to re-open the trial of Mubarak, who lodged an appeal against his life sentence. Egyptians were split on the decision; some were saying that the court would "free" Mubarak from his life sentence and others were arguing that Morsi was just fulfilling the promise he had made to those who called for a new trial for the deposed president, because he does deserve capital punishment. On the second anniversary of the revolution, clashes erupted in many major cities in the country between Morsi's opponents and security forces in which more than seventy people were killed, with army chief Abdul Fattah el-Sisi cautioning that these political strikes were pushing the state to the brink of collapse. Late in February, Morsi pushed forward the date of the start of parliamentary elections to April 22. The main opposition, the National Salvation Front, declared a boycott of the poll.

Over those eight months of stagnated transition, revolt mounted against Morsi (and the Brotherhood) due to his haughty disdain for working-class citizens and civil liberties. Lately, I have witnessed some Egyptians shying away from saying the word "revolution"; their optimistic projections in 2011 have been shattered. Yes, the picture of the country's first freely elected president has been tarnished in the minds of many Egyptians who are today shouting that they need a leader, not a preacher, and that Islamist cronyism must end. Morsi will not remain in office for long; in fact, I anticipate that he will be pushed out of office—possibly by the army—prior to the end of 2013. He has been employing the same techniques Mubarak used, such as invoking emergency law, to crush popular unrest. It would be foolish to believe those who are propagating the notion today that Egyptians are vying for a Mubarak-like "secular" autocrat to rule them. The people, especially the younger generation, in the Land of the Nile have tasted freedom and there is no going back for them. They have no nostalgia for the old order—for a renewed dictatorship—and they will not rest until they have their "bread, freedom, social justice, and human dignity." Our hearts are with them.

Egyptian society is not rebelling against Islam but against decades of dictatorial rule. And yes, one cannot rule out that remnants of the Mubarak regime may be fuelling division among Egyptians (possibly with assistance from Saudi Arabia which wants to keep its citizens from rebelling against the King) on the hope that they come back in office or continue their corruption in the North African state. I have also heard Egyptians claiming that America is behind this and referring to former Secretary of State Condoleezza Rice's "creative chaos" aphorism.

No one knows the truth. What we know is that Morsi's term is finished; he is in Mubarak's moment. Even if he retreats from his decisions, Egyptian youth will not stop their opposition to him and to the Brotherhood affiliates holding power. The country is certainly in for tougher times and will witness more spasms of violence, but justice will eventually win out. Egyptians will enjoy the fruit of their struggle in the not too distant future, simply because they know the way to Tahrir Square.

Dedication

This book is dedicated to my beloved grandmother, Haneim, who died a year after the revolution, in July 2012, at the age of ninety, after battling illness for two years. Even on her death bed, she always prayed for Egypt and "its youth"—for a better future for them and all the voices that have called for end to injustice in the Arab world.

She constantly held great hope for the future of post-revolution Egypt. At a time when Egyptians were living in disillusionment because many of the events that were happening around them were incomprehensible, she always advised her large family "not to worry" because Egypt would be safe. She loved the revolutionary voices in her family and they loved her; she loved Egypt and Egypt loved her. She was a very kind woman indeed, a symbol of motherhood, of Egypt, and she met her illness with great courage.

Though illiterate, my grandmother frequently engaged in debates on politics, and I never saw her weep — except once, when I told her that there are mothers in many parts of Egypt who continue to shed tears for the loved ones they lost in the January 25, 2011, Revolution, and they want justice for them. Sitting in the balcony of her residence in a remote village located seventy miles north of Cairo, and with a breeze of fresh air coming from the Nile River close-by, she raised her hands up high in the sky as if she was trying to reach the stars and prayed that justice be served for the "martyrs of the revolution." This was her wish, and I saw her pronounce it; I heard her call for justice so that we all live in a world that tolerates people who voice different views than ours or call for the downfall of dictatorial regimes.

And, yes, she supported Mohamed Morsi and denounced Ahmed Shafiq during the presidential elections, though she agreed that Morsi would not last for long in the post-revolution upheaval.

Minutes before her death, she whispered: "Daughters! Where are you?" Her four daughters, who were sitting on the bed next to hers, rushed to her side. She refused to say she was in pain, or that she was dying (because Egypt cannot die), and she again raised her hands up—but this time not so high—and she paid farewell to our world, to her beloved Egypt, to her kingdom.

The passionate ninety-year-old woman died, but Egypt will live. "Egypt will cross this hurdle as it has done with others," she once told me, while tightly pressing on my hand. May the soul of my grandmother rest in peace and may her wishes come true. May the world unite to help insure that trials be held for those who killed, or contributed to the extermination of, hundreds of people in cold blood during the eighteen-day Egyptian revolution. May all the mothers who lost their sons, daughters, and husbands during the Arab Spring obtain justice for them—justice that comforts their souls.

BIBLIOGRAPHY

Amin, Galal. Egypt and Egyptians in Mubarak's Age (1981-2008). Cairo: Merit, 2009). [In
Arabic]

Brooks, David. "Huntington's Clash Revisited." *The New York Times*, March 3, 2011, http://www.nytimes.com/2011/03/04/opinion/04brooks.html (accessed March 5, 2011).

El-Bendary, Mohamed. The Egyptian Press and Coverage of Local and International Events. Lanham, MD: Lexington Books, 2010.

El-Bendary, Mohamed. *The "Ugly American" in the Arab Mind: Why Do Arabs Resent America*. Dulles, VA: Potomac Books, 2011.

El-Hakim,Tawfiq. *The Revolution of Youths*. Cairo: Misr Bookstore, 1975. [In Arabic.]

Gharbal, Mohamed Shafiq. *The Formation of Egypt Across Ages*. 2nd ed. 1957. Reprint, Cairo: The General Egyptian Book Organization, 1996. [In Arabic.]

Hamdan, Gamal. *Egypt's Personality: A Study of the Ingenuity of the Place*. Cairo, Egypt: Dar Al-Hilal, 1967. [In Arabic.]

Hamed, Raof Abbas. Forty Years on the July Revolution: An Historical Study. Cairo: Al-Ahram Center for Political and Strategic Studies, 1992. [In Arabic.]

Hammad, Ahmed Samir. "The Assumed Arab Groups on the Internet: An Analytical Study of the Dimensions of Arab Social Networking on the Web." Ph.D. Dissertation, Al-Azhar University, 2011. [In Arabic.]

Howeidy, Amira. "Between Two Constitutions." *Al-Ahram Weekly*, March 10, 2011.

Huntington, Samuel. *The Clash of Civilization and the Remaking of the World Orders*. New York: Simon and Schuster, 1966.

Issa, Salah. *Constitution in the Rubbish Bin*. Cairo: Cairo Center for Human Rights Studies, 2001. [In Arabic.]

Kirkpatrick, David D. "A Nobelist Has an Unfamiliar Role in Protests." *The New York Times*, January 28, 2011. http://www.nytimes.com (accessed July 26, 2011).

Kirkpatrick, David, and Steven Erlanger. "Egypt's New Leader Spells Out Terms for U.S.-Arab Ties." *The New York Times*, September 21, 2012. http://www.nytimes.com/2012/09/23/world/middleeast/egyptian-leader-mohamed-morsi-spells-out-terms-for-us-arab-ties.html?pagewanted=all&_r=0 (accessed September 28, 2012).

Kotb, Ahmed. "Cyber-Adverts Show Great Potential." *Al-Ahram Weekly*, January 27, 2011, http://www.weekly.ahram.org.eg/2011/1033/ec5.htm (accessed December 12, 2011).

Moussa, Salama. *The Book of Revolutions*. Cairo: Salama Moussa Printing and Distribution, 1954. [In Arabic.]

Rugh, William A. *The Arab Press*. New York: Syracuse University, 1979.

Samuelson, Robert J. "Democracy in America." MSNBC.COM, November 13, 2000. March 21, 2011. http://www.msnbc.com/news/485465.asp (accessed November 13, 2000).

United Nations, *World Population Prospects: The 2010 Revision*. http://esa.un.org/unpd/wpp/index.htm (accessed May 15, 2011).

U.S. State Department, *Bureau of Public Affairs*, November 10, 2010. http://www.state.gov/r/pa/ei/bgn/5309.htm (accessed May 17, 2011).

ENDNOTES

1 This is according to figures released by various news agencies.

2 Elections to the 508-member People's Assembly, or lower house of Parliament, was set between November 28 and January 10, 2012; elections to the Shura Council, or upper house of parliament, was set between January 29 and March 11, 2012.

3 *Radio and Television*, March 12, 2011, 92–93.

4 BBC World, April 12, 2011.

5 See U.S. State Department, Bureau of Public Affairs, November 10, 2010, http://www.state.gov/r/pa/ei/bgn/5309.htm (accessed May 17, 2011); United Nations, World Population Prospects: The 2010 Revision, http://esa.un.org/unpd/wpp/index.htm (accessed May 15, 2011); Population Council, http://popcouncil.org (accessed, May 15, 2011).

6 According to Amina El-Naqkash, editor of the party paper *Al-Ahali*, more than 40 percent of Egyptians live below the level of poverty. See *Al-Ahali*, February 2, 2011, 7.

7 *Radio and Television*, March 12, 2011, 92.

8 *Radio and Television*, March 12, 2011, 92.

9 See *Al-Shorouk Al-Jadeed*, March 22, 2011.

10 *Sabah El-Kheir*, March 1, 2011, 6.

11 Mohamed Ali Pasha (1769-1849) governed Egypt from 1805 to 1848.

12 United Nations, World Population Prospects: The 2010 Revision, http://esa.un.org/unpd/wpp/index.htm (accessed May 15, 2011).

13 Gamal Hamdan, *Egypt's Personality: A Study of the Ingenuity of the Place* (Cairo, Egypt: Dar Al-Hilal, 1967), 295. [In Arabic.]

14 Ibid, 13.

15 Al-Oula, June 7, 2011.

16 Led by Saad Zaghlul (1985-1927), the 1919 Revolution was a nationalist one seeking independence and the founding of constitutional and parliamentary life in Egypt. Zaghlul was the first elected prime minister and his government was established in 1924, a year after the constitution was formed. It was known as the "government of the people."

17 Championed by Colonel Ahmed Urabi Pasha (1841-1911), the 1882 Revolution against Khedive Tawfiq was a pro-democracy that established a constitution and called for equality for people of all faiths living in Egypt at the time. The Urabi Pasha resistance forces were defeated whilst British troops invaded and occupied Egypt in the same year. Urabi Pasha coined a popular phrase often echoed when Egyptians refer to him: "We have been created free, and we will not be enslaved after today."

18 A lawyer and journalist, Mustafa Kamil (1874-1908) was a popular Egyptian nationalist who called for Egypt's independence from British occupation. Among his popular sayings which are often quoted is: "If I were not an Egyptian, I would have wished to be one."

19 *Alwafd*, March 22, 2011, 10.

20 *As-Safir*, May 23, 2012, 8.

21 The only strong support that President Barack Obama had shown toward the Tunisian Revolution was in his State of the Union address on January 25 in which he said the United States backs Tunisia as a nation "where the will of the people proved more powerful than the writ of a dictator. And tonight, let us be clear: **the United States of America stands with the people of Tunisia, and supports the democratic aspirations of all people."**

22 *Radio and Television*, March 12, 2011, 92.

23 On that day President Mubarak made the first of the three televised speeches he delivered during the eighteen day revolution.

24 See *Al-Akhbar*, February 3, 2011, 16.

25 This is according to the ONTV television program "O Tube" broadcast on December 31, 2011. [In Arabic.] See also *Al-Ahram*, April 27, 2012, 5 (Friday Section). [In Arabic.]

26 Naila Hamdy, "Arab Citizen Journalism in Action: Challenging Mainstream Media, Authorities and Media Laws," *Westminster Papers in Communication and Culture* 6, no. 1 (2009), 94.

27 *El-Osboa*, January 31, 2011, 15.

28 This is according to a report by Egypt's Ministry of Communications and Information Technology released in March of 2011, and which stated that Internet users have increased in the North African state by 28 percent in 2010. For more on this see "Internet Users in Egypt Increase 28 Percent Last Year," *Al-Masry Al-Youm*, March 30, 2011 www.almasryalyoum.com/en/node/380145 (accessed December 12, 2011).

29 See http://bikyamasr.com/58693/how-the-arab-spring-has-transformed-journalism (accessed July 22, 2011).

30 See Ahmed Kotb, "Cyber-Adverts Show Great Potential," *Al-Ahram Weekly*, January 27, 2011, www.weekly.ahram.org.eg/2011/1033/ec5.htm (accessed December 12, 2011).

31 *Akhbar El-Yom*, January 29, 22.

32 Ahmed Samir Hammad, "The Assumed Arab Groups on the Internet: An Analytical Study of the Dimensions of Arab Social Networking on the Web," February, 2011, Al-Azhar University Department of Media and Journalism. Ph.D. Dissertation. [In Arabic.]

33 Egyptians are big mobile phone users with an estimate of sixty five million of the country's eighty five million population own mobiles.

34 Al-Shorouk Al-Jadeed, January 29, 2.

35 *Al-Shorouk Al-Jadeed*, March 5, 2011, 14.

36 *Al-Fagr*, March 14, 2011, 15.

37 *Al-Ahram*, March 12, 2011, 10.

38 *Radio and Television*, March 12, 2011, 92.

39 *Radio and Television*, March 12, 2011, 39.

40 *Al-Gomhuria*, March 9, 2011, 13.

41 *Alwafd*, March 13, 2011, 20.

42 *Alwafd*, March 22, 2011, 10.

43 *Al-Shorouk Al-Jadeed*, March 22, 2011, 7.

44 *Al-Akhbar*, February 3, 2011, 17.

45 The general strike by textile workers at factory in the Delta-town of Mahalla on April 6, 2008, was in demanded of better pay and gave birth to the pro-democracy movement.

46 With highly-educated cyberspace members, the independent Egyptian group has been pushing for political reform in Egypt.

47 Ghonim joined the protesters at Tahrir Square from the day it began on January 25. A couple of days later, he disappeared and his family looked for him everywhere—even at the "autopsy". He was kidnapped by the Egyptian secret police without any notification made to his family. After exerted efforts, which reached to the minister of interior, Ghonim was released on February 7. On the same night, Mona El-Shazli of the popular television show "10 p.m." hosted him in an interview which many Egyptians watched and were shaken by his "honesty" and the tears he shed for the lives of his follow comrades who died during the demonstration. The day Mubarak resigned, Ghonim was interviewed from Cairo by CNN and tweeted: "Mission accomplished."

48 During the revolution, Tahrir became the number-one searching topic on the Internet.

49 Almost all of the Facebook pages asked Egyptians to accept the referendum results no matter what their position were.

50 The Mohamed Ali dynasty ruled Egypt for almost a century and a half. It was formed of ten kings, beginning with Mohamed Ali (1805-1848) and ending with King Farouq I whom leaders of the Revolution drove to surrender his throne to his son Fouad II, then a child, on 26 July 1952. In mid-1953, the Republic of Egypt declared the demise of Fouad II.

51 The 1996 press law states that board members must include editors of national press establishments, editors of partisan newspapers, the current chairperson of the Journalists Syndicate and four former chairpersons of the Syndicate of Journalists, and public figures concerned with the press to be selected by the Shura Council.

52 *Sabah El-Kheir*, March 1, 2011, 6.

53 There were also party newspapers founded prior to the 952 Revolution, which nationalized the Egyptian press, and dating back to the end of the nineteenth century. Some went out of business by World War II, others were launched with the establishment of the 1923 Constitution and lasted until the Revolution.

54 This figure was cited by one of the paper's former founders, Hisham Kassem, in an interview with the Egyptian television station ONTV on February 22, 2011.

55 The paper was first launched as a weekly on the Internet in October 2008.

56 The one-party system was eliminated by the constitutional amendments undertaken by President Anwar Sadat. The National Democratic Party, which a president served as its head, ruled Egypt from that time until President Hosni Mubarak resigned on February 11, 2011.

57 William A. Rugh, *The Arab Press* (New York: Syracuse University, 1979).

58 It was dissolved in March by a decision from the Supreme Council of the Armed Forces.

59 *Sabah El-Kheir*, March 1, 2011, 6.

60 For more on the Egyptian press see: Mohamed El-Bendary, *The Egyptian Press and Coverage of Local and International Events* (Washington, DC: Lexington Books, 2011).

61 *Radio and Television*, March 12, 2011, 38-39.

62 *Al-Ahram* ["Youth of January 25" section], March 25, 2011, 4.

63 *Alwafd*, March 13, 2011,1.

64 On January 16, 1953, the Free Officers issued a decree dissolving political parties.

65 Late in 2011, the New Wafd Party publicly declared that it holds no political ties with the Freedom and Justice Party.

66 *Radio and Television*, March 12, 2011, 93.

67 *Al-Ahram*, March 22, 2011, 10.

68 *Al-Ahram* ["Youth of January 25" section], March 25, 2011, 4.

69 In fact, over the past two decades there has been a staggering rise in the number of transitional Arab satellite television stations. This boom is attributed to the Iraq war of 1991 when Arabs learned about Iraq invasion of Kuwait via CNN. According to a 2010 report by the Arab States Broadcasting Union, there are 696 free Arab satellite television stations, most of which are privately owned. This shows an increase of 16 percent from the union's report released in 2008. More than 80 percent of these stations are broadcast in Arabic and 599 are privately owned. Most of these stations focus on entertainment, religion, sports, and television episodic series. For more on the Egyptian and Arab media, see Mohamed El-Bendary, *The "Ugly American" in the Arab Mind: Why Do Arabs Resent America* (Dulles, VA: Potomac Books, 2011).

70 *Radio and Television*, March 12, 2011, 95.

71 The Mubarak government ordered the revocation of Al-Jazeera's services on January 30

72 *Al-Ahrar*, January 31, 2011, 3.

73 *Al-Gomhuria*, January 31, 2011, 3.

74 *Al-Fagr*, March 14, 2011, 15.

75 *Al-Fagr*, March 14, 2011, 15.

76 *Al-Masry Al-Youm*, March 10, 2011, 15.

77 Al-Masria, March 25, 2011.

78 *Radio and Television*, March 12, 2011, 39.

79 *Radio and Television*, March 12, 2011, 40—41.

80 Quoted in David D. Kirkpatrick, "A Nobelist Has an Unfamiliar Role in Protests," *The New York Times*, January 28, 2011, www.nytimes.com (accessed July 26, 2011).

81 Our use of the word "press" throughout this book refers to the print media, mainly newspapers.

82 For more on the Egyptian press, see Mohamed El-Bendary, *The Egyptian Press and Coverage of Regional and International Events* (Lanham, MD: Lexington Books, 2010).

83 *Al-Ahram Al-Masae*, January 29, 2011, 2.

84 *Al-Ahram Al-Masae*, January 29, 2011, 3.

85 *Al-Ahram*, January 29, 2011, 11.

86 *Al-Masry Al-Youm*, January 29, 2011, 7.

87 *Al-Masry Al-Youm*, January 29, 5.

88 Al-Shorouk Al-Jadeed, January 29, 2.

89 *Al-Masry Al-Youm*, January 29, 2011, 7.

90 Article 76, which was amended by Mubarak in 2005, makes it extremely difficult for a candidate outside the NDP to run for the presidency. Article 77 does not restrict the number of years a president can stay in office.

91 *Al-Masry Al-Youm*, January 29, 2011, 17.

92 *Al-Shorouk Al-Jadeed*, January 29, 2011, 13.

93 *El-Dostour*, January 29, 2011, 6.

94 *Al-Shorouk Al-Jadeed*, January 29, 2011, 13.

95 *Al-Shorouk Al-Jadeed*, January 29, 2011, 15.

96 *Al-Masry Al-Youm*, January 29, 2011, 18.

97 *Al-Masry Al-Youm*, January 29, 2011, 20.

98 *Al-Shorouk Al-Jadeed*, January 9, 2011, 4.

99 *Alwafd*, January 29, 2011, 12.

100 *Alwafd*, January 29, 2011, 16.

101 *Alwafd*, January 29, 2011, 5.

102 *Alwafd*, January 29, 2011, 1.

103 *Alwafd*, January 29, 2011, 1.

104 Khaled Said is a twenty-eight-year-old who was tortured to death by police in Alexandria.

105 *Alwafd*, January 29, 2011, 12.

106 In an endeavor to protest his poor living standards, the man, owner of a small restaurant, set himself on fire in front of the Egyptian Parliament building on January 17, 2011. Some Egyptians said that he shouted statement against the SSIA before setting himself on fire. His act was the latest of a number North Africans employing self-immolation as a means of dissent.

107 On the day before the Friday of Anger, El-Sherif blamed the Nazif government and said his party is willing to engage in dialogue with the protesters and to address the complaints of youth. But he made no concessions and stressed, "The minority does not force its will on the majority."

108 Heads of state universities are appointed by a presidential decree.

109 For more on this see *Alwafd*, January 29, 2011, 9.

110 The AUC professor made that comment in *Al-Masry Al-Youm* on January 29, 2011, 17.

111 Suleiman is a seventy-four-year-old who headed the country's Intelligence Service since 1993. It is said that he became a close ally of Mubarak after he saved the Egyptian president's life in 1995 when he demanded that he ride in an armored car in Ethiopia. Mubarak escaped the assassination attempt unhurt.

112 *Al-Gomhuria*, January 29, 2011, 12.

113 *Al-Ahram Al-Masae*, January 29, 2011, 16.

114 *Al-Gomhuria*, January 29, 2011, 3.

115 *Al-Ahram*, January 29, 2011, 15.

116 *Akhbar El-Yom*, January 29, 2011, 22.

117 *Al-Masry Al-Youm*, January 29, 2011, 7.

118 *El-Dostour*, January 29, 2011, 12.

119 *Al-Shorouk Al-Jadeed*, January 29, 2011, 13.

120 *Al-Masry Al-Youm*, January 29, 2011, 18.

121 *Al-Shorouk Al-Jadeed*, January 29, 2011, 13.

122 *Al-Masry Al-Youm*, January 29, 2011, 4.

123 *Al-Masry Al-Youm*, January 29, 2011, 5.

124 *Alwafd*, January 29, 2011, 4.

125 *Alwafd*, January 29, 2011, 10.

126 *Alwafd*, January 29, 2011, 12.

127 *Alwafd*, January 29, 2011, 12.

128 *Alwafd*, January 29, 2011, 16.

129 *Alwafd*, January 29, 2011, 5.

130 *Al-Ahram*, January 29, 2011, 8.

131 *Al-Gomhuria*, January 29, 2011, 18.

132 *Akhbar El-Yom*, January 29, 22.

133 *Akhbar El-Yom*, January 29, 2011, 27.

134 *Al-Ahram*, January 29, 2011, 12.

135 *Al-Ahram*, January 29, 2011, 24.

136 *Akhbar El-Yom*, January 29, 14.

137 *Al-Shorouk Al-Jadeed*, January 29, 2011, 13.

138 *El-Dostour*, January 29, 2011, 6.

139 *Al-Shorouk Al-Jadeed*, January 29, 2011, 3.

140 *Al-Masry Al-Youm*, January 29, 2011, 20.

141 *Al-Masry Al-Youm*, January 29, 2011, 5.

142 *Al-Masry Al-Youm*, January 29, 2011, 20.

143 *Alwafd*, January 29, 2011, 12.

144 *Alwafd*, January 29, 2011, 10.

145 *Alwafd*, January 29, 2011, 12.

146 *Alwafd*, January 29, 2011, 12.

147 *Alwafd*, January 29, 2011, 5.

148 *Alwafd*, January 29, 2011, 10.

149 *Al-Ahram*, January 29, 2011, 11.

150 *Akhbar El-Yom*, January 29, 2011, 14.

151 *Al-Masry Al-Youm*, January 29, 2011, 19.

152 *Al-Masry Al-Youm*, January 29, 2011, 20.

153 *Al-Masry Al-Youm*, January 29, 2011, 7.

154 *Al-Masry Al-Youm*, January 29, 2011, 2.

155 *Al-Masry Al-Youm*, January 29, 2011, 7.

156 *Al-Masry Al-Youm*, January 29, 2011, 17.

157 *Alwafd*, January 29, 2011, 10.

158 *Al-Ahram Al-Masae*, January 29, 2011, 4.

159 In a statement on February 4, 2011, Ali Khamenei, Iran's supreme religious leader, referred to the revolution in Egypt as a "sign of Islamic awakening in the world following the victory of the Islamic revolution in Iran."

160 *Al-Ahram*, January 29, 2011, 15.

161 *Al-Gomhuria*, January 29, 2011, 19.

162 *Al-Ahram Al-Masae*, January 29, 2011, 12.

163 *Akhbar El-Yom*, January 29, 2011, 14.

164 *Al-Ahram Al-Masae*, January 29, 2011, 12.

165 *Al-Gomhuria*, January 29, 2011, 19.

166 Almost all of the well-established magazines in Egypt, including *Sabah El-Kheir*, are owned by the state.

167 *Al-Ahram*, January 29, 2011, 10.

168 *Al-Ahram*, January 29, 2011, 11.

169 *Akhbar El-Yom*, January 29, 2011, 22.

170 *Al-Ahram*, January 29, 2011, 11.

171 *Akhbar El-Yom*, January 29, 2011, 15.

172 *Al-Shorouk Al-Jadeed*, January 29, 2011, 4.

173 *Al-Shorouk Al-Jadeed*, January 29, 2011, 13.

174 *Al-Masry Al-Youm*, January 29, 2011, 18.

175 See Simon Tisdall, "Hosni Mubarak: Egyptian 'Pharaoh' Dethroned Amid Gunfire and Blood," *The Guardian*, February 11, 2010, www.guardian.co.uk (accessed February 12, 2011).

176 *Akhbar El-Yom*, January 29, 2011, 22.

177 *Al-Ahram*, January 29, 2011, 8.

178 *Akhbar El-Yom*, January 29, 2011, 27.

179 *Akhbar El-Yom*, January 29, 2011, 14.

180 *Al-Gomhuria*, January 29, 2011, 3.

181 *Al-Ahram*, January 29, 2011, 11.

182 *Al-Masry Al-Youm*, January 29, 2011, 17.

183 *El-Dostour*, January 29, 2011, 6. Members of the banned Muslim Brotherhood party often ran as independent candidates in parliamentary elections.

184 *Al-Shorouk Al-Jadeed*, January 29, 2011, 3.

185 *Al-Shorouk Al-Jadeed*, January 29, 2011, 13.

186 *Alwafd*, January 29, 2011, 1.

187 *Alwafd*, January 29, 2011, 10.

188 *Akhbar El-Yom*, January 29, 2011, 22.

189 *Al-Ahram*, January 29, 2011, 11.

190 *Akhbar El-Yom*, January 29, 2011, 14.

191 *Al-Shorouk Al-Jadeed*, January 29, 2011, 3.

192 *Al-Gomhuria*, January 29, 2011, 19.

193 *Akhbar El-Yom*, January 29, 2011, 14.

194 *Al-Ahram*, January 29, 2011, 11.

195 *Al-Ahram*, January 29, 2011, 7.

196 *Akhbar El-Yom*, January 29,2011 22.

197 *Al-Gomhuria*, January 29, 2011, 17.

198 *Al-Masry Al-Youm*, January 29, 2011, 17.

199 *Al-Shorouk Al-Jadeed*, January 29, 2011, 15.

200 See *Alwafd*, January 29, 2011, 12.

201 The New Wafd Party won five seats in Parliament in the 2005 elections. In the 2010 elections that number increased by only one seat. The members of the banned Muslim Brotherhood who ran as independent members won eighty eight seats in 2005 and only one seat in 2010. The NDP's seats increased from three hundred and thirty in 2005 to four hundred and twenty in 2010 from the total four hundred forty ordinary seats contested in Parliament. It is worth mentioning here that in June 2011, the New Wafd Party declared that it is to ally with the newly-established political wing of the Muslim Brotherhood known as the Freedom and Justice Party.

202 *Al-Ahram*, January 29, 2011, 11.

203 This practice of theft was still going on, even as this book was delivered to the publisher.

204 NDP was headed by Hosni Mubarak and his forty-six-year-old son, Gamal, chaired its influential Policies Secretariat.

205 Dream2, February 24, 2011.

206 Al-Hayat, February 1, 2011.

207 *Al-Ahram*, January 31, 2011, 13.

208 *Al-Ahram*, January 31, 2011, 10.

209 *Al-Masry Al-Youm*, January 31, 2011, 5.

210 *Al-Ahrar*, January 31, 2011, 12.

211 *El-Osboa*, January 31, 2011, 3.

212 *Al-Masry Al-Youm*, January 31, 2011, 13.

213 *El-Osboa*, January 31, 2011, 3.

214 *Al-Shorouk Al-Jadeed*, January 31, 2011, 2.

215 *Al-Masry Al-Youm*, January 31, 2011, 13.

216 *El-Osboa*, January 31, 2011, 14.

217 *Al-Shorouk Al-Jadeed*, January 31, 2011, 4.

218 *El-Osboa*, January 31, 2011, 6.

219 *Al-Masry Al-Youm*, January 31, 2011, 13.

220 *Al-Shorouk Al-Jadeed*, January 31, 2011, 4.

221 *Al-Shorouk Al-Jadeed*, January 31, 2011, 2.

222 *Al-Gomhuria*, January 31, 2011, 4.

223 *Al-Masry Al-Youm*, January 31, 2011, 8.

224 Ikhnaton who ruled in the eighteenth century dynasty (1353—1336) established Aten as the main, principal monotheistic god of Egypt.

225 *Al-Masry Al-Youm*, January 31, 2011, 13.

226 *Al-Masry Al-Youm*, January 31, 2011, 13.

227 *Al-Shorouk Al-Jadeed*, January 31, 2011, 3.

228 *Al-Gomhuria*, January 31, 2011, 15.

229 *Al-Gomhuria*, January 31, 2011, 1.

230 *Al-Shorouk Al-Jadeed*, January 31, 2011, 9.

231 *Alwafd*, January 31, 2011, 4.

232 *Al-Ahram*, January 31, 2011, 4.

233 *Alwafd*, March 12, 2011, 10.

234 There was a fierce debate going on among the nine countries that border the Nile—the Nile Basin Initiative (NBI)—over the issue of sharing waters. Egypt, which faces possible water shortage due to climate change and overconsumption, is dependent on the Nile and was watching closely the construction of the hydroelectric dam in East Africa.

235 *Alwafd*, February 19, 2011, 11.

236 *Al-Ahram*, January 31, 2011, 11.

237 In his interview with ABC's Christiane Amanpour on February 3, 2011, Mubarak said "I am fed up. After 62 years in public service, I have had enough. I want to go."

238 I heard some Egyptians claim, however, that Zewail holds U.S. citizenship as well as Egyptian.

239 In an interview with CNN on February 1, ElBaradei said Mubarak will "not only be a lame duck president but a dead man walking" if he does not pay attention to his people's demands and immediately step down. He denounced him as "a dictator who doesn't want to

listen to the voice of the people." In an interview with the pan-Arab Al-Arabiya TV station, ElBaradei made similar remarks and deplored Mubarak's decision to continue his term.

240 *Al-Akhbar*, February 3, 2011, 17.

241 *Al-Shorouk Al-Jadeed*, February 3, 2011, 7.

242 *Al-Ahali*, February 2, 2011, 6.

243 *Al-Gomhuria*, February 3, 2011, 5.

244 *Al-Akhbar*, February 3, 2011, 16.

245 *Al-Akhbar*, February 3, 2011, 19.

246 *Al-Ahram*, February 3, 2011, 11.

247 *Al-Ahram*, February 3, 2011, 4.

248 *Al-Gomhuria*, February 3, 2011, 16.

249 *Alwafd*, February 3, 2011, 5.

250 Al-Shorouk Al-Jadeed, February 3, 14.

251 *Alwafd*, February 3, 2011, 16.

252 *Al-Masry Al-Youm*, February 3, 2011, 13.

253 *Al-Masry Al-Youm*, February 3, 2011, 10.

254 *Alwafd*, February 3, 2011, 19.

255 Al-Shorouk Al-Jadeed, February 3, 5.

256 *El-Dostour*, February 3, 2011, 13.

257 *Al-Shorouk Al-Jadeed*, February 3, 2011, 14.

258 Al-Shorouk Al-Jadeed, February 3, 13.

259 Al-Shorouk Al-Jadeed, February 3, 2.

260 *Al-Masry Al-Youm*, February 3, 2011, 8.

261 *Al-Ahali*, February 2, 2011, p. 7.

262 *Al-Masry Al-Youm*, February 3, 2011, 13.

263 *Alwafd*, February 3, 2011, 16.

264 *Al-Shorouk Al-Jadeed*, February 3, 2011, 13.

265 *Al-Masry Al-Youm*, February 3, 2011, 15.

266 *Alwafd*, February 3, 2011, 16.

267 *Al-Shorouk Al-Jadeed*, February 3, 2011, 13.

268 *Al-Masry Al-Youm*, February 3, 2011, 8.

269 *Al-Masry Al-Youm*, February 3, 2011, 13.

270 *Al-Ahrar*, February 3, 2011, 12.

271 *Al-Masry Al-Youm*, February 3, 2011, 5.

272 *Al-Ahrar*, February 3, 2011, 10.

273 *El-Dostour*, February 3, 2011, 5.

274 *El-Dostour*, February 3, 2011, 13.

275 *Alwafd*, February 3, 2011, 16.

276 *Al-Masry Al-Youm*, February 3, 2011, 2.

277 *Al-Masry Al-Youm*, February 3, 2011, 10.

278 *Al-Ahram Al-Masae*, February 3, 2011, 2.

279 *Al-Gomhuria*, February 3, 2011, 4.

280 *Al-Akhbar*, February 3, 2011, 5.

281 *Al-Akhbar*, February 3, 2011, 20.

282 See, for example, *Al-Akhbar*, February 3, 2011, 16; *Al-Ahram*, February 3, 2011, 10.

283 *Al-Gomhuria*, February 3, 2011, 1.

284 *Al-Akhbar*, February 3, 2011, 17.

285 *Al-Akhbar*, February 3, 2011, 17.

286 *Al-Akhbar*, February 3, 2011, 2

287 Article 76 hinders individuals from becoming presidential candidates and Article 77 grants the president the power stay in office forever.

288 *Al-Gomhuria*, February 3, 2011, 1.

289 *Al-Akhbar*, February 3, 2011, 20.

290 *Al-Ahram*, February 3, 2011, 11.

291 *Al-Akhbar*, February 3, 2011, 19.

292 *Al-Ahram*, February 3, 2011, 17.

293 *Al-Gomhuria*, February 3, 2011, 5.

294 *Al-Ahram*, February 3, 2011, 10.

295 *Al-Ahram Al-Masae*, February 3, 2011, 11.

296 *Al-Akhbar*, February 3, 2011, 17.

297 *Al-Ahram Al-Masae*, February 3, 2011, 11.

298 *Al-Gomhuria*, February 3, 2011, 14.

299 *Al-Akhbar*, February 3, 2011, 16.

300 *Al-Gomhuria*, February 3, 2011, 14.

301 *Al-Gomhuria*, February 3, 2011, 14.

302 *Al-Gomhuria*, February 3, 2011, 13.

303 The only positive reference of the police was made in *Al-Masry Al-Youm* (February 3, 2011, 7). The independent paper pointed out: What took place over the past a few days is nothing but a "conspiracy" to hurt the image of police officers and plant division between them and the public.

304 *El-Dostour*, February 3, 2011, 5.

305 *Al-Ahrar*, February 3, 2011, 5.

306 *Al-Masry Al-Youm*, February 3, 2011, 10.

307 *Al-Masry Al-Youm*, February 3, 2011, 14.

308 *Alwafd*, February 3, 2011, 16

309 *Al-Masry Al-Youm*, February 3, 2011, 13.

310 *Al-Ahali*, February 2, 2011, 13.

311 *Al-Shorouk Al-Jadeed*, February 3, 2011, 13.

312 *Al-Masry Al-Youm*, February 3, 2011, 11.

313 *Al-Ahram*, February 3, 2011, 18.

314 *Al-Gomhuria*, February 3, 2011, 13.

315 *Al-Akhbar*, February 3, 2011, 16.

316 *Al-Gomhuria*, February 3, 2011, 13.

317 *Al-Akhbar*, February 3, 2011, 18.

318 *Al-Gomhuria*, February 3, 2011, 13.

319 ONTV, March 24, 2011.

320 *El-Dostour*, February 3, 2011, 13.

321 *Al-Masry Al-Youm*, February 3, 2011, 2.

322 *Al-Akhbar*, February 3, 2011, 17.

323 *Al-Gomhuria*, February 3, 2011, 16.

324 *Alwafd*, February 3, 2011, 16.

325 *Al-Shorouk Al-Jadeed*, February 3, 2011, 13.

326 *Al-Masry Al-Youm*, February 3, 2011, 8.

327 *El-Dostour*, February 3, 2011, 5.

328 *Al-Shorouk Al-Jadeed*, February 3, 2011, 14.

329 *Al-Ahrar*, February 3, 2011, 5.

330 *El-Dostour*, February 3, 2011, 13.

331 *Al-Ahram*, February 3, 2011, 4.

332 *Al-Akhbar*, February 3, 2011, 5.

333 *Al-Gomhuria*, February 3, 2011, 5.

334 *Al-Akhbar*, February 3, 2011, 17.

335 In his interview with Christiane Amanpour of ABC News on February 3, Mubarak noted that he was "fed up" with being president but that he could not step down for concern of spreading disorder in Egypt.

336 BBC Arabic. February 3, 2011.

337 For the full speech, see *Washington Post*, "Hosni Mubarak's Speech to the Egyptian People: 'I Will Not . . . Accept to Hear Foreign Dictations,'" February 10, 2011, http://www.washingtonpost.com/wp-dyn/content/article/2011/02/10/AR2011021005290_pf.html (accessed February 12, 2011).

338 *Al-Masry Al-Youm*, February 12, 2011, 13.

339 *El-Dostour*, February 13, 2011, 2

340 *Al-Masry Al-Youm*, February 13, 2011, 4.

341 *Alwafd*, February 14, 2011, 10.

342 *Al-Masry Al-Youm*, February 12, 2011, 4.

343 *Al-Masry Al-Youm*, February 13, 2011, 2.

344 Dream, February 11, 2011.

345 *El-Dostour*, February 13, 2011, 4.

346 *Al-Shorouk Al-Jadeed*, February 13, 2011, 2.

347 *Al-Masry Al-Youm*, February 13, 2011, 17.

348 *Al-Masry Al-Youm*, February 14, 2011, 2.

349 *Al-Masry Al-Youm*, February 13, 2011, 19.

350 *El-Dostour*, February 14, 2011, 12.

351 *Al-Masry Al-Youm*, February 14, 2011, 15.

352 *El-Dostour*, February 14, 2011, 4.

353 *Al-Shorouk Al-Jadeed*, February 13, 2011, 14.

354 *Al-Masry Al-Youm*, February 13, 2011, 2.

355 *El-Dostour*, February 13, 2011, 12.

356 *Al-Masry Al-Youm*, February 13, 2011, 17.

357 *Al-Masry Al-Youm*, February 13, 2011, 17.

358 *El-Dostour*, February 13, 2011, 12.

359 *Al-Masry Al-Youm*, February 12, 2011, 4.

360 *Al-Masry Al-Youm*, February 14, 2011, 15.

361 *El-Dostour*, February 14, 2011, 12.

362 *Al-Shorouk Al-Jadeed*, February 14, 2011, 3.

363 *El-Dostour*, February 13, 2011, 2.

364 *Al-Shorouk Al-Jadeed*, February 14, 12.

365 *Al-Masry Al-Youm*, February 13, 2011, 6.

366 *Al-Shorouk Al-Jadeed*, February 13, 2011, 4.

367 *El-Dostour*, February 14, 2011, 12.

368 *Al-Shorouk Al-Jadeed*, February 14, 14.

369 *Al-Masry Al-Youm*, February 14, 2011, 6.

370 *El-Dostour*, February 14, 2011, 2.

371 *El-Dostour*, February 14, 2011, 12.

372 *Al-Masry Al-Youm*, February 14, 2011, 5.

373 *Al-Shorouk Al-Jadeed*, February 14, 2011, 2.

374 *Al-Masry Al-Youm*, February 14, 2011, 16.

375 *Alwafd*, February 12, 2011, 1.

376 *Al-Ahrar*, February 12, 2011, 1.

377 *Alwafd*, February 13, 2011, 20.

378 *Al-Ahrar*, February 12, 2011, 3.

379 *Alwafd*, February 13, 2011, 4.

380 *Al-Ahrar*, February 13, 2011, 8.

381 *Alwafd*, February 13, 2011, 13.

382 *Al-Ahrar*, February 14, 2011, 8.

383 *Al-Ahrar*, February 14, 2011, 3.

384 *Al-Ahrar*, February 14, 2011, 8.

385 *Alwafd*, February 14, 2011, 5.

386 *Alwafd*, February 14, 2011, 16.

387 *Alwafd*, February 14, 2011, 1.

388 *Al-Ahrar*, February 14, 2011, 8.

389 *Alwafd*, February 14, 2011, 12.

390 *Al-Ahrar*, February 14, 2011, 3.

391 *Al-Ahrar*, February 14, 2011, 3.

392 *The Guardian* story, it should be stated, quoted the figure from one individual it interviewed and that figure was later reported on as exaggerated. See Phillip Inman, "Mubarak Family Fortune Could Reach $70bn, Says Expert," February 4, 2011, http://www.guardian.co.uk/world/2011/feb/04/hosni-mubarak-family-fortune (accessed February 14, 2011).

393 *Akhbar El-Yom*, February 12, 2011, 14.

394 See, for example, *Al-Ahram*, February 14, 2011, 17.

395 *Al-Ahram*, February 13, 2011, 7.

396 *Al-Ahram*, February 13, 2011, 7.

397 *Al-Gomhuria*, February 14, 2011, 15.

398 *Al-Ahram*, February 14, 2011, 17.

399 See, for instance, *Al-Gomhuria*, February 13, 2011, 2.

400 See, *Al-Gomhuria*, February 13, 2011, 14.

401 *Al-Ahram*, February 13, 2011, 2.

402 *Al-Akhbar*, February 14, 2011, 13.

403 *Al-Akhbar*, February 13, 2011, 20.

404 *Al-Ahram*, February 13, 2011, 19.

405 *Al-Akhbar*, February 13, 2011, 20.

406 *Al-Gomhuria*, February 13, 2011, 14.

407 *Al-Ahram*, February 13, 2011, 11.

408 *Al-Akhbar*, February 13, 2011, 17.

409 *Al-Akhbar*, February 14, 2011, 15.

410 *Al-Gomhuria*, February 14, 2011, 15.

411 *Al-Ahram*, February 14, 2011, 4.

412 *Al-Ahram*, February 14, 2011, 5.

413 See *Al-Akhbar*, February 14, 2011, 15.

414 *Al-Gomhuria*, February 14, 2011, 13.

415 *Al-Ahram*, February 14, 2011, 2.

416 *Al-Ahram*, February 14, 2011, 4.

417 *Al-Akhbar*, February 14, 2011, 13.

418 *Al-Ahram*, February 14, 2011, 6.

419 *Al-Ahram*, February 14, 2011, 7.

420 *Al-Ahram*, February 14, 2011, 10.

421 *Al-Ahram*, February 14, 2011, 7.

422 *Al-Akhbar*, February 14, 2011, 13.

423 *Al-Ahram*, February 14, 2011, 9.

424 *Al-Ahram Al-Masae*, February 14, 2011, 15.

425 *Al-Akhbar*, February 14, 2011, 13.

426 *Al-Ahram*, February 14, 2011, 10.

427 *Sabah El-Kheir*, April 12, 2011, 3.

428 Salama Moussa, *The Book of Revolutions* (Cairo, Egypt: Salama Moussa Printing and Distribution, 1954), 146. [In Arabic.]

429 Mohamed Shafiq Gharbal, *The Formation of Egypt Across Ages* (Cairo: The General Egyptian Book Organization, 1996/1957). [In Arabic.]

430 Moussa, The Book of Revolutions, 8.

431 Pasha is a title of a Turkish officer of high rank

432 *Alwafd*, March 13, 2011, 10.

433 *Al-Ahram*, February 14, 2011, 10.

434 *Alwafd*, February 13, 2011, 1.

435 *El-Dostour*, February 13, 2011, 4.

436 *Al-Masry Al-Youm*, March 10, 2011, 17.

437 *El-Dostour*, March 22, 2011, 12.

438 *Al-Masry Al-Youm*, March 10, 2011, 15.

439 *Al-Gomhuria*, February 13, 2011, 14.

440 *Al-Ahram*, February 13, 2011, 6.

441 Dream, February 11, 2011.

442 *Al-Ahrar*, February 13, 2011, 8.

443 *El-Dostour*, February 13, 2011, 4.

444 *Al-Ahrar*, February 14, 2011, 8.

445 *Al-Gomhuria*, February 13, 2011, 13.

446 *Al-Akhbar*, February 14, 2011, 18.

447 *Al-Shorouk Al-Jadeed*, February 14, 2011, 13.

448 See *Al-Ahrar*, February 13, 2012, 3.

449 *El-Dostour*, February 14, 2011, 2.

450 *Alwafd*, February 14, 2011, 10.

451 *El-Dostour*, February 14, 2011, 12.

452 In general, under Mubarak's rule state newspapers enjoyed much more freedom than state television stations which served as a propaganda tool for his regime.

453 Mohamed El-Bendary, The Egyptian Press and Coverage of Local and International Events (Lanham, MD: Lexington Books, 2010).

454 Al-Masria, March 5, 2011.

455 *Al-Ahram*, February 14, 2011, 10.

456 See *Al-Akhbar*, February 13, 2011, 18.

457 *Al-Ahram*, February 14, 2011, 10.

458 *Al-Akhbar*, February 13, 2011, 18.

459 See what presidential candidate Hamdeen Sabahi said in his interview with Mahmoud Saad on Al-Nahar on May 16, 2012, and *Horria and Adala* newspaper, May 13, 2012, 10.

460 *Al-Masry Al-Youm*, February 13, 2011, 20.

461 Al-Nahar, April 3, 2012.

462 See *Al-Shorouk Al-Jadeed*, May 13, 2012, 19.

463 See *Al-Akhbar*, February 13, 2011, 5.

464 Human Rights Watch, "Egypt: A Year of Attacks on Free Expression: Halt Assaults on Journalists; Repeal Laws that Curb Speech," February 11, 2012, http://www.hrw.org/news/2012/02/11/egypt-year-attacks-free-expression (accessed 8 April 2012); Reporters Without Borders, "Journalists and Bloggers Among 12 People Who Could Face Military Trial," March 9, 2012, http://en.rsf.org/egypt-journalists-and-bloggers-among-12-09-03-2012,42045.html (accessed April 8, 2012); Amnesty International, "Promises: Egypt's Military Rulers Erode Human Rights," November 22, 2011. http://www.amnesty.org.uk/uploads/documents/doc_22167.pdf (accessed April 8, 2012).

465 *Al-Masry Al-Youm*, February 13, 2011, 17.

466 See *Al-Masry Al-Youm*, March 3, 2009, 20.

467 *Sabah El-Kheir*, October 1970.

468 *Al-Masry Al-Youm*, March 22, 2011, 20.

469 *Al-Wafd*, March 12, 2011, 10.

470 The Constitution states that Sharia (Islamic law) is the foundation of the law of Egypt.

471 Al-Hayat, March 28, 2011.

472 The Quran says, " . . . their [Muslims'] affair is a matter of consultation among them" (Surah 42:38).

473 Headed by Colonel Ahmed Urabi Pasha (1841-1911), the 1882 Revolution against Khedive Tawfiq (who governed Egypt from 1879-1892) was a pro-democratic one that aimed at restricting the power of the khedive and acknowledging the election of delegates.

474 A 1954 constitution draft (which was aimed at turning Egypt into a liberal democracy) was also written but was never introduced. It was formed by a committee of fifty members, including some of the greatest minds of the legal system at the time most notable of whom was Abdel Razeq El-Sinhowri who—based on the recommendation of the Leadership Council of the Revolution—chaired the committee. That draft constitution disappeared and was discovered in the rubbish in a forgotten room in the Arab League in Cairo in 2002 by the distinguished Egyptian journalist Salah Issa, editor of the weekly paper *Al-Qahira* (Arabic for "Cairo"), and it was was published in a book in 2001 titled: *Constitution in the Rubbish Bin*. Based on Issa's account, the officers of the July Revolution abandoned the draft constitution.

475 Similar to the way the national media reacted during the 2011 Revolution, some newspapers also submitted to the regime and British rule during the 1919 Revolution and the years that followed. Among the newspaper that was under government influence in the

period prior to WWI was *El-Moayed*—which was a voice of Khedive Abbas II—while *El-Moqatam* reinforced the polities of the British occupier. This phenomenon of having a press system that supports either side continued until the 1952 Revolution, with its press organization mechanism making all papers the voice of authority and resulting in what was known as the national press. For more on this, see Younan Labib Rizq, "The Fall of the Libertarian Experiment in Egypt," in *Forty Years on the July Revolution: An Historical Study*, ed. Raof Abbas Hamed (Cairo: Al-Ahram Center for Political and Strategic Studies, 1992). [in Arabic.]

476   Raof Abbas Hamed, "The Road to the Revolution," in *Forty Years on the July Revolution: An Historical Study*, ed. Raof Abbas Hamed (Cairo: Al-Ahram Center for Political and Strategic Studies, 1992), p. 19. [In Arabic.]

477   *Al-Masry Al-Youm*, March 22, 20.

478   *Al-Fagr*, March 14, 2011, 14.

479   It is important to note here that those political parties were products of the rise of a rich elitist group; many of its members were land owners. They used their money to exercise influence on the political decision-making process.

480   Raof Abbas Hamed, "The Road to the Revolution," in *Forty Years on the July Revolution: An Historical Study*, ed. Raof Abbas Hamed (Cairo: Al-Ahram Center for Political and Strategic Studies, 1992), p. 17. [in Arabic.]

481   Ahmed El-Sherbini, "Economic and Social Development," in *Forty Years on the July Revolution: An Historical Study*, ed. Raof Abbas Hamed (Cairo: Al-Ahram Center for Political and Strategic Studies, 1992), p. 125. [In Arabic.]

El-Dostour, March 12, 2011, 4.

482   Ahmed Zakaria El-Shelq, "The Ideological Foundations of the New Political System and Political Arrangements," in *Forty Years on the July Revolution: An Historical Study*, ed. Raof Abbas Hamed (Cairo: Al-Ahram Center for Political and Strategic Studies, 1992), p. 20. [In Arabic.]

483   Article 2 states: "Islam is the religion of the state, the Arabic language is the official language, and Islamic Sharia is the source jurisdiction."

484   It is worth mentioning here that right before his resignation from Office (on February 10, 2011) Mubarak stated that he had requested that Articles 76, 77, 88, 93, and 181 be amended and that Article 179 be abolished.

485   *Al-Masry Al-Youm*, March 12, 2011, 4.

486   *Al-Mehwar*, March 16, 2011.

487   Quoted in Amira Howeidy, "'Between Two Constitutions,'" *Al-Ahram Weekly*, March 10, 2011, 5.

488   See for, example, *Al-Masry Al-Youm*, March 22, 2011, 20.

489   Following the establishment of the committee, I heard more than one Egyptian on the street speaking of a "deal" between the SCAF and the Muslim Brotherhood, which later became the Freedom and Justice Party.

490   Nile News, April 12, 2011.

491   *Al-Masry Al-Youm*, March 22, 2011, 16.

492   *Al-Shorouk Al-Jadeed*, March 22, 2011, 11.

493   *Al-Shorouk Al-Jadeed*, March 22, 2011, 13.

494   For example, only 27 percent of registered voter balloted on the constitution amendment referendum in March 2007.

495 *Alwafd*, March 22, 2011, 10.

496 *Al-Ahram*, March 22, 2011, 10.

497 *Al-Ahram*, March 22, 2011, 11.

498 *Alwafd*, March 22. 2011, 12.

499 *Al-Masry Al-Youm*, March 12, 2011, 4.

500 *Al-Masry Al-Youm*, March 22, 2011, 5.

501 *Alwafd*, March 13, 2011, 1.

502 *Al-Ahram* ["Youth of January 25" section], March 25, 2011, 4.

503 *El-Dostour*, March 22, 2011.

504 *Al-Shorouk Al-Jadeed*, March 22, 2011, 4.

505 Article 82 states: "If on account of any temporary obstacle the President of the Republic is unable to carry out his functions, he shall delegate his powers to a vice-president . . ."

506 See *Al-Shorouk Al-Jadeed*, March 22, 2011, 4.

507 Established in Belgrade in 1961 in an emerging bipolar world, the Non-Aligned Movement consists today of one hundred and eighteen member nations who view themselves as not aligned with or against any major power bloc. The product of the leaders of the five countries of Yugoslavia, India, Ghana, Egypt, and Indonesia, the aim of the organization has been to ascertain "the national independence, sovereignty, territorial integrity and security of non-aligned countries."

508 *El-Dostour*, March 22, 2011, 11.

509 *Al-Masry Al-Youm*, March 12, 2011, 7.

510 *Al-Ahram*, March 22, 2011, 21.

511 *Al-Fagr*, March 14, 2011, 14.

512 *Al-Ahram*, March 22, 2011, 3.

513 On May 27, 2011, and in the largest protests since the toppling of Mubarak, hundreds of thousands of protesters poured into Tahrir Square and thousands others in major Egyptian cities demanding an end to military trials of civilians, implementing a new constitution before parliamentary elections (In mid April a court suspended the one-hundred constitutional committee entrusted with drafting a new constitution), and put on trial those involved in killing protesters during the eighteen-day revolution.

514 "January 25 Revolution and Changing the Political System in Egypt—Ambitions and Challenges," seminar, International Center for Future and Strategic Studies, Cairo, May 23, 2011.

515 *Sabah El-Kheir*, April 12, 2011, 34.

516 The Shafiq government was asked by SCAF to resign in response to people's demands.

517 The $145 million sum was cited in an article in *Al-Ahram*, March 22, 2011, 3.

518 In an interview with *Al-Ahram* on March 22, Serageldin said that Mrs. Mubarak served as an honorary head of trustees. See *Al-Ahram*, March 22, 2011, 3.

519 *Al-Mehwer*, April 13, 2011.

520 See *Al-Fagr*, March 14, 2011, 11.

521 See *El-Dostour*, March 13, 2011, 7.

522 Al-Dafa served as ambassador to Spain from 1982 to 1988 and to Egypt from 1988 to 1993. While serving in Cairo, Ambassador Al-Dafa was also Qatar's permanent representative to the Arab League.

523 *Al-Fagr*, March 14, 2011, 02.

524 *Al-Fagr*, March 14, 2011, 02.

525 During those days in which every Egyptian was talking about government corruption, I got a message on Mobile that read: "If your apartment has turned into a palace, short cash have become in abundance, you then must certainly be a minister or a high-ranking official in Egypt."

526 *Sabah El-Kheir*, April 12, 2011, 8—9.

527 Al-Salafiya (or Salafism in English) is an Islamic reform movement founded in Egypt by Mohamed Abduh (1849-1905).

528 CBC, August 3, 2011.

529 *Al-Shorouk Al-Jadeed*, August 4, 2011, 4.

530 *Al-Akhbar*, August 4, 2011, 6.

531 Al-Oula, August 3, 2011.

532 Al-Masriya, August 3, 2011.

533 *Alwafd*, August 4, 2011, 10.

534 *Al-Tahrir*, August 4, 2011, 10.

535 *Sibhah* (or rosary) is formed of a chain of beads and used for the glorification of God (Allah) after prayer by counting His names in a process known as *tasbih*.

536 El-Youm El-Sabaa, August 4, 2011, 10.

537 El-Youm El-Sabaa, August 4, 2011, 2.

538 *Al-Shorouk Al-Jadeed*, August 4, 2011, 2.

539 There was one article in the state press that, nonetheless, referred to Mubarak as the "accused former president" and which we coded under the "former" president category. There were also three articles (two in the independent press and one in the state press) which made reference to Mubarak as the "accused" but without attaching the words "former" or "deposed/ousted" to it and hence we did not code them.

540 The full Surah reads: "So today We will save you in body that you may be to those who succeed you a sign. And indeed, many among the people, of Our signs, are heedless."

541 *Al-Messa*, August 4, 2011, 16.

542 *Al-Ahram*, August 4, 2011, 6.

543 *Al-Akhbar*, August 4, 2011, 20.

544 *Al-Akhbar*, August 4, 2011, 6.

545 *Al-Akhbar*, August 4, 2011, 20.

546 *El-Youm El-Sabaa*, August 4, 2011, 13.

547 *Al-Shorouk Al-Jadeed*, August 4, 2011, 4.

548 *El-Youm El-Sabaa*, August 4, 2011, 5.

549 *Alwafd*, August 5, 2011, 11.

550 *Alwafd*, August 4, 2011, 11.

551 See Mohamed Shafiq Gharbal, *The Formation of Egypt Across Ages*, 2nd ed. (1957; rep., Cairo: The General Egyptian Book Organization, 1996). [In Arabic.]

552 *Al-Akhbar*, August 4, 2011, 20.

553 *Al-Ahram*, August 4, 2011, 11.

554 *Alwafd*, August 4, 2011, 10.

555 *Al-Tahrir*, August 4, 2011, 5.

556 *Al-Akhbar*, August 4, 2011, 2.

557 *Al-Masry Al-Youm*, August 4, 2011, 21.

558 *Al-Masry Al-Youm*, August 4, 2011,4.

559 *Al-Ahram*, August 4, 2011, 7.

560 Al-Tahrir, August 4, 2011, 4.

561 Al-Akhbar, August 4, 2011, 6.

562 In an interview with Al-Nahar TV station on May 26, 2012, the then-final presidential runner Mohamed Morsi stressed that those who carried the atrocious attack on the Two Saints Church in were member of the security apparatuses.

563 Al-Masry Al-Youm, August 4, 2011, 4.

564 Al-Akhbar, August 4, 2011, 20.

565 Al-Tahrir, August 4, 2011, 14.

566 El-Youm El-Sabaa, August 4, 2011, 1.

567 Al-Shorouk Al-Jadeed, August 4, 2011, 4.

568 Al-Akhbar, August 4, 2011, 6.

569 Al-Tahrir, August 4, 2011, 10.

570 Al-Akhbar, August 4, 2011, 6.

571 Al-Tahrir, August 4, 2011, 11.

572 Alwafd, August 4, 2011, 15.

573 El-Youm El-Sabaa, August 4, 2011, 5.

574 Al-Tahrir, August 4, 2011, 3.

575 Al-Shorouk Al-Jadeed, August 4, 2011, 7.

576 Al-Tahrir, August 4, 2011, 14.

577 Al-Messa, August 4, 2011, 2.

578 Al-Shorouk Al-Jadeed, August 4, 2011, 4.

579 Alwafd, August 4, 2011, 16.

580 Al-Shorouk Al-Jadeed, August 4, 2011, 2.

581 Al-Messa, August 4, 2011, 2.

582 Alwafd, August 5, 2011, 4.

583 Al-Ahram, August 4, 2011, 11.

584 Al-Ahram, August 4, 2011, 11.

585 Al-Tahrir, August 4, 2011, 5.

586 Al-Shorouk Al-Jadeed, August 4, 2011, 4.

587 Al-Hayat, January 15, 2012.

588 In the months that followed the revolution, the Muslim Brotherhood established the Freedom and Justice Party, which later published a daily party paper. This has added the number of daily party papers in Egypt to two.

589 The elections were repeated on January 14 and 15 in four constituencies due to "fraud" allegations.

590 The well-organized group, established in 1928 and outlawed since 1954, is known among Egyptians for its social welfare programs. The group won only 1 seat in the 2010 parliamentary elections (as opposed to 88 seats in 2005 elections) of the total 518 parliamentary seats. Many political analysts denounced the 2005 elections as "rigged" elections.

591 As-Salafiya (or Salafism in English) is an Islamic reform movement founded in Egypt by Mohamed Abduh (1849-1905).

592 The Law was not passed and Ahmed Shafiq was not disqualified.

593 Aboul Fatouh wrongfully stated this, but there is no statement—according to the knowledge of this researcher—in the peace treaty which mandates that the treaty be revised every five years.

594 See Al-Shorouk Al-Jadeed, May 13, 2012, 9.

595 *Al-Akhbar*, May 13, 2012, 14.

596 *Al-Gomhuria*, May 13, 2012, 2.

597 *Al-Tahrir*, may 13, 2012, 5.

598 Dream2, May 11, 2012.

599 ONTV May 11, 2012.

600 *Al-Hurria Wal Adalah* (Freedom and Justice), May 12, 2012, 7.

601 Quoted in *Al-Shorouk Al-Jadeed*, May 12, 2012, 7.

602 Al-Shabab, May 13, 2012.

603 Quoted in *Al-Shorouk Al-Jadeed*, May 13, 2012, 8.

604 *Al-Gomhuria*, May 12, 2012, 5.

605 *Al-Akhbar*, May 13, 2012, 22.

606 *Akhbar El-Yom*, May 12, 2012, 4.

607 *Akhbar El-Yom*, May 12, 2012, 22.

608 *Al-Akhbar*, May 13, 2012, 6.

609 *Al-Akhbar*, May 13, 2012, 16.

610 *Al-Akhbar*, May 13, 2012, 17.

611 *Akhbar El-Yom*, May 12, 2012, 4.

612 *Al-Masry Al-Youm*, May 13, 2012, 5.

613 *Al-Masry Al-Youm*, May 13, 2012, 21.

614 *Al-Tahrir*, May 12, 2012, 16.

615 *Al-Tahrir*, May 13, 2012, 16.

616 *Al-Shorouk Al-Jadeed*, May 12, 2012, 7.

617 *Al-Masry Al-Youm*, May 13, 2012, 5.

618 *Al-Masry Al-Youm*, May 12, 2012, 5.

619 *El-Youm El-Sabaa*, May 12, 2012, 2.

620 *Al-Tahrir*, May 12, 2012, 16.

621 *Al-Masry Al-Youm*, May 13, 2012, 5.

622 *El-Youm El-Sabaa*, May 12, 2012, 2.

623 *Al-Tahrir*, May 12, 2012, 10.

624 *Al-Shorouk Al-Jadeed*, May 13, 2012, 2.

625 *Al-Masry Al-Youm*, May 13, 2012, 21.

626 *Al-Masry Al-Youm*, May 12, 2012, 7.

627 A nonpartisan organization named the Citizens' Debate Commission was founded in 2004 because it claimed that the Commission on Presidential Debates failed to meet voters' demands.

628 *El-Youm El-Sabaa*, May 13, 2012, 12.

629 *El-Dostour*, May 12 29, 2012, 2.

630 *Al-Akhbar*, May 13, 2012, 16.

631 *Al-Gomhuria*, May 13, 2012, 12.

632 *Al-Tahrir*, May 13, 2012, 16.

633 We must stress, however, that once results were declared complaints of election fraud were filed by Aboul Fatouh and presidential candidate Hamdeen Sabahi who ranked third in election results.

634 *Al-Masry Al-Youm*, May 13, 2012, 21.

635 *Al-Masry Al-Youm*, May 12, 2012, 7.

636 *Al-Shorouk Al-Jadeed*, May 12, 2012, 7.

637 *Al-Akhbar*, May 13, 2012, 4.

638 Many of us who studied politics and mass communication in America often heard about the marvelousness and genuineness of the 1858 debates between Abraham Lincoln and Stephen Douglas.

639 *Al-Hurria Wal Adalah*, May 12, 2012, 7.

640 Quoted in *Al-Shorouk Al-Jadeed*, May 13, 2012, 8.

641 Quoted in *El-Youm El-Sabaa*, May 12, 2012, 8.

642 Quoted in *Al-Shorouk Al-Jadeed*, May 13, 2012, 8.

643 See Robert J. Samuelson, "Democracy in America," MSNBC.COM, November 11, 2000. http://www.msnbc.com/news/485465.asp (accessed November 13, 2000).

644 *Al-Tahrir*, May 13, 2012, 13.

645 *As-Safir*, May 23, 2012, 8.

646 Al-Nahar, May 19, 2012.

647 *Al-Akhbar*, June 26, 2012, 11.

648 *Al-Gomhuria*, June 26, 2012.

649 *Al-Akhbar*, June 26, 2011, 17.

650 *Al-Gomhuria*, June 26, 2012, 2.

651 *Al-Ahram*, June 26, 2012, 24.

652 *Al-Akhbar*, June 26, 2011, 17.

653 In his inauguration speech on June 30 Morsi proclaimed "a new Egypt, the second republic," adding: "Today the Egyptian people have founded a new life, with true freedom and true democracy."

654 *Al-Ahram*, June 26, 2012, 11.

655 *Al-Gomhuria*, June 26, 2012, 16.

656 *Al-Gomhuria*, June 26, 2012, 16.

657 *Al-Ahram*, June 26, 2012, 24.

658 *Al-Akhbar*, June 26, 2012, 17.

659 *Al-Ahram*, June 26, 2012, 10.

660 *Al-Akhbar*, June 26, 2012, 12.

661 *Al-Ahram*, June 26, 2012, 2.

662 *Al-Akhbar*, June 26, 2012, 4.

663 *Al-Ahram*, June 26, 2012, 4.

664 *Al-Massa*, June 26, 2012, 4.

665 *Al-Ahram*, June 26, 2012, 10.

666 *Al-Gomhuria*, June 26, 2012, 15.

667 *Al-Ahram*, June 26, 2012, 11.

668 *Al-Gomhuria*, June 26, 2012, 15.

669 *Al-Ahram*, June 26, 2012, 5.

670 *Al-Ahram*, June 26, 2012, 10.

671 *Al-Massa*, June 26, 2012, 11.

672 *Al-Gomhuria*, June 26, 2012, 7.

673 *Al-Massa*, June 26, 2012, 15.

674 *Al-Akhbar*, June 26, 2012, 12.

675 *Al-Ahram*, June 26, 2012, 11.

676 *Al-Gomhuria*, June 26, 2012, 14.

677 *Al-Ahram*, June 26, 2012, 22.

678   *Al-Gomhuria*, June 26, 2012, 15.

679   *Al-Gomhuria*, June 26, 2012, 15.

680   *Al-Akhbar*, June 26, 2012, 15.

681   *Al-Massa*, June 26, 2012, 2.

682   *Al-Massa*, June 26, 2012, 16.

683   *Al-Gomhuria*, June 26, 2012, 15.

684   *Al-Akhbar*, June 26, 2011, 17.

685   *Al-Gomhuria*, June 26, 2012, 2.

686   *Al-Akhbar*, June 26, 2012, 16.

687   *Al-Massa*, June 26, 2012, 5.

688   *Al-Akhbar*, June 26, 2011, 15.

689   *Al-Akhbar*, June 26, 2012, 16.

690   *Al-Gomhuria*, June 26, 2012, 2.

691   *Al-Ahram*, June 26, 2012, 10.

692   *Al-Gomhuria*, June 26, 2012, 15.

693   *Al-Masry Al-Youm*, June 26, 2012, 21.

694   *Al-Masry Al-Youm*, June 26, 2012, 20.

695   *El-Youm El-Sabaa*, June 26, 2012, 4.

696   See *Al-Tahrir*, June 26, 2012, 5.

697   *El-Youm El-Sabaa*, June 26, 2012, 13.

698   *Al-Masry Al-Youm*, June 26, 2012, 24.

699   *Al-Tahrir*, June 26, 2012, 10.

700   *Al-Tahrir*, June 26, 2012, 6.

701   *El-Youm El-Sabaa*, June 26, 2012, 13.

702   *Al-Tahrir*, June 26, 2012, 10.

703   *Al-Masry Al-Youm*, June 26, 2012, 24.

704   *Al-Shorouk Al-Jadeed*, June 26, 2012, 4.

705   *Al-Shorouk Al-Jadeed*, June 26, 2012, 18.

706   *Al-Shorouk Al-Jadeed*, June 26, 2012, 4.

707   *El-Youm El-Sabaa*, June 26, 2012, 2.

708   *El-Youm El-Sabaa*, June 26, 2012, 13.

709   *Al-Masry Al-Youm*, June 26, 2012, 20.

710   *El-Youm El-Sabaa*, June 26, 2012, 13.

711   *El-Youm El-Sabaa*, June 26, 2012, 4.

712   *Al-Masry Al-Youm*, June 26, 2012, 24.

713   *Al-Masry Al-Youm*, June 26, 2012, 5.

714   *El-Youm El-Sabaa*, June 26, 2012, 4.

715   *El-Youm El-Sabaa*, June 26, 2012, 13.

716   *Al-Masry Al-Youm*, June 26, 2012, 21.

717   *El-Youm El-Sabaa*, June 26, 2012, 13.

718   *Al-Masry Al-Youm*, June 26, 2012, 24.

719   *Al-Masry Al-Youm*, June 26, 2012, 21.

720   *Al-Tahrir*, June 26, 2012, 10.

721   *Al-Shorouk Al-Jadeed*, June 26, 2012, 15.

722   *El-Youm El-Sabaa*, June 26, 2012, 2.

723   *Al-Masry Al-Youm*, June 26, 2012, 7.

724 *Al-Shorouk Al-Jadeed,* June 26, 2012, 14.

725 *Al-Masry Al-Youm,* June 26, 2012, 4.

726 *Al-Masry Al-Youm,* June 26, 2012, 6.

727 *Al-Masry Al-Youm,* June 26, 2012, 21.

728 *Al-Shorouk Al-Jadeed,* June 26, 2012, 15.

729 *Al-Masry Al-Youm,* June 26, 2012, 4.

730 *Al-Shorouk Al-Jadeed,* June 26, 2012, 18.

731 *Al-Masry Al-Youm,* June 26, 2012, 24.

732 *Al-Shorouk Al-Jadeed,* June 26, 2012, 4.

733 *Al-Masry Al-Youm,* June 26, 2012, 21.

734 *Al-Masry Al-Youm,* June 26, 2012, 24.

735 *Al-Tahrir,* June 26, 2012, 10.

736 *Al-Masry Al-Youm,* June 26, 2012, 24.

737 *Al-Tahrir,* June 26, 2012, 15.

738 See *Al-Tahrir,* June 26, 2012, 5.

739 *Al-Masry Al-Youm,* June 26, 2012, 7.

740 But there are other constitutional decrees which SCAF issued dating back to February 2011 that should have been also nullified.

741 Bruce K. Rutherford, *Egypt after Mubarak: Liberalism, Democracy, and Islam in the Arab World* (New Jersey: Princeton University Press, 2008).

742 Galal Amin, *Egypt and Egyptians in Mubarak's Age (1981-2008)* (Cairo: Merit, 2009), 5, 30, 65. [In Arabic]

743 Tawfiq El-Hakim, *The Revolution of Youth* (Cairo, Egypt: Misr Bookstore, 1975). [In Arabic.]

744 Mohamed Shafiq Gharbal, *The Formation of Egypt Across Ages,* 2nd ed. (1957, repr., Cairo: The General Egyptian Book Organization, 1966), 12. [In Arabic.]

745 See *Al-Masry Al-Youm,* June 26, 2012, 24.

746 *Al-Ahram,* May 13, 15, 17, 2011.

747 See Samuel Huntington, *The Clash of Civilization and the Remaking of the World Orders* (New York: Simon and Chuster, 1966).

748 David Brooks, "Huntington's Clash Revisited," *The New York Times,* March 3, 2011, www.nytimes.com/2011/03/04/opinion/04brooks.html (accessed March 5, 2011).

749 Interview with Al-Masria, March 5, 2011.

750 *Al-Ahram,* May 13, 2011.

751 *Radio and Television,* March 12, 2011, 93.

752 Nile Family, June 20, 2012.

753 The Marxist-Leninist viewpoint stated that imperialism is the expansion of the capitalist system to its highest phase, with monopoly being its most important feature.

754 *Al-Ahram,* March 22, 2011, 12.

755 *Al-Ahrar,* February 14, 2011, 10.

756 *El-Fagr,* March 14, 2011, 7.

757 The Morsi administration, though, has given a facelift, a beautification, to Tahrir in August and September.

758 Al-Azhar is a religious institution established in the tenth century.

759 *El-Youm El-Sabaa,* June 26, 2012, 13.

760 *Al-Masry Al-Youm,* October 1, 2012, 8.

761 David Kirkpatrick and Steven Erlanger, "Egypt's New Leader Spells Out Terms for U.S.-Arab Ties," *The New York Times*, September 21, 2012,

http://www.nytimes.com/2012/09/23/world/middleeast/egyptian-leader-mohamed-morsi-spells-out-terms-for-us-arab-ties.html?pagewanted=all&_r=0 (accessed September 28, 2012).

762 The U.S. media reported that Morsi asked for the delay and not Washington. See Nancy A. Youssef and Amina Ismail, "Anti-Morsi Protesters Besiege Palaces as Egyptian Constitution Crisis Worsens," *The State*, December, 5, 2012,

http://www.thestate.com/2012/12/04/2544019/protesters-storm-presidential.html (accessed December 6, 2012).

INDEX

Issa, Ibrahim, 60, 106, 144

J

Japanese, 170, 198
Jasmine Revolution, See Tunisian revolution
Jews, , 90
Jordan, 14, 196
Journalists, 3, 8, 13, 22, 25, 27, 32, 37, 38, 42, 45, 47, 49-53, 55, 61, 63, 68, 76, 82, 85, 94, 96, 99, 101-107, 115, 119, 138, 143, 144, 154, 170, 174, 177, 179, 204, 207, 208, 222, 232
judiciary, 90, 119, 132, 136, 140, 145, 148, 153, 173, 179, 183-186, 191, 211, 212
justice system, 135, 148

K

Kamel, Mustapha, 98, 116
Kamil, Mustafa, 9, 220
Kennedy, John F., 151
Kerry, John, 8, 122
Kifaya, 27, 110, 115

L

Lamb, David, 1
Lebanon, 47, 54, 75, 76, 79, 80
legislative authority, 152, 189
Lewis Greiss, 7, 25, 202
Libya, 7, 14, 48, 196, 197, 204, 209
Lotus Revolution, 196

M

Mahfouz, Naguib, 9, 195
Mansur, Anees, 78
martyrs, 78, 86, 104, 110, 139, 143, 144, 155, 157, 172, 173, 175, 178, 181, 182, 195, 202, 215
Marzouki, Moncef, 6
Maspero, 28, 33, 54, 84, 105, 152
Matar, Gamil, 72
Mehwar, 81
Middle East News Agency (MENA), 26, 46, 49, 52, 53
military, See army
minister of interior, 3, 40, 48, 59, 77, 111, 132, 142
monopoly, 100, 183, 201, 204, 241
Montasser, Salah, 75
Morocco, 14, 24, 146, 196

morsheed, 179, 181, 191
Morsi, Mohamed, 13, 149, 153, 171, 198, 216, 236
Moussa, Amr, 15, 121, 151, 178, 211
Moussa, Salama, 98, 218, 232
Mubarak, Gamal, 81, 92, 95, 132, 133, 191, 199
Mubarak, Hosni, 1, 13, 19, 36, 58, 61, 64, 67, 75, 76, 83, 91, 94, 99, 115, 131, 139, 151, 165, 171, 193, 222, 225, 226, 229
museum, 8, 55, 62, 66, 68, 70, 83
Muslim Brotherhood, 3, 27-30, 39, 50-52, 60, 94, 101, 112, 120, 121, 123-125, 127, 153-160, 162, 169, 171, 176-179, 181-187, 190, 191, 200, 205, 207-209, 226, 234, 237
Muslims, See Islamists, Muslim Brotherhood

N

Nafah, Hassan, 38, 124
Nafie, Ibrahim, 60, 75, 94, 128
Naguib, Mohamed, 118, 203
Nasser, Gamal Abdel, 19, 26, 44, 71, 87, 98, 117, 139, 147, 175, 198, 204, 211
National Democratic Party (NDP), 5, 19, 20, 25, 26, 28-30, 38, 39, 44-46, 50, 52, 58, 70-72, 81, 92-95, 103, 109-111, 115, 119, 126, 132, 133, 136, 140, 176, 222, 223, 226
National Progressive Unionist Party, 29, 30, 37, 90
Nazi, 102
Nazif, Ahmed, 6, 19, 40, 43, 111, 132
New Wafd Party, 28-30, 37, 55, 77, 86, 90, 91, 222, 226
New Zealand, 110
Nile News, 31, 32, 102, 121, 234
Nixon, Richard, 151

O

Obama, 10-12, 66, 76, 79, 80, 83, 94, 102, 165, 209-211, 220
Oman, 7, 14, 196
ONTV, 30, 31, 33, 36, 78, 154, 221, 222, 229, 237
Ottoman., 98, 194

P

Palestine, 79, 80, 101, 210